south of the clouds

Exploring the
Hidden Realms of China

st. martin's press ☙ new york

south
of *the* clouds

S e t h   F a i s o n

www.stmartins.com

Except as noted, all photographs are by the author.

Library of Congress Cataloging-in-Publication Data

Faison, Seth.
     South of the clouds : exploring the hidden realms of China / by Seth Faison.
        p. cm.
     ISBN 0-312-30640-7
     EAN 978-0312-30640-3
     1. China—Social conditions—1976- I. Title.

HN733.5.F34 2004
951.05'8'092—dc22

                                                              2004048380

First Edition: October 2004

10 9 8 7 6 5 4 3 2 1

For Siobhan

contents

south
of *the* clouds

TERRA-COTTA

Over the centuries, the farmers who tilled the dry soil in Lin Tong County, a bleak patch of China near a turn in the Yellow River, told their young about ghosts lurking underground. A boy named Yang listened to his grandfather tell stories at evening gatherings around a communal fire, and one favorite tale concerned an unfortunate ancestor who dug too deeply in the earth and saw the face of a ghost, half hidden in the dirt. The ancestor was cursed with a life of bad luck, Grandfather Yang said, for disturbing the slumber of an old spirit. The earth was to be respected, and feared.

In the 1940s, when Yang was still a boy, Communist cadres arrived in the area and opened a rudimentary school. Yang learned to read, a skill his father and grandfather never possessed. Yang was taught to value science and reject superstition. He was taught that workers, not gods, were the masters of fate. But Yang's parents were reluctant to let go of the ancient lore. Yang's father warned his boy not to ignore the gods who governed rainfall and the health of the family cow.

Yang left school at age sixteen to farm the family plot. It was tiresome work, but he had little choice, living in a rural area. When family farms were merged to create a commune, as they were all over China in the 1950s, Yang had to work under a brigade leader, a man who knew little of farming. Yang had a stubborn streak and bristled at taking direction from another man. In those days, however, there was no option. At Yang's commune, farming yields fell steadily. In the early 1960s, there was not enough food to go around, and Yang sometimes had to fight for scraps to feed his children. Although Lin Tong was located twenty miles from Xi'an, at one time the distinguished capital of China, the region retained few signs of its illustrious history. It was poor, and its people were hungry.

In 1974 Lin Tong suffered a bad drought. Yang, then thirty-six, was sent with another farmer to dig a well. They settled on a spot in the middle of a broad plain, where the wheat fields had gone fallow. It was dry and dusty. Yang and his comrade started digging. They worked at a Communist pace, taking turns. One dug for half an hour while the other sat. They took long breaks. To Yang, it was another day of wasted work. Still, they labored on. At about noon on the third day, Yang hit something hard with his shovel. "At first I thought I hit a brick, but when I scraped away the dirt, it was the length of a full body," Yang said later. He pulled the torso-shaped piece of clay out of the ground, puzzling at the ornate warrior's tunic over the chest. Yang and his partner walked back to their brigade to tell their leader. The leader could not be bothered to see for himself and told the two men to ignore the discovery and get back to work. Other neighbors came to take a look. Some were scared, recalling the old stories of ghosts in the ground, and urged Yang to rebury it. Yang would not. He was not afraid of ghosts. If his find was a historical relic, maybe it would earn him a small reward. His family needed the money. Yang put the long chunk of terra-cotta in the back of a three-wheeled cart and hauled it to the county headquarters a few miles away.

When Yang got there, a county official impatiently listened to Yang's tale. He tried to send Yang away, saying the office was busy with "political study," where Mao-suited cadres sat around a table and took turns reading aloud from *People's Daily.* Yang insisted that someone look at his discovery. The official reluctantly let Yang dump the piece in a storeroom in the back, where it remained until an official from the Xi'an Relics Bureau came to look at it. This man guessed that the piece was one hundred years old and didn't regard it as anything special. Yang was back at his commune. He was given no reward and sent to another site to dig a well.

An archaeologist from Xi'an heard about the discovery and came to examine it. He reasoned that the design of the clay warrior's outfit meant that the relic was from a far earlier time. Soon archaeologists from Beijing began investigating. When they went to look at the site where Yang's shovel hit the relic, and did more digging, they discovered that it was only inches from a buried doorway. Digging further, they saw that the doorway led to an underground vault. The more they dug, the more they found. Hundreds of buried warriors lay in long rows, as well as terra-cotta horses and a bronze replica of an emperor's chariot, The vault eventually measured nearly a hundred yards long. Behind it lay three more vaults, and the army of buried clay figures totaled more than six thousand. There was only one conclusion: the warriors were intended for the tomb of Qin Shi Huang, the first emperor of China.

Qin Shi Huang was a conqueror. He inherited a modest, mountainous kingdom as a young man, vanquished a neighboring area and then another and another, eventually merging them into a grand empire in 221 B.C.E. Qin's name, pronounced "chin," became the origin of the word *China,* as his country would come to be known in the West. Qin considered his nation the center of the world, and *Zhong Guo,* or Central Kingdom, is what the Chinese call it today. Qin was a tyrant. He executed officials who questioned his judgment, and devised strict ways to control his subjects, like punishing the entire family of anyone suspected of committing a crime. He distrusted scholars and orchestrated a massive burning of books to keep them from reading texts he did not like. At the same time, he established a common system of writing with Chinese characters, a system that endures today. Qin envisioned and began constructing the Great Wall, a project that would take centuries. He created a strong and centralized Chinese state, concentrating power in the hands of one man and demanding submission from all others, giving Chinese culture its cautious, conservative, and politicized nature.

Qin planned an elaborate tomb, grander than any that had come before. He ordered the sculpting of life-sized warriors, an army of them, to surround his final resting place. It was a tremendous job, and the warriors were still being built when Qin died in

207 B.C.E. at age fifty-two. Qin's son ascended to the throne, but the empire crumbled a year later, when rebels sacked the capital and torched the site where the terra-cotta warriors were still being assembled. The warriors were buried in burning rubble. Archaeologists later found that the mixture of compressed earth and ash preserved the terra-cotta warriors well. They lay underground, undisturbed, for more than two thousand years, while wars and rebellions came and went on the land above.

After Farmer Yang hit that first warrior with his shovel, the site was fully excavated. It opened to the public in 1981 and was recognized as one of the greatest archaeological finds in the world. No one knows how many farmers digging in the fields of Lin Tong stumbled onto other pieces in centuries past, only to rebury them out of fear, as Yang's ancestor did. It took one stubborn farmer to bring a terra-cotta warrior out into the open, and access to archaeologists and their science to bring along the other six thousand.

China is a country haunted, and nourished, by its past. Old fears and antiquated habits hold great power. Chinese culture, for all its glorious achievements, is burdened with a tendency toward caution and a wariness of anything that threatens the established authority. Conforming, relying on old teachings, and controlling youthful impulses are staples of the Chinese way. Although Chinese architecture and poetry and cuisine have attained illustrious heights by mixing tradition and innovation, China's society is also riddled with conventions that breed close-mindedness and privacy. People are circumspect. Even in times of rapid change, much remains hidden.

China is a land of secrets. Political decisions are still made behind the thick walls of secluded compounds. Social intercourse relies on elaborate rules, and allusion and suggestion are preferred to directness or confrontation. Friends and colleagues often keep significant aspects of their lives secret from one another. Sex is practiced with discretion. Spiritual traditions are elusive and hard to pin down. Outsiders trying to describe China often circle back to the same word: inscrutable.

As a young man, I saw China as many Westerners do: an endless sea of indistinguishable faces. I knew China was an ancient civilization and the world's most populous country, but I had a hard time discerning any sense of humanity in the people I saw in newspaper photographs. When I was twenty-five, casting about for direction, China had just begun to open its doors to Westerners after decades of seclusion. I had grown up in a comfortable home in Brooklyn, New York, and my Waspy youth was a safely predictable sequence of schooling, summers at the beach, and orderly dinner-table conversation. I wanted a challenge. Going to the far side of the world to learn a difficult language fit my bill. China looked secretive, and that attracted me.

There was something more that drew me, too. China looked like a feminine culture. Chinese women were delicate, lithe, and small-breasted, while Chinese men appeared somewhat effeminate. Social interaction in China seemed soft and gentle, and averse to confrontation. Growing up surrounded by sisters, I was a friendly and gentle boy, not tough or strong. I never felt particularly masculine. In China, I sensed that my soft side would be an asset, not a drawback. Once I got there, I felt safe and unthreatened among Chinese people. I knew innately how to talk to them. I felt at home among Chinese people in the same way I was usually more comfortable around women than around men. I could sympathize with how un-comfortable many Chinese people felt with the rougher edges of Westerners, just as I was uncomfortable with macho men. I knew without thinking how to assure a Chinese woman or man that I was not threatening. It gave me a sense of power. In China, my Western appearance made me feel masculine in a way I had not felt in the West. Among Chinese, I looked tall and strong. I was more of a man, without trying.

Westerners often carry misguided notions about China. Today, some see China as a serious military power that might threaten the United States. Others see a country on the brink of dissolution, torn by the strains of overpopulation and corruption. Those views are invariably alarmist or wishful thinking, or some combination. Over the years, I came to see that China is so big and complicated that anyone can find evidence for any argument: China is friendly, China is threatening, China is reserved, China is expansionist, China is masculine, China is feminine. Those arguments usually say more about the arguer than they do about China.

When I first went there in 1984, China was still recovering from the nightmare of leftist rule, a period known as the Cultural Revo-lution. Many people were afraid to speak to a Westerner, much less befriend one. State-run stores had surly clerks and empty shelves. Telephones were scarce. Travel was an ordeal. Still, I found myself drawn to the hidden sides of this beguiling nation. As I spent years there, learning how to speak and find my way through Chinese idiosyncrasies and cultural habits, I gradually became able to probe more deeply. I pursued Chinese women. I became a journalist and used my calling card to peek into the mysteries of Chinese politics, the netherworld of underground business, and remote corners of the vast countryside. Uncovering secrets became my domain.

As a journalist, I had another mission: writing about China as a nation of individuals, not a monolith. In newspaper articles, I wanted to tell stories that captured the flavor of people's lives. I was determined to show how China's growing economy was bringing openness and diversity, and not fueling a consolidation of Communist power, as many in the West mistakenly believed. I tracked the way the authorities were reluctantly relinquishing control over the lives of Chinese citizens. I watched China undergoing a transformation from a stagnant and tightly restricted police state in the early 1980s into a chaotic and semi-modern country at the turn of the century, an immeasurably freer place to live.

When I sat down to write this book, sixteen years after I had arrived, I wanted to tell the story I knew best: my own. I wanted to convey how China came alive in my moments of interaction with those willing to show me a hidden realm. A cute cafeteria worker introduced me to nightlife in Xi'an. A gregarious policeman told me about murder in the countryside. A political activist guided me through the hidden drama behind Tiananmen Square. A sleazy businessman in Guangzhou tried to snow me, but instead went to jail for saying too much. A voluptuous executive in Shanghai taught me about the secret sex lives of married women. A transgendered choreographer opened my eyes to my own true nature.

All through my travels I was searching, for what I was not sure. I intuitively homed in on secret aspects of Chinese culture, as though the act of uncovering them would satisfy my intellectual and emotional yearnings. I came to see that my ultimate quest involved a spiritual issue I had to encounter all on my own. And I found my answer on a hilltop in the most secret land of all, Tibet.

I was always collecting stories, human threads that colored little sections of the complex quilt I was traveling across. During my first year, studying Chinese in Xi'an, I visited the site of terra-cotta warriors in Lin Tong on several occasions. In those days, official guides told visitors that the warriors had been discovered by a farmer looking for a well, but said nothing more. The formal telling of that story did not mention Farmer Yang by name or say how difficult it was for him to get anyone to recognize the discovery. I wondered about that man.

Years later, when I was living in Shanghai as a correspondent for the *New York Times,* I heard that the manager of a tourist shop at the terra-cotta warrior site had hired the farmer who had discovered the first warrior to sit inside and sign glossy coffee table books. That meant Farmer Yang was available to talk to anyone who walked up to his table. I wanted to go and meet him, to hear how he actually made his discovery. Besides, going to look for him offered me an excuse to visit Xi'an again, for the first time in years.

After a flight from Shanghai, I took a cab from the airport into Xi'an. The road bustled with trucks and tourist buses and taxis, a congested contrast to the lonesome roads and simple poverty of Xi'an as I remembered it from 1984. Flashy signs advertised Coca-Cola and Korean Airlines. The sidewalks were peopled with men in colorful polo shirts and women in tight miniskirts. When my taxi arrived at the terra-cotta warrior site, I barely recognized it. New restaurants and tourist shops selling T-shirts and trinkets, including imitation warriors three inches tall, surrounded the entrance. Hawkers stood outside each storefront, raucously competing for business.

I pushed my way past the sellers and went inside the main vault. It was still covered by a simple airplane hangar of a roof. I was entranced once again by the sight of a whole army of clay soldiers, arranged in long rows, their individually carved faces the color of earth. Staring down at the open pit of warriors, I could not help but muse about the passage of time, wondering what the surrounding area looked like two thousand years ago, when these clay men were crafted. It had been fourteen years since my first visit to the site, a blink of the eye in the longer scheme of history.

I inquired at a tourist shop where to find Farmer Yang. A clerk behind the counter looked at me blandly and asked, "Which one?" It took me a moment to recognize the problem. In China, the rush to market capitalism meant that every good business idea was swiftly and shamelessly copied. In this case, once Farmer Yang was hired to sign coffee table books, a competing tourist shop had hired another farmer named Yang, who claimed that it was *he* who had actually discovered the terra-cotta warriors. The managers of the two stores each insisted that theirs was the true discoverer and accused the other of commercial subterfuge. The authorities at the site did nothing to settle the dispute, busy counting their money at the gate. But I wanted to figure out which Yang was real.

I walked into a store displaying a prominent sign: THE MAN WHO DISCOVERED THE TERRA-COTTA WARRIORS, YANG QUANYI. A short, kind-looking old man sat on a wooden bench. He was bald but for a few days' stubble on his head and chin. He wore a plain white shirt and green slacks. He smiled as I approached, and when I addressed him in Chinese, he invited me to sit down next to him on his bench. He seemed intrigued that a tall blond American could speak his language. When I asked if we could *pian yi pian,* local slang for hanging out together, he laughed heartily and put his hand on my shoulder. I assumed a conspiratorial whisper and asked how much they paid him to sit there all day. Yang looked over his shoulder before leaning forward to mumble, "Not enough." "How much?" "Just 280 yuan," he said, about thirty-five dollars. "A day?" "A month." I grimaced in sympathy.

When I asked Yang to describe what it was like the day he found the soldiers, he leaned forward to whisper again. "I found the soldiers," he said. "Don't believe what other people tell you."

I asked again how he had found the soldiers. Yang studied my face. "You speak Chinese very well," he said. "Where did you study?" I answered, then tried another tack. Why did he say not to believe what others said? Would someone lie about who made such an important discovery? "It's hard to say," he said. Hard to say. A common phrase in Chinese, often used when one wants to avoid answering a question. I had expected Yang to call his competitor a liar, but instead he was trying to change the subject. Suspicious, I pushed a little harder. I asked what he showed people when they asked for proof of his discovery. Yang looked at me blankly. Two Chinese tourists walked up and presented him with a book to sign. Yang engaged them in conversation, and I stepped aside. I didn't mind. I would be back. But first I wanted to find the other Yang.

He sat in another shop a few doors down. There was no sign this time, but a young woman behind a counter pointed him out to me, the man sitting alone in a row of coffee table books. He stood to greet me as I approached. He was taller and stronger-looking than his rival. A worn blue Mao suit hung on his broad frame. His full name was Yang Zhifa. I took a seat beside him. He had a peasant's habit of grunting to signal assent, instead of speaking. At first, he needed encouragement to say anything more than a short sentence. His fingernails were dirty, he was unrefined, and he gave me the feeling he would sit and talk as long as I wanted.

Yang's eyes came alive when I asked about the day of discovery, twenty-four years earlier. I listened carefully, keeping my eye on his as he spoke, encouraging him to keep going. He told me about hitting the first fragment with his shovel. He told me about the reluctant county official, who had been busy with "political study." He didn't seem to mind when I asked all kinds of questions, digging into his family background, his grandfather's old stories, the work conditions in his commune, and unearthing the exact sequence of events before and after his discovery. Yang eventually told me enough that I could piece together, with some later help from an archaeologist in Beijing, the whole tale of how the terra-cotta warriors emerged from their resting place underground. It was clear that this was the Yang who had made the discovery. I looked at him with renewed respect, putting a face on the man I had heard about all those years earlier.

I asked Yang Zhifa about the other Yang, and he sighed wearily.

"If he can claim he found it, so can you," Yang said. "You really want to know the truth? Ask him what time of day the discovery was made. Eh? Ask him what day and what time, and see what he says."

I bid him good-bye and went back to the first store. I wanted to give Yang Quanyi a second chance to prove himself. He was sitting alone again and acted friendly when he saw me approach again. I told him I had spoken with his competitor, who suggested asking what time of day the discovery was made. Now Yang Quanyi's face showed discomfort. He tried to change the subject again. I brought him back.

"Aaaaah, the date and time were not so important," he said dismissively. "I was the one who found the arrows and swords beside the soldiers." But not the first soldier? No, Yang admitted, he may not have been present "at the first moment" of discovery. But there were six farmers who helped dig up early pieces, he said. His explanations and justifications slowed to a mumble as he watched the expression of doubt grow on my face.

After leaving the terra-cotta warrior site, I stopped a mile away at the actual grave of Qin Shi Huang. It had still not been excavated. I had to remind myself that the terra-cotta warriors had been intended to surround this tomb but were buried in their ancient warehouse before they could be deployed. Qin's tomb was a simple hill whiskered with grass, about 125 feet in altitude. It looked unsuitably plain for the burial place of China's first emperor, a man with such a powerful impact on history. As I climbed the hill, I wondered whether any riches still lay within, or if they all had been looted in the years or centuries after Qin was buried. No one knew the answer, because local authorities have prevented Chinese archaeologists from excavating the site, arguing that China did not yet possess the technology to preserve the site when opening it. But an archaeologist in Beijing told me the real reason appeared to be political. The local authorities did not like the way that outside scientists had taken over and controlled the excavation of the terra-cotta warrior site. The bosses did not want the same thing to happen to Qin's actual tomb, and so it remained buried. Like so much of China, ancient and modern, what lies inside the site remains a mystery.

On the way back to Xi'an, I asked my driver to pull over by a roadside cart for something to eat. I sat on a tiny wooden stool at a small table, where an old woman served *jing gao,* a local specialty made with sticky rice and sweet dates. It was an old favorite from my student days. Biting into its soft crunch, a tangy fragrance triggered a cascade of memories of my time in Xi'an. Cold mornings on dusty streets. The old green army coat I wore to an unheated class-room every day. Sitting outside at little food stalls with Chinese friends. Back in those days, the secrets of China drew long shadows in my mind. So much was hidden. I was young and earnest, willing to try anything, and quite ready for my first adventure.

chapter one

BIG NOSE

When I stumbled out of the train station in Xi'an, the late-afternoon sky looked vividly clear and blue. I felt dazed from a bumpy thirty-hour train ride from Hong Kong. My lower back ached, but I could not feel the ground beneath my feet as I walked. I was a hazy bundle of excitement and apprehension. My gaze fixed on the brilliant, limitless autumn sky.

A broad, muddy square stretched out before me, crowded with horse-drawn carts, rickety old trucks, and dirty buses. Simple houses on the far side of the square looked the color of earth, tawny and cinnamon. Old signs, browning with age, hung outside plain-looking storefronts. The air smelled dusty and sour. Thousands of Chinese men and women moved in and out of the train station in a tangled mass. Most of them looked like farmers from the countryside, with bronze weather-beaten faces and faded blue or green Mao jackets, bits of mud dried on their cuffs.

I put down my bags at one corner of the square outside the station. Two old men wearing threadbare Mao jackets stopped to stare at me, evidently curious about a Westerner. The men stood so close I wondered if they were going to reach out and touch my blond hair. I was anxious about talking to commoners. I had been warned that people in Communist China were sullen and would be afraid to speak to foreigners. The men spoke to each other about me as if I were not there.

"Da bizi zhen da," said the man with the scruffy white beard. "That big nose is really big."

I laughed involuntarily, surprising the men, who laughed too. "Big nose," the local term for Westerner, fit me well since I have a substantial beak. The man with the white beard seemed intrigued that the "big nose" could speak some Chinese. He offered me a cigarette, and I accepted, eager to please, even though I did not smoke. It was filterless, and I coughed on the first puff, eliciting even more laughter. That drew more listeners. In minutes, a crowd of nearly a hundred people crowded around me tightly, mouths agape. I felt as awkward as a novice movie star, attracting attention for my looks alone.

"Why did you come to China?" asked the bearded man.

"To meet you," I replied. Uproarious laughter.

Cheerful smiles on peasant faces, the easy bonding of laughter, friendly conversation. Relief flushed down to my toes. After worrying that I would feel like a caged animal in China, I was welcome at the train station. It softened my anxiety.

Riding on a clunky old bus toward the university where I had enrolled for a year, I looked out at the teeming sea of Chinese cyclists and pedestrians who packed the city streets. Millions of people, everywhere. In the pallid afternoon light, all the storefronts had the same dull look of simplicity and poverty. The bus weaved its way through a crowded intersection, headed for a towering monument with an imperial Chinese roof, jade green eaves sloping majestically on four sides. I learned later that it was the city's South Gate, built by an emperor intent on intimidating all comers with the size of his impenetrable front door. An enormous wall, forty feet high and wide enough on top for six horse-drawn chariots to trot side by side, surrounded the entire city. Xi'an had been one of the most cosmopolitan cities in the world during the Tang Dynasty of 618–907, the terminus of the fabled Silk Road, before a long slide toward obscurity. Still, centuries later, the wall remained. As my bus entered the darkness of a long tunnel that cut through that wall, I wondered about the multitudes who had passed the same way over the past thousand years, courtiers who rode hundreds of miles on horseback to bow before an emperor, Communist soldiers promising to "liberate" the city from its feudal past, Red Guards chanting fanatical leftist slogans.

Outside the city wall, the road grew wider as the sidewalks disappeared. My bus headed toward the outskirts of the city. In the foot traffic, I noticed a barefoot young boy in rags hauling a wooden cart piled high with three or four long, heavy slabs of concrete. The boy leaned hard into a worn leather shoulder strap as he inched forward, sweat darkening his clothes. He could not have been more than ten years old. I craned my neck to watch him as the bus passed. After he fell from sight, I spotted another boy with a similar load, and then another. The road was crowded with farmers and tradesmen riding donkey-drawn carts, and filthy old trucks that lurched in the ruts of the road, choking out black clouds of exhaust. But I fixed my eyes on those young boys, sweating like medieval slaves. I wondered how many pennies a day they earned for their labor.

At Shaanxi Teachers University, the austere campus of gray brick buildings included a dormitory for foreign students. It had been built for the Vietnamese in the 1960s, when China and North Vietnam were allied in a war against the United States. By the time I got to China, in 1984, the notion of Asian solidarity had surrendered to an interest in making money. Universities enrolled foreign students who could pay to learn Chinese. Ten Americans and fifteen Japanese shared the rooms along two pea-green hallways with dim lightbulbs. I washed my laundry by hand in a cast-iron sink where my fingers pruned up in the cold water. It was primitive, but I didn't care about amenities. I was in China.

I became bewitched by China in college, when I fell for a classmate named Deborah Wang. She was learning Chinese, the language of her parents. She gave me a Chinese name, Fei Liangshi, by randomly picking three Chinese characters she liked. She went to China to study for a year and wrote me letters with engaging descriptions of Chinese villages, long train rides, and abandoned graveyards. Across thin pages of rice paper, she drew Chinese calligraphy, graceful emblems of timeworn beauty. I found myself drawn to these symbols of a faraway culture, intrigued that a written language could look so mysterious and meaningful. I started reading about China, its history of ruthless tyrants, its sophisticated intellectual traditions, and its vast peasantry. When Deborah returned to America, we split up, but she had already planted the seed in my mind. I signed up to study Chinese in Xi'an.

In my first weeks in Chinese class, Teacher Wang furrowed her dark eyebrows whenever I opened my mouth. I had to distinguish the four tones of Mandarin Chinese and remember which word went with which tone. Teacher Wang insisted that I get every tone right. She was patient and persistent. So many words sound the same in Chinese that one false tone can alter the meaning of an entire sentence. *Mao* could mean cat, hair, leader of China, crude, hat, or appearance, depending on its tone and context. *Hui* could mean return, meeting, regret, or kindness. I knew some basic Chinese from a summer program in Taiwan, and I could begin a conversation easily, as I had that first day at the train station. Since Chinese avoids annoying grammatical rules like conjugations or tenses—very sensibly, I thought—I could get through simple greetings without a problem. Yet I quickly ran aground as soon as a discussion became sophisticated.

The hardest part was learning vocabulary. There was no shortcut to learning Chinese characters. I had to memorize them, which was time-consuming and exhausting. I had to learn and forget a word ten to twenty times before I could hold on to it. Outside of my daily classes, I spent hours each day hunched over a simple textbook at a small desk, my legs squeezed underneath. At times, I yearned to be back studying high school French, where "the difference" was translated as *la différence*. In Chinese, it was *bu yi yang*. Looking up a word in a Chinese dictionary, by counting the strokes and laboriously scanning long lists of characters, was an ordeal in itself. I often got dizzy with frustration, and went outside for a walk to escape the torture. Seeing street signs in Chinese characters and struggling to decipher their meaning would renew my determination, sending me back to my desk. The payoff, accumulated painstakingly, was the charm and subtlety that lay within Chinese characters. I came to admire the balance built into each one. I learned how to pick out basic symbols, used like building blocks in complex characters. The symbol for water, for instance, is one part of the character for soup, alcohol, and coffee. The symbol for tall is one part of building, skyscraper, and tower. I loved the discovery one day that *an,* the word for peace, is the symbol of a woman alone under a roof. I imagined a house in the woods during a snowy winter night, with only a woman inside, peaceful and quiet. Teacher Wang frowned. More likely, she suggested, the character reflected the perspective of a man in ancient China. A man has peace only when he owns a home and owns the woman inside.

The student cafeteria at Shaanxi Teachers University was a dark, desolate, unheated cavern with gaping holes in the roof. At mealtime, I joined the crush of students in Mao jackets or worn army coats, each carrying a bowl and chopsticks in hand. In the darkness, with long snaking lines of students waiting for food, the place looked like a refugee camp. One line inched forward to a giant vat of rice, where steam rose so thick that it was sometimes hard to see the cafeteria workers in dirty smocks ladling out spoonfuls. Another line was for a choice of slop—boiled vegetables, sour tofu, or chunks of fat with a scrap of meat hanging off one end. Everything tasted a few days old. A few dilapidated, dirty benches occupied the far end of the cafeteria. Most students either squatted on their haunches to slurp the meal quickly or carried their bowls to eat back in a dormitory. No one spoke. I hoped to make friends in the cafeteria, but I always went back to my dormitory alone.

After a few days, I started making asides to the cafeteria workers as they put food in my bowl. Most looked askance, baffled by a tall blond "big nose" babbling in primary-school Chinese. But there was one woman whose wide eyes peeked out from beneath a drooping white surgeon's cap, who laughed at a joke I made about the food she was serving. The next day, I went back to take whatever she dished out, just for another shot at a laugh. She smiled broadly when I approached and asked my name. When I told her, "Fei Liangshi," she laughed hard, dropping her serving spoon. She told another worker, and he laughed as well. I knew I had a funny-sounding Chinese name, chosen for me by my college girlfriend, who had not realized that it was a synonym for wasted crops. On a tall and skinny guy like me, that was an unfortunate name. When the worker got over her laughter, she said she would call me *Xiao Fei,* or Little Fei, a casual form of address that tactfully avoided my full name. She told me her name was Shu. "Call me Little Shu," she said.

I went back to Shu's table every day. She always gave me a smile. She was sweet and plain, talking easily and sometimes picking her nose and inspecting her snot as we spoke. One day, she took me aside and asked quietly if I wanted to go out to a dance in the evening. I had been told that there was no nightlife in Communist China and was excited by the thought of venturing into a secret world of dancing and dating. Besides, I could escape the drudgery of my ordinarily deskbound evening, wrestling with Chinese characters. I could not help wondering, too, if I might get somewhere with Shu. Most Chinese women I saw on the street looked away when I tried to meet their gaze. Now that Shu asked me out, my mind began to gallop, envisioning possible scenarios.

I met Shu at the front gate of the university after dark. She had exchanged her cafeteria whites for a dark blue turtleneck and a London Fog–style raincoat. It looked like she had also combed her hair. She smiled as I approached on a bicycle and nodded toward the main road. Wordlessly, we set out, riding side by side. It was almost pitch-dark. When a truck passed us, its dim headlights illuminated a few donkey-drawn carts and peasant farmers walking in the road. Shu remained silent. I wondered whether she was having second thoughts about taking a foreigner out for an evening.

I followed Shu toward a street corner with overhead lights, which looked like an oasis in the blackness. On the sidewalk was a small night market, where food carts peddled noodles and assorted gruel for pennies a bowl. Shu parked her bicycle and stepped away, saying she was going to look for someone. As I watched her wander off into the small crowd, I momentarily felt like a small boy, wondering if his mother will ever come back. It was a feeling I often had those early days in Xi'an. But Shu had left me with her bicycle, so I told myself she had to return. Before she did, a slender man with a pencil-thin mustache walked up.

"Where's Little Shu?" he asked nonchalantly, as though I must be the foreigner he had been told about. He offered me a cigarette, but I felt shy, not sure who he was, and said no. He took my refusal without a pause and lit his own. Shu wandered back in a moment and told me her friend's name was Wu. "We already met," Wu said to her. She spoke to him in a muted voice. They did not touch, but I could sense that they were close.

We rode out on the main road again, three astride. My notion of romance with Shu evaporated, but I felt glad to be included in an outing at night. Shu and her friend murmured to each other as we rode toward the city's South Gate. As we pedaled inside the long tunnel under the gate, the sounds of our three rickety bicycles echoed loudly. We parked at a fenced-in lot where hundreds of other bikes were lined. An old watchwoman wearing a thick padded army coat held out her hand without looking up, and Wu dropped in a two-cent fee. A man with thick glasses inadvertently knocked over a bicycle at the end of one row and, like a domino, it knocked down fifty more bicycles, including ours. Shu's face contorted in anger as she cursed the man, using words I did not understand. I was surprised that a gentle-looking woman could erupt so suddenly. Wu put his arm around her shoulder and led her away, leaving the man behind to re-right the bicycles one by one.

We walked a block to our destination, a run-down movie theater. I wondered if I was being taken to see a film, rather than the promised dance. Wu bought our tickets for about twenty-five cents apiece, deftly refusing my efforts to pay for myself. We stepped inside the theater lobby, and I saw that it had been converted to a dance floor. The lights were dim, and the room smelled musty. An eight-piece string-and-horn band was playing 1940s tunes with the grace of a clunky washing machine. On the floor, men waltzed with women, men with men, women with women. The waltz was charmlessly called "three-step" in Chinese. Men and women who went to their day jobs in dull green or blue Mao jackets now wore Western jackets and floor-length skirts as they glided across the room.

Dancing had been banned in China during the days of political extremism in the 1960s and '70s, denounced by leftists as a symbol of bourgeois decadence. In Xi'an, dancing had quietly reappeared in the early 1980s. There was no change in the law. Old restrictions were simply no longer enforced. The manager of a movie theater could allow ballroom dancing in the lobby as long as it was not advertised and was kept discreet and orderly. One had to know where to go, or be taken by someone who did.

Inside the lobby, Wu asked if I would dance with him. I didn't know what to say. Dancing with a man was not what I expected. Besides, I did not know how to dance the "three-step." Wu did not believe me. The only Westerner in the place, he said, ought to know how to dance a Western dance. Ignoring my protests, Wu took my hand and led me firmly out onto the floor. Wu patiently showed me the same steps over and over, and acted unfazed when I kept stepping on his toes. I felt self-conscious, trying hard to keep up and to ignore the stares of other dancers. I was relieved when the tune came to an end, and I could let Shu take a turn with her boyfriend. They glided off together like a pair of expert figure skaters.

After a few more dances, Shu asked me to teach her how to dance disco, a word she murmured like a taboo. I was happy to show her something I knew. I took her to the middle of the dance floor and showed her how to move side to side, shake her hips, swing her arms. Other dancers stopped and stared, then created a circle around us, cheering as we danced. Pretty soon the entire dance floor enveloped us. Wu tried to step in to get us to stop. At first I thought he wanted to keep another man from dancing with his girlfriend, but he looked quite nervous. Shu rebuffed him while the others kept cheering us on. The louder they got, the more nervous Wu became. He pleaded with Shu to stop. Once we got outside, away from the crowd, he murmured to me, "Too dangerous."

A year before I arrived in Xi'an, a political campaign to fight "spiritual pollution" had been launched by leaders in Beijing, a throwback to the days of the Cultural Revolution. During the campaign, disco dancing was singled out as an evil to be banned. Ballroom dancing was now permissible, but disco was considered degenerate. I learned that four young men in Xi'an had been arrested for disco dancing and sentenced to seven years in prison. Evidently, a handful of "criminals" had to be identified and punished in every province to justify the campaign. By the time I went to that dance in Xi'an, the ban on disco had not been formally lifted, but the campaign had blown over and most of the dancers that night figured it was not dangerous anymore. Wu was not sure.

K ill the chicken to scare the monkeys" is a common Chinese saying. Arbitrary punishment fells the unlucky ones but is intended to intimidate the larger populace. For the authorities, the unjust jailing of a few could keep a greater number under control. No one could say what "spiritual pollution" actually meant, or why what had been innocuous one day—disco dancing—became a punishable crime without warning. Leaders in Beijing issued orders, and everyone else was accustomed to following them, no matter how irrational. Disco dancing lost its taboo a few years later. The debate over spiritual pollution moved on to other targets.

After that evening, I worried that Shu might keep her distance from me, but she still had a smile when I saw her in the cafeteria. Shu pulled me aside again one day and whispered conspiratorially, "I want you to meet someone." I was automatically interested, having few chances to meet a Chinese woman who would go on a date with me. "You already know her," Shu added. I could not imagine whom she meant, and Shu would not tell me. She simply made me promise to come out again that Friday evening.

On Friday evening, I cycled to a small hotel twenty minutes from the university. When I walked in the hotel restaurant, I saw Shu and Wu sitting with a young woman. Her name was Ping, one of my students in the English class I had begun teaching two nights a week. I had not paid much attention to her in class. Now she smiled demurely, with dimples in her cheeks. I looked at her more carefully. She was small, with straight hair that fell to her waist. To my surprise, she was my age, twenty-five, though she could have passed for fourteen. I was aware of Shu and Wu watching the two of us closely, as though looking for sparks. I was looking for them myself. Ping praised me as a great teacher. Her words rang hollow, and I could tell she was saying so to be polite. Still, my mind lurched ahead. I asked where she lived. She had a one-room apartment at her place of work, which meant she did not live with her parents. "She has freedom to come and go," interjected Shu, meaning: she could invite a man over if she wished.

Soon I could sense that Ping was working up her courage to ask me something. She hesitated, as if afraid to ask so directly. I had to coax it out of her. Finally, her question came: "Can you change money?" I felt deflated. She wanted American dollars, in exchange for Chinese renminbi, or people's money. I looked at Shu, whose expression said nothing. Ping explained that she wanted to buy a cassette player, and the price would be 20 percent cheaper if she could pay in American currency. It was not the first time I had been asked to "change money." I had been learning that in China friends constantly did favors for each other. In a culture of scarcity, where obtaining basic consumer goods often required ingenuity and effort, friends had to rely on each other. Now I saw that Ping's flirtation had been a cover for her real interest. I felt a gulf between me and my three friends at the table. I was looking for romance, and they wanted hard currency.

Meeting women in China was difficult, a negotiation I did not understand. Most of the women I saw on the streets of Xi'an looked drab, wearing faded Mao suits over shapeless and sexless bodies, since displays of beauty or individuality were still frowned upon. Eyeglasses were uniformly ugly, with square plastic frames. Shoulder bags were all green canvas, army-issue. Wearing a colored ribbon in the hair was considered racy, as was wearing a skirt. People who dressed too well opened themselves to questioning or teasing by their peers or leaders.

Still, in every somber crowd, I noticed one or two women whose gaze lingered on mine. A few women showed me a faint smile or a friendly nod, hinting at their curiosity. The signs were subtle, yet they nourished me. I came to scan every crowd, on the lookout for a sign in a woman's eyes that she had noticed me. That faint connection, in a moment's glance as I passed a woman on the street, felt like a tiny heartbeat, an opening into a hidden world I could not yet see. Maybe those women were simply intrigued by the sight of a Westerner, though I wondered if something else in my face caught their attention. I felt tall and strong and distinctive-looking, compared with the Chinese men surrounding me. I liked being noticed. Yet I did not know how to progress from a friendly glance to a conversation. I was bewildered about the rules of conduct between the sexes. The landscape for romance, with Communist rules and restrictions still so strong, looked gray. All I had to go on were those hints of color, almost hidden in the little glances I gathered on the street.

Courting rituals in China still followed old-fashioned patterns. In a Chinese family, tradition dictated that parents made decisions about whom their children would marry. Financial and social considerations weighed heavily; a son's or daughter's wishes did not count for much. In the old society, a bride was carried to the wedding ceremony on a sedan chair, a silk veil over her face to be removed in the bridal chamber, the first time she and her husband would see each other. When romance bloomed outside prescribed boundaries, a young man and woman would be chided by family elders, who typically dismissed love as an impractical fantasy, provoking tears and arguments and sometimes suicide. Those who bristled under the control of their parents inevitably repeated the pattern when they became parents themselves.

When Mao Zedong and the Communists came to power in 1949, they criticized the old practices as a negation of individual will and proclaimed that comrades in a socialist state would make their own choices. But it was not easy to break old patterns. In some families, children continued to be fixed up by their parents. Some Communist officials even made matches themselves, intruding in the personal lives of those ranking below them "for the good of the Party." During the 1960s, many young city folk were exiled to the countryside and married comrades from the countryside, only to see the marriage founder when times changed and a move back to the city magnified cultural differences. By the time I got to Xi'an, some men and women chose their own mates, though many allowed their parents the power of a veto. Many more families continued to control the marriages of their sons and daughters, either to angle for money or social position or simply to exert control. Coupling outside of family approval required careful discretion.

One evening, I walked into the TV room of my dormitory building and saw a pretty young woman sitting alone watching the evening news. She was friendly, spoke English well, and made me laugh with a crack about the vapid nature of government news. She wore an attractive cotton jacket, tapered to her slender figure. Her hair was in pigtails, like that of many university students, but her eyes were lively and intelligent. Her skin was creamy and soft-looking, strikingly different from the raw, wind-burned skin on so many faces in Xi'an. Her name was Huang, a teacher of English at the university. I was smitten.

Huang was curious about all things American and asked me a lot of questions. In exchange, she explained many oddities of Chinese life in terms I could understand. She told me why Chinese people refuse a gift three times before accepting (no one wanted to seem too eager to want, in a culture of want) and why so many people I met asked if I would be their English teacher (a way to express respect, even if they had no expectation of ever seeing me again). Most people I met in Xi'an were cautious and polite in the presence of a Westerner. Huang seemed charmingly spontaneous. When she took me on a bicycle ride through the countryside one day, I looked over at her in the dusky sunlight, surrounded by golden wheat fields, and her hair seemed to take on an auburn sheen.

Huang and I fell into a daily routine of meeting outside my dormitory at lunchtime to walk together to the cafeteria, joining the parade of others. I tried to ignore Shu's stares when she saw us there, but I felt a little guilty, now that I had moved on to a new friend. Huang and I talked nonstop about books and movies and cultural habits, about everything. Our kinship felt natural. At times, she seemed to anticipate my thoughts. One afternoon when we sat together on an outdoor bench in a secluded area, I became intensely aware of our two bodies, close but not touching. I wanted to take her hand but sensed that the time was not right. Huang was drawn to me, but she kept a distance. She would not let me visit her dorm room, nor would she ever come to mine. We each had roommates and perhaps she feared gossip, or perhaps she was afraid of what might happen if we were alone together. When I asked her about past boyfriends, she deflected the question. I told myself to be patient. We have time, I thought.

Huang told me she grew up in a house full of books, the daughter of university professors. When the leftist frenzy of the 1960s closed all the schools, she stayed home and read. When entrance exams for university admission started again in 1978, Huang's parents fretted that it might be a one-time chance, that schools might be unpredictably closed down again. Even though Huang was only fifteen and ought to have waited two more years before taking the exam, her parents forced her to take it early. She passed but did not excel as she had hoped. She was assigned to a mediocre university in Xi'an. Her parents were satisfied that she would get any university education, but Huang was bitter at losing her shot at a top school like Beijing University, a stepping-stone to a good career. Now she felt stuck in a lousy city as an English teacher, looking for a way out. I fantasized about marrying her as a way to save her. "You have to plan your big decisions carefully," she said once, in counterpoint to her usual spontaneity. I wondered if I should try to become part of her plan.

We rode bicycles together, exploring Xi'an. We followed a path that circled the city wall, and Huang pointed out the places where its enormous gray bricks were crumbling, vandalized by poor residents. She took me sampling the street food outside the Big Goose Pagoda, watching my facial reaction to skewered lamb and crispy black balls of tofu. We parked our bicycles and walked down long tree-lined avenues. When we went to a restaurant, Huang would fight her way through the crowd around the window where orders were placed while I would secure two seats together at a large round table, often needing to shove and elbow my way forward. Department stores were all state-run in those days, uniformly dreary, poorly lighted, and ill-stocked. Years of Communist-induced scarcity seemed to have conditioned store clerks to answer *"mei you,"* meaning "there are none," no matter what was requested. One clerk answered *"mei you"* when I pointed at the jar of yogurt sitting in plain view on a shelf behind her. Huang showed me how polite persistence could wear down even the most stubborn saleswoman. When it came to buying a more precious commodity, like a bicycle or a train ticket, Huang explained that one needed to find a "back door," a secret connection. *Mei you* sometimes meant "not now, but maybe later if you try a back door."

One day in December, Huang disappeared. She did not come for lunch, and there was no answer when I knocked at her dorm room. When I went back the next day, a woman in a neighboring room said Huang had gone to Beijing, a day's train ride away. I felt strangely empty in Xi'an without Huang but told myself she'd probably be back in a few days. Days became weeks, and I did not hear from Huang before New Year, when I traveled to Beijing myself to visit American friends studying there. I spent days exploring the city, visiting the Forbidden City and the Great Wall. In outdoor crowds of Chinese faces, I sometimes wondered if I might see Huang. I knew we were in the same city but did not know how close or far apart. One evening I returned to the guest house where I was staying to be told that Huang had come looking for me. I was touched that she had gone to some effort to find me. But I felt intensely frustrated, missing her by a few hours, stymied by the strangeness of a land with few telephones, with habits of friendship I did not yet understand. When I returned to Xi'an a week later, I found a short letter Huang had slipped inside my desk, so that no one else would see it. She wrote that she had been accepted at a university in California and had left immediately to study there. "I got married," she also wrote. Three words. They opened another mansion-sized mystery in my mind.

A friend of Huang's told me that Huang's family had pressured her to marry a man from a military family in Beijing with privilege and access. Huang wanted a chance to study in America, and she knew she had a better chance of getting an exit visa if she were married, not single, on the theory that going to America while her husband stayed behind would give her an incentive to return. She agreed to marry so that she could go to America alone.

Many Chinese students plotting an escape overseas kept their plans secret, knowing that jealousy and competition among fellow students could prompt a classmate to inform on him or her, even if it meant fabricating a story. Maybe that was why Huang was so secretive, I thought. Yet I was hurt that she had not confided in me. She had been laying out this plan over the months I was getting to know her. Maybe she was unsure if it would go through. Maybe she was ashamed to be taking part in an arranged marriage. There seemed to be so much about China I did not yet understand. And now Huang was gone, so I had no one to ask.

chapter two

ENCOUNTERS WITH THE POLICE

One chilly winter night, I boarded a train bound for Kaifeng, an old city in central China. I climbed into a third-class car. It was dimly lighted and humid and overflowing with farmers who smelled like damp soil and sour garlic. All seats were taken, and there was little standing room. I squeezed into a spot in the aisle where I could at least hold on to the corner of a hard wooden seatback. When the train jerked forward, I fell back against an old woman, who looked up in horror at me. Other passengers stared as though I were an animal in the zoo. I tried to strike up a conversation with a man in a gray Mao jacket, but he gazed back in silence. After thirty minutes, I was miserable. I could not see how I would survive an overnight trip, eight hours long, standing. A plump man sitting near me must have seen the look on my face, and he leaned forward to suggest I try the dining car. After mealtime, he said, the staff in the dining car sometimes let passengers ride there, for a small fee. I took his advice, pushing my way through several long third-class cars, each one as crowded as the last. When I arrived at the dining car, I saw a handful of passengers scattered between a dozen little tables with white plastic tablecloths. It was bright and clean. A train attendant in a blue uniform told me it cost $1.20 for a seat, which seemed a bargain. I got my own table. The light overhead allowed me to read. I opened *A Farewell to Arms,* Hemingway's tale of war and romance in Europe. The story seemed distant and thin compared with the rich scenery of China passing outside the train windows.

Restless, I strolled to the far end of the dining car, where a man in a dark blue business suit sat alone. He had a large, square face with a strong jaw and deep-set eyes and a pug nose. A handkerchief peeked out of his breast pocket. He nodded in greeting and invited me to sit down. His name was Wu. He pushed a cigarette toward me. Chinese men all seemed to smoke in those days, and after a few months in China I was smoking, too. Wu told me he was heading home to Guangzhou, a city in the south, near Hong Kong. He worked for a trading company in Xi'an but hated the city. Xi'an's people were crude and its food inedible, he said. He asked how I could stand it. I told him it was the only place in China I had been. Wu laughed.

"Pathetic," he said. "You must come to Guangzhou."

Wu turned to the train attendant, who was watching us talk, and asked him to bring two beers. "We're off duty," the attendant said. I assumed off duty meant off duty. But Wu cajoled the attendant, saying that just two bottles would be harmless, saying it would be rude to deny the foreigner, saying it was such a long train ride, saying whatever he could think of until the attendant finally gave in. We got the beer. It was cold and refreshing, and our conversation grew more lively. Wu asked what I thought of Chinese women. I told him I found them attractive, but that few would talk to me. "They don't dare," Wu said. "You're a foreigner."

Wu said he would never touch a woman in Xi'an because they were mostly cultureless bumpkins. Women in Beijing or Guangzhou were more appealing, he insisted. "At least they know how to dress." Wu made me laugh, and doing so seemed to release some of my frustration in Xi'an: the difficulty of buying anything, the struggle of learning Chinese, the slow pace of daily life. The cold beer and relaxed conversation, after my distress in third class, made me feel anything was possible. I looked at Wu as a new friend, someone I could get to know in Xi'an. When he suggested that we trade addresses and phone numbers, I agreed. We vowed to meet up in Xi'an someday and go out for a meal.

It got late. I went back to my seat at the other end of the dining car. I nodded goodnight to Wu, who was smoking another cigarette. Then I took a cue from other passengers and leaned forward to rest my head on my arms, crossed against the tabletop. It was not easy to sleep, but after a while I began to doze.

I woke to a firm tap on my shoulder. I looked up, groggy. A police officer in a green uniform was standing before me. He told me to follow him. I assumed he was going to offer me a sleeper in first class, since foreigners were treated with privilege in those days, not expected to endure the indignities of the masses. I followed the officer through another train car before he showed me into a tiny compartment with a small table and two stools. He asked me to sit. He closed the door and sat down himself. His face was about ten inches from mine.

"So, you speak Chinese pretty well," he said.

I felt annoyed. Had he awakened me to make conversation?

"So, you act pretty friendly," he continued.

I looked down and saw that he held Wu's ID card in his hand, slapping it against his thigh like a coveted possession. My sleepy head started clearing rapidly.

"Why don't you show me that piece of paper he gave you?" the officer asked.

I looked him in the eye. I felt like I was looking at Big Brother. Wu's address, a scribble on a scrap of paper, was my own coveted possession. I almost said I had lost it. But doing so might get Wu in deeper trouble, since I would be denying possession of something the officer could find in my pocket easily. I tried to make light of it, saying I often exchanged addresses with people I met, and that refusing to do so would be impolite. I pulled the slip of paper from my pocket and handed it to him, saying again that it meant little. But inside, I felt as though I was giving in.

"Did he give you anything else?" the officer asked.

"No," I said, pretending to conscientiously search my pockets, to appear cooperative. "Are you sure?" the officer asked firmly. Yes, I was sure. He looked over the address, checking against the one on Wu's ID card. I watched him in silence. The interrogation infuriated me. Did he really think Wu and I were conspiring against the Chinese state? Or was this just his power game, enjoying his ability to wield authority? This officer looked young, not yet thirty years old, but he acted confident. He held the confiscated slips of paper like little pieces of treasure that could be turned in for a reward. He looked me in the eye again and smiled. I felt ill.

"Why do you want this slip of paper?" I asked. He took a moment to respond.

"You're a foreign student, right?" he asked back. "You meet students at your school and make friends, right?" I nodded. "That's permitted. But when you are traveling, you must be careful. You don't know these people." He motioned toward the dining car. "It is best not to be concerned with them." He looked at me sternly, the smile gone from his face. "Don't concern yourself with them." Then the smile came back. "You understand, don't you?"

I recognized the officer's tone. It was the same tone I heard from Chinese officials at my university when they rejected my request for a more flexible class schedule, or from the clerk in a department store where I asked for a larger size undershirt. It was the tone of authority, a firm, bland, unforgiving tone. It pretended to know what was best for everyone, it demanded compliance, and it knew that most people would quickly succumb, trained for centuries not to challenge authority. The tall strand of grass gets lopped off. I wanted to have the courage, or the recklessness, to challenge this officer. But I did not. I succumbed, just like the other passengers on the train. That decision burned inside me.

"What if I kept this address, and called this man in Xi'an?" I asked. "What is the harm?"

The officer's smile disappeared again.

"China needs stability," he said. "It is best if you have no contact."

He showed me back to the dining car. As I took my seat, I saw Wu at the far end. He raised his eyebrows, as if to say, What can you do? I wanted to go talk with him, to compare notes from our respective interrogations, but feared I had already caused enough damage. I sat down to try to sleep but could not. I felt violated, sad to have lost a friend I had not yet really made.

China needs stability. The phrase echoed in my mind. I latched on to it, rolled it over, played it back again and again. China needs stability, so we will decide who you can make friends with. We will decide where you can go and what you can say. During my time in Xi'an, I had heard many people say that China was not ready for democracy because "China needs stability." People said it so often, it almost sounded logical. It was a line the authorities drummed into everyone's head, a clever bit of manipulation, playing on people's fear of change by stressing the need for stability. After decades of civil war and political turmoil, many Chinese people had an understandable anxiety about change, and instead desired political continuity. Countless Chinese people expressed a mystical-sounding fear of *luan,* or chaos, often saying that a non-Chinese could not possibly understand. China needs stability.

I came to see what a hollow mantra it was. Of course China needed stability. However, the Communist Party had provided almost no stability, with unending political turmoil, economic devastation, and a famine that killed more than twenty million people. So why did everyone accept that line, China needs stability? The Confucian ethic, where seniority and rank outweigh reason, and Communist rule, so brutal and dehumanizing, taught people to keep their heads down. At times I wondered if it made a nation of cowards, unwilling to stand up on matters of principle. Why didn't anyone have the guts to say no?

The truth was, I could understand those cowardly habits of mind because I had them myself. I feared confrontation. I usually felt more comfortable at the rear of a crowd than at the front. I often noticed the way most Chinese people went to some length to avoid conflict, and I aspired to do the same myself. In many circumstances, I liked that element of Chinese culture. In others, where the authorities were unreasonable or unjust, I resented that willingness to bend. When I recognized it in myself, as I had on the train, I felt defeated by it.

When I got back to Xi'an and told a friend named Gao about my interrogation, he clucked his disapproval. Gao was a university professor whose balding head and thick glasses gave him the look of a scholar, and he often assumed the air of a know-it-all. He had firm ideas about right and wrong even if, true to his Chinese heritage, he would bend when confronted by authority. For me, Gao took on a role of chief explainer of Chinese culture, often delivering lectures over an evening cup of tea in the one-room apartment he shared with his wife, near my dormitory.

"It's about power," Gao said. He suggested I try to look at the incident through the prism of the work unit, or *dan wei,* a basic building block of life in Communist China, set up after the revolution in 1949 and modeled on the system of the Soviet Union. Gao taught in the geography department, where his life was controlled by his department head, the chief of his *dan wei.* Gao's job, his housing, his vacation, even his plans to have a child were in the hands of his boss. Even though Gao and his wife agreed to comply with China's one-child policy, they had to get permission from Gao's boss in order to get pregnant. Gao's boss monitored the menstrual cycles of Gao's wife and other women in the *dan wei,* keeping a chart posted on the wall of the department's family-planning office, like other bosses all over China. Every urban resident in China was assigned to a *dan wei.* In theory, it gave the Communist authorities an efficient way to provide employment, housing, and health care to its citizens. In practice, the *dan wei* system offered mediocre care but excellent control over political dissent and social disorder. It also gave *dan wei* chiefs an unlimited scope for meddling in the private lives of their employees.

Gao told me about the time he got in a fistfight in a restaurant over who was first in line for a table. When the police came to break it up, the first question they asked was, What is your *dan wei*? Gao tried to slink away without telling, but the officer insisted. Gao showed his identification card, and the police copied down his name and his work unit. Within a week, Gao's *dan wei* chief summoned him to talk about the incident. It was not serious enough to earn any punishment, just a potential demerit. Gao's chief lorded it over him with subtlety, like a poker chip that could be cashed in at a later date. Gao wanted a transfer to the history department at his university, and he knew that the file at his *dan wei* contained a record of the incident in the restaurant. His chief could cite it as an excuse to block the transfer or to extract a "present" from Gao. "If you have a lousy chief, you're in big trouble," Gao said. It all depended on one's *dan wei*.

To outsiders, China often looks like a monolithic police state. The ruthless way the authorities stamp out political dissent suggests a large well-oiled machine, able to locate and execute anyone at will. The network of *dan wei,* together with the culture of obeying authority, gives the police efficient tools to monitor people's behavior. Yet all those chains of authority are composed of human beings. When an order comes from above, it has to be carried out by a flesh-and-blood man or woman. Individual officers have no choice but to follow instructions, but that does not mean they agree. Behind the stern-looking faces of police officers in the street, so hard and emotionless, stand human beings with hopes and fears like everyone else. During my time in Xi'an, I had not imagined having a real conversation with anyone in the police, a secret part of Chinese society. But then I met an officer who was quite human.

At a dumpling house near Xi'an's city wall, a place I frequented for its tasty, greasy pot-stickers, I fell into conversation with a man named Lu. He was just five feet tall and given to drinking beer in large plastic mugs. He complained that no woman would have him because he was too short. I saw Lu at the dumpling house several times, and we often shared a beer. One night he said he wanted me to meet someone. He would not say whom, but suggested I follow him on my bicycle. We rode together down Liberation Street, the main thoroughfare in Xi'an, turned down a small backstreet, then turned again into an alleyway so narrow that I had to follow Lu single file. We went past a row of gray brick homes with roofs sloping down so low and close together that I was afraid my shoulder might catch on one as we rode by. It was dark, and only a few homes had lights over their doorways. Stacks of cabbage stood in tall piles outside each door. Lu eventually slowed and hopped off his bicycle. I followed. He turned to me and placed a finger over his lips to signal silence, lest we attract the attention of neighbors. There may not have been any rule banning a foreigner from visiting one's home, but there was no need to draw notice.

A bamboo curtain shielded the doorway. Lu pushed it aside and stepped in without knocking. Inside, his friend stood to greet us. A tall and strong man, he had a tired but friendly face, lined lightly with wrinkles. His name was Wang. His wife nodded hello from a small kitchen, where she was cooking in a wok over a single flame. I could see pots piled high in the stone sink, under a single faucet. It was a one-and-a-half-room dwelling. A double bed was pushed against a wall, with a coarse bedsheet and a thick cotton blanket folded into a square, so that the bed could serve as a couch during the day. Wang insisted that Lu and I sit in the room's only two chairs, and he took a small stool for himself. Wang's daughter, who was eighteen months old, waddled around in thick cotton clothing, slit open at the crotch so that she could relieve herself on the clay floor. One of the walls was crumbling, patched over in several places with cardboard and newspaper.

Wang wore a white shirt, open at the collar, and olive green trousers with a single red stripe on the outside of each pant leg, worn by police officers. As I glanced around, I saw a police jacket hanging on the back of the front door. Wang was a police officer. "You're not afraid?" he asked. "No, no, no," I said, concerned that my face was flushed. I had never spoken to a police officer in China, and I was indeed afraid. Yet Wang seemed friendly, and he was also curious. At first, he asked simple questions: Why had I come to China? Did I like Chinese food? Were chopsticks a problem? He soon moved to questions he seemed more interested in: Does everyone in America really have a car? Are there really gunfights in city streets every day? Were drugs available on every street corner? Do black people all live in poverty? He listened intently to my answers and, unlike most people I spoke with in China, seemed to appreciate my efforts to describe American life in an honest way that took account of its flaws, including its racism. "Black people in America are probably treated like minorities are in China," Wang observed. I knew that China's Muslim, Tibetan, and Mongolian citizens faced discrimination, even though Chinese usually insisted that everyone in China was treated the same, no matter their race. When I discussed America with Chinese people, they seemed to assume that black Americans were mostly criminals. Wang was an exception.

Wang's wife served us a meal of braised tofu, sautéed spinach, roasted peanuts, rice, and flatbread. Wang apologized for the modest meal, a show of humility meant to imply that an honored guest deserves better. But after the slop I had been eating at the university cafeteria, this meal was delicious. Wang's wife did not sit with us, but instead sat on the corner of the bed and picked up her knitting. The baby daughter waddled back and forth from parent to parent. Wang rose at one point and went out with an empty thermos, full of beer when he returned a few minutes later. He showed me a custom by looking me in the eye and holding out his beer glass in a silent toast before taking a slug. When he wanted to take a drink, everyone had to join him.

After dinner, as we sipped tea, Wang spoke openly of China's shortcomings. "Our country is trying to reform now, but it was badly damaged from so many years of political upheaval," he said. "Our living standards are still so low." He gestured at the crumbling wall of his living room. "We were told for years that socialism would bring us prosperity. But what really happened? There was one political campaign after another." Leaders accused each other of wrongdoing, scrapping for power, he said, while the nation stagnated. Poverty was justified as morally superior to capitalism. Wang snorted his disapproval. His voice started to rise as he recounted Mao's notion, put forth when Wang was a child in the 1950s, that China would surpass Great Britain in fifteen years. Instead, radical politics drove China further into poverty and ignorance. One-party politics was to blame, Wang argued, because it eliminated public participation. "The Communist Party only represents itself!" His face grew red and he banged his fist on the small table, rattling the leftover dinner dishes. His wife stopped knitting and looked at him. Wang took a breath. Then he told me his story, a story of the Cultural Revolution.

It started with Mao Zedong, who led the Communist army to victory in 1949. Mao was a brilliant campaigner and a terrible administrator. He preferred bold, sweeping actions to the details of governing. His plan for mass industrialization in the 1950s failed so miserably that it provoked a famine. Mao was humiliated, and his lieutenants forced him to share power with moderates, including a commander named Deng Xiaoping, who was more of a pragmatist. Mao grumbled that revolutionary energy was being sapped by China's bureaucracy. In 1966, when infighting heated up between radicals and moderates, Mao saw his moment and launched a campaign based on the ideal of radical egalitarianism. Mao called it the Cultural Revolution, though it was not cultural at all. It was a time of political frenzy. Every workplace was ordered to abolish ranks and to expose "rightists." Hospitals expelled doctors, and surgery was performed by orderlies, who wound up maiming and often killing vulnerable patients. Factories shut down, and workers held political meetings instead of working. Schools and universities were closed. Students formed bands of Red Guards who destroyed homes and offices and temples, burning books and historic relics. More than a million people died in the turmoil. Mao was worshiped like a God, and he ousted his moderate rivals, including Deng and Liu Shaoqi, China's president, who was later found dead in a closet where he had been locked, languishing in his own excrement. Mao's writings were printed in small red books that were memorized like religious gospel. All over China, people were ordered to act selflessly for the greater glory of Chairman Mao. A headline in the *People's Daily* summed up the mood in 1966: "Great Chaos Everywhere, the Situation Is Excellent."

Once the Red Guards outlived their usefulness, Mao called on the People's Liberation Army to restore order in cities. Millions of teenagers were sent to the countryside to "learn from the peasants," whether they had participated in the mayhem or not, and Wang was sent to a rural part of Shaanxi Province, about two hundred miles north of Xi'an. At first, Wang resented having to live in a shack with several other teenagers, without heat or hot water. Yet he also found an unexpected freedom, living away from family and school, hanging out with people his own age all day long.

One of the other boys in his group, who was sixteen years old, liked to ride a cow in the field. It irritated the local commune leader, who told the boy not to do so. The boy obeyed for a time, but then took to riding the cow again when he thought the commune leader was not around. But the leader noticed and was angry at being ignored. He came to call with a knife in his hand. The boy thought he was bluffing. They scuffled, and the leader knifed the boy in the gut. There was no way to get to a hospital, so the boy bled to death. The commune leader filed a report to his superior, giving his own guilt-free version of events. The commune leader went unprosecuted, untarnished. Wang and three other boys tried to protest. They got nowhere. As long as a political leader was protected by a superior, he literally could get away with murder.

By the time Wang returned to Xi'an, after five years in the countryside, he had missed years of schooling. He took a university exam but failed to make the top five percent, which was required for enrollment. He was assigned to a job with the police and had been there for six years. He spent most days in an office, copying forms in triplicate, effectively a clerk. Now thirty-four, he was stuck in a bureaucratic system with little chance to shift jobs. To Wang, the Communist Party structure operated on a simple hierarchy: "Connections first, subservience second, merit third." I asked about the court system. Wang said many of those arrested for serious crimes were "tried" and executed within a week of their arrest. Most were guilty, he guessed, but some were not.

"At least I have a family," Wang said, lifting his daughter off her feet and swinging her overhead before placing her on his lap. His wife looked up from the cutting board, smiling faintly. Wang stood and put on his policeman's jacket, saying he had to go out. His mother was ill, he explained, and he had to ride a bicycle across town to see that she got to bed all right. It would take him about an hour to ride there and an hour to ride back. "I must go, but I leave you with my wife and my good friend," he said by way of good-bye. Lu and I shared another cup of tea, but said little.

When I saw Lu at the dumpling house, I asked him to take me to see Wang again. *"Bu fang bian,"* Lu said. Not convenient. I had heard this phrase often. It was a conversation stopper. It could mean anything from "I don't feel like taking you there," to "He told me never to bring you by again," or even "He's being investigated for having a foreigner in his house and he's in big trouble." Maddeningly vague, it threw a blanket of secrecy over the matter at hand. I tried to ask Lu the reason, but he changed the subject. I was tempted to try to find Wang's home on my own, but doubted I would be able to find my way through the maze of back alleys.

I never saw Wang again, but I often thought of him when I heard people generalize about the evil nature of China's police. Years later, as a reporter, I saw plenty of evidence of the brutality of China's criminal justice system, with its callous disregard for human life. The system perpetrated it. The culture condoned it. The despotic power accorded to the chief of a *dan wei* allowed it to thrive. Yet individuals, policemen like Wang, hated it.

Wang's story about the Cultural Revolution lingered in my mind. When I met people on long train rides with idle time for conversation, I often asked how their families fared during the Cultural Revolution. Many of them deflected the question, mouthing the new Party line that leftist extremism had been a mistake and that reforms were putting the nation back on track. To ordinary Chinese people, even a nationwide political movement was to be kept secret from outsiders.

Every once in a while, however, I encountered someone who would talk. Maybe they responded to my gentle, indirect way of posing questions. Perhaps I caught them in the right mood. The stories, once they started, were gripping. A schoolteacher told me how his father, a printer, was sent to the countryside for questioning his boss's judgment on how many pamphlets to print. With little money, his mother starved herself to make sure her three children could eat. When she caught a cold, she died. The boss was promoted. "That was the Cultural Revolution," he said. I met a university instructor who admitted she had enjoyed the power she wielded as the leader of a faction of the Red Guard and regretted her use of it. She once led an attack on the home of a classmate she did not like. "I told everyone that her father was a reactionary," the instructor said. "I didn't have any evidence. I made it up." The Red Guards broke into the girl's apartment, smashing antiques, tearing down bookshelves, and burning the books in a bonfire. "That is a crime that I will always carry with me," she said.

The scars of the Cultural Revolution were still fresh. I tried to think of a political movement in America that was comparable to the Cultural Revolution, but McCarthyism looked like a day at the playground next to what had happened in China. I sometimes asked people why so many had gone along with it. It was a question no one answered well. Some said they had been swept up in the excitement and had truly believed in the religion of Mao. Others said they had been forced, with no choice but to go along. I sensed that the real answer lay somewhere in the mix of Chinese idiosyncrasies: the Confucian tradition of obeying authority, the vulnerability to following the crowd, the Communist expertise at political control.

Still, most days I felt a sense of wonder of living in China. I rose each morning savoring the utter unpredictability of my coming day, not knowing who I would meet and what stories I would hear. As I grew better able to speak Chinese, I collected tales more easily. I also became addicted to spending hours at my desk each day studying classical Chinese, enchanted by ancient poetry that wove vivid images into a remarkably concise line of Chinese characters. The more I knew about Chinese language and culture, the more Chinese people seemed to appreciate me. I yearned for their pats on the back, their recognitions. When my first year in China came to a close, I signed up for a second.

chapter three

OLD MAN YANG

Sauntering through an art museum one afternoon, I noticed a short woman with an oval face. She wore a maroon scarf sprinkled with glitter, a risqué item of clothing in China in 1985. I sidled up next to her as she looked at a painting and asked what she thought. "No good," she said, glancing at me and walking away. I watched her go, to see if she would look back over her shoulder. She did. I followed her. We looked at several more paintings, easing into conversation. I kept it going as we exited the museum together, then asked her casually if she would accompany me to a noodle shop. She agreed. When we took seats at a small wooden table, other customers stared, examining a woman willing to sit alone with a big nose. She did not look at them directly, but the staring bothered her. *"Bu wenming,"* she said. Uncivilized.

Her name was Li. She had a bowl haircut, fleshy cheeks, and narrow eyes, and was small, about a foot shorter than I. She walked in short steps, like a Japanese woman. Sitting in the noodle shop, she gave me long, knowing glances that suggested an open mind. She displayed none of the opportunism I smelled in many of the women who befriended me, looking for foreign currency or access to an American passport. I got the sense that she was curious about the Other. She wanted to know what a white guy smelled like. Maybe she wanted a taste of the forbidden. I certainly did.

Now in my second year in China, I was learning to navigate. Traveling often, I got the hang of how to wangle train tickets, how to chat up restaurant staff for a seat in an overcrowded dining room, how to talk my way into a room in a "full" Chinese hotel. My hard work at learning Chinese was paying off, making it easier to befriend people who would help me see behind the thick curtains of Chinese society, to understand how things really worked. Yet I was still having trouble getting close to a woman.

Toward the end of our first meeting, Li started to ask me a question but hesitated. I prodded her. Finally she asked, "What is your blood type?" I thought I had misheard her. My blood type? Did she want me to donate some blood? I told her I thought my type was A but was not really sure. She smiled. I asked why she wanted to know. She smiled demurely. I pressed her. Finally she told me that in China, when men and women look for a mate, one of the main criteria is blood type, seen as reflecting a person's character. Asking one's blood type was the Chinese equivalent of asking one's astrological sign. Type A blood was preferred, considered a sign of strong character. Type B was second best, type AB was mediocre, and type

O was considered the worst. I laughed out loud as she explained the system. She looked at me as though I was doubting the existence of Santa Claus.

Li worked in China's aviation bureaucracy, assigned a job she had no say in, like everyone else in those days. On her first day at work, she was given a desk and some stationery, but nothing to do. Office mates spent the day reading a newspaper, drinking tea, and chatting. After a week, bored, Li brought a book to work. Her boss noticed and took her aside to say it was not proper. Reading the newspaper was acceptable, he said, but a book suggested that she was not working. She pointed out that she had not been given any work. Be patient, he replied. When I met her, Li had been there three years. She had not yet been given anything to do.

Li and I got together regularly, going for walks in a park, visiting museums, eating in noodle shops. Whenever Li wanted time off from work, she simply told her boss, *"Wo you shi,"* or, "I have a thing." In practice, it meant "I have a personal matter," the equivalent of suggesting a doctor's appointment or a family emergency. No further explanation was needed. Li did not have to lie that her mother was sick or say anything else. She would tell her boss, "I have a thing," and he would nod sympathetically. I was impressed how easily she could skip out on work. Whenever I proposed meeting for an afternoon or even a whole day, Li could be sure to get the time.

One afternoon as we strolled in a park, I asked Li about this magic phrase. Was there some deeper allusion I wasn't grasping? Some story from ancient Chinese history that would explain it? Li thought about it, then said that "I have a thing" was deliberately vague. In a politically sensitive society, there was a premium on vagueness. It had become a socially acceptable way to excuse oneself, from a day at work, from an uncomfortable date, from almost anything. Even in ordinary conversation among friends, "I have a thing" was employed all the time. In reality, it could mean anything from "I have an errand to run," to "I'm busy," to "I feel like going home," to "I'm going off to see my foreign boyfriend." In a culture of overpopulation and poverty, where people live in close quarters, there is an extra need for private space. If it is unattainable physically, it is hoarded mentally. I often imagined my Chinese friends with hidden compartments in their minds, keeping parts of their lives secret from those closest to them.

Whenever Li met me in the daytime, I asked her what she had said to her boss. I knew the answer but always laughed when she told me, "I have a thing." I repeated it back to her over and over, playing with the uncountable number of different meanings. The day came when Li turned down my suggestion that we meet the following evening. "I have a thing," she said. I looked her in the eye. She was not being sarcastic; she was serious. I could not resist asking, what thing? Li looked at me as if I had asked her weight. "You don't ask that question," she said curtly. No justification, no explanation. She would not even hint at it. The wall went up.

It came down again, soon enough. A week later, Li took me for a meal in a restaurant that closed, as most did in those days, by 8 P.M. Then she led me to a park where several couples snuggled closely on benches in a dark, secluded area. It was winter, and the night air was chilly. But when we sat down on a park bench, Li leaned up against me. I felt nervous and vulnerable, sitting in plain view. Li told me to relax. The only people around us were all doing the same thing. She took my hand and guided it inside her overcoat.

After a few trips to that park, Li and I needed a place to go, a place with four walls. She lived with her parents, so that wouldn't work. I lived in a dorm watched by a doorman, so that was out, too. Li had a friend with an apartment that was vacant during the day; maybe her friend would give us the key for an afternoon. The friend agreed at first, but when Li mentioned that I was a foreigner, the friend rescinded the offer. We were stuck. We were going to have to be daring. I began to scrutinize the dormitory where I lived.

The dorm had a little room just to the left of the entrance, where a little man was posted twenty-four hours a day. It was called the *chuan da shi,* or communications room. It was where announcements were posted, mail was delivered, and the building's one telephone was located. In theory, this little room was where the school authorities communicated with the dorm residents. In practice, it was a guard station. The little man was a guard. The rule was that any Chinese visitor had to stop in the communications room and sign in. The police checked the list once a week and made a note of anyone who came too often. What was too often? No one could say. When a brave friend of mine was signing in, the little man hinted to him that too many visits to a foreigner could be bad for one's career. The little man was a local version of Big Brother. He was the dirty, ill-cut fingernail at the end of the long arm of the state. Sometimes I saw him as evil. But mostly I saw him for what he was, a Chinese man with a job to do. I could fight him, or I could work with him.

We called him Old Yang. He had a white crew cut and a puffy, bloated face that made his eyes look like slits, so narrow I sometimes wondered if he could see out of them. Yang was in his late fifties, but looked twenty years older than that. He was crusty in the morning, often mumbling at low volume. Since I could not stomach the cold noodles and vinegar served at breakfast in the cafeteria, my morning ritual involved buying a cake the size of a hockey puck at a corner store and bringing it back to the communications room to have with a cup of instant coffee and powdered milk. I would chat with Yang, if his mood allowed. It was good practice for my Chinese, speaking with a grizzled old man who mumbled. I grew to like Yang. I laughed at the way he mimicked the constant bowing and stiff walking style of the Japanese students in the dorm. Sometimes I filled Yang's thermos at the hot water pump, since his bad knee did not like the stairs.

As I got more friendly with him, Yang told me pieces of his story. He had been a soldier in the Korean War. At first, Yang talked about being a patriotic soldier, humble and committed, fighting the good fight against treacherous Americans. As I got to know him better, Yang's descriptions of the war began to change. He complained about having to risk his life, being ill-prepared, trudging hundreds of miles in grass slippers, even in winter. Yang pointed out that he began adulthood by fighting Americans and was ending it by guarding them. "Life's a fart," he often said.

Yang often pretended to stare absentmindedly out the window while he was actually eavesdropping on telephone calls. A couple of times, he recited back to me the time and place I had arranged to meet a friend the week before, surprising me with his memory. I don't know if he passed on that kind of information to the police, but I assumed that he did. He didn't know English, so he couldn't understand what I said when I called my family in New York on Christmas Eve. But he could tell without asking how far from home I felt when I hung up the phone. He put his hand on my shoulder, telling me that he was away from home for three years during the war without a chance to communicate with his family. "At least you have the telephone," he said.

I was not sure how much I could trust Yang, but he knew me well enough to consider doing me a favor, the currency of friendships in

China. One morning when I sat alone with Yang in the communications room, I told him a story, sketching a hypothetical situation where a man watching a door turned his back for a moment, when it was necessary. Whether or not anyone passed in or out of the door at that moment, he did not know. But he could honestly say that he had not seen anyone inappropriate pass through the door. "How did he know when to turn his back?" Yang asked. "He just knew," I said. "Someone suggested that he look out the window." "OK," Yang said. I thought I saw him wink, though it was so fast I was not sure. I was afraid to ask too directly, afraid he would say no.

Li was skeptical when I explained the situation. "How do you know he won't tell the police?" she asked. I didn't know. I couldn't say what could happen to Li if we were caught. She guessed that her *dan wei* chief would criticize her, but it would not be the end of the world. She would not lose her job. But I could not evaluate the risk rationally. I wanted to get Li inside my room. She was willing, so I thought it worth taking a chance.

It was about 8 P.M. when Li and I approached my dorm building. She was anxious but excited by the risk. She waited outside. I sucked in my stomach and walked into the communications room. Yang was alone. "It's time," I said. Yang looked quizzical. "Time to look out the window," I said. He looked at me as though he had no idea what I was talking about. "Go ahead," I said. "Look out the window." "What's out the window?" Yang asked, sounding innocent. And then he turned to look, as though he expected to see an elephant standing out there. I stepped back outside and motioned to Li. She darted past Yang's door while he was still gazing out the window into the darkness. "What's out the window?" he asked again. "Nothing," I said. "Nothing at all."

During our time together, Li sometimes observed that I was in

China "temporarily," an indirect way of inviting me to talk about whether we had a future. I usually responded that I did not know how long I would be around. When summer came, I felt simultaneously relieved and sorry that the school year was ending. It was time for me to move on. I had achieved my goal of learning to speak and read Chinese, and had enjoyed the romantic innocence of my time as a student in Xi'an, but I felt ready to find a job. I was not sure where or how to find one and had made no plans, but I knew I wanted to stay in Asia. I did not know what to say to Li. When she asked what I was going to do, I simply said I didn't know. She had noticed that I seemed to love writing in a journal, "You need a job writing," she said.

chapter four

THE HONG KONG STANDARD

After two years in China, I visited Hong Kong to ponder my next step. Hong Kong looked like a shiny jewel to me. I was mesmerized by the efficient bustle of urban streets, brimming with British executives in pinstriped suits and Cantonese women in miniskirts. After the draining poverty and slow pace of rural China, I felt enlivened simply by walking into the lobby of the sumptuous Mandarin Hotel. I consumed countless newspapers and magazines, having lived without them for two years. I delighted in seeing American movies in a theater with soft, cushy seats and an operatic sound system. I relished the anonymity of walking down a street without being stared at, since there were plenty of Westerners around. I was enchanted by the Star Ferry and rode back and forth across Hong Kong harbor for two cents a ride, smelling the salt air and gazing at the lighted skyscrapers and neon advertisements in bright Chinese characters, set against the steep hill called Victoria Peak.

I was taken by the idea of finding a job in Hong Kong, an escape from the harshness of life in China. I made a few halfhearted attempts to look for work with American companies that did business in China, but I was not really interested in buying and selling. When people asked what did interest me, my mind went blank.

A friend who worked for the *Wall Street Journal,* Adi Ignatius, suggested I try journalism. I was fascinated by newspapers, having grown up in a home that worshiped the *New York Times.* I liked writing but felt timid about the notion of working as a journalist myself. The all-knowing tone of newspaper articles intimidated me. How could I possibly ever know enough to write that way? Adi assured me that lesser minds than mine had succeeded in journalism. The most important tools for a journalist, he suggested, were common sense and energy. An ability to write came in handy, too. I felt confident in those areas. But how was I going to get a job? I had no experience and no clips, no printed examples of my writing. "Lie," Adi said. "It's Hong Kong. Everyone lies."

I cooked up a fictional resume and with it got an interview at the Hong Kong *Standard,* an English-language newspaper. It was not a particularly impressive place. The managing editor, Henry Parwani, had sleepy, dark eyes and a vague, lackadaisical manner. His tie was stained with coffee, and a breakfast crumb was positioned inexplicably on his collar. He asked me a few questions but did not seem to be listening to my answers. He noisily sucked his teeth and kept gazing out the window, lost in thought. Things were disorganized at the *Standard,* as I could see from the front page, with its incomprehensible headlines and grammatical errors.

Parwani, the second-ranking editor, seemed barely competent. But I will always be grateful to Henry Parwani. He gave me my start in journalism.

Parwani walked me through the newsroom, past rows of messy desks strewn with Chinese- and English-language newspapers, where a mix of Chinese and Western reporters and editors worked idly on clunky black telephones and cheap-looking computers. A yellowed sign hung on the wall: READ YOUR STORY AGAIN. IS IT FAIR? IS IT ACCURATE? Parwani introduced me to the news editor, a Canadian named Brian Power. He had a bewildered look but was friendly. He parked me at a vacant desk. I was a reporter.

I did not have the first idea what to do. I picked up a Chinese-language newspaper and glanced at it, noisily turning the pages and hoping that someone would notice that I could read Chinese. I picked up the telephone and called the three people I knew in Hong Kong, to make it look like I was working. I wondered if I was making a big mistake, trying a job in journalism, at which I had no experience, in a city I scarcely knew. Having faked my way into the *Standard,* I worried that I would somehow be exposed. A real reporter would know what to do, leaping in with energy, to make a good first impression. Was I expected to produce an article on my first day? I had no idea. To ask anyone would reveal me as an imposter.

Soon a desk editor tapped on my shoulder and asked what I was doing. "Just calling around," I said weakly. He handed me a sheet of paper, mumbling that there might be a story in it. A travel agent was offering a promotional airfare, a $99 ticket for a flight from Hong Kong to Los Angeles. I called and set up an interview. At the end of the day, I wrote a story. It was not much, as news goes. But then, neither was most of what was printed in the *Standard* every day. The next morning I eagerly opened a copy of the paper. There was my story, printed on page 3. I can do this, I thought.

I found a small apartment on the sixth floor of a narrow tenement with no elevator. The bedroom was tiny, the kitchen was tinier, and the bathroom fit only a toilet and a sink the size of one hand, with a showerhead hanging from the ceiling. There was no hot water, so I learned the masochistic pleasure of starting my day with a cold, electrifying rush.

My neighbor, Ah Wong, was a matronly woman with a puffy face and teased hair. She invited me for dinner the day I moved in, offering me a seat on a stool at the table she shared with her twin thirteen-year-old daughters, skinny little girls who were afraid to look me in the eye. Ah Wong served snake soup and fried rice, and complimented my ability with chopsticks. She helped me buy a refrigerator for the street price, warning me that as a *gwei-lo,* or foreign devil, I would have been charged three times as much if I had gone alone. I bought a dresser, a bookshelf, and a small double bed at a used furniture store, all delivered within the hour by a crew of recent immigrants from China, who carried the bed up six flights only to find that it would not fit through my narrow front door. No problem. They sawed it in half and reassembled it inside in minutes. I felt as content as a little bird, padding his own nest.

Hong Kong was still a British colony, a holdover from days of Empire when pink-skinned men came from Europe, trading opium and silk and tea, and grabbing land. By the mid–1900s, colonialism had become politically outdated and had essentially disappeared from Asia. Hong Kong was an anomaly. Ninety-five percent of the population was Asian, mostly refugees from Communist China, but they were ruled by British men who wore white wigs in court and favored lawn bowling and cricket. When I arrived in 1986, the

British had recently agreed to return Hong Kong to China in 1997. But how that handover would occur was still foggy, as was China's promise to preserve Hong Kong's freewheeling ways. The culture of Hong Kong was built on uncertainty about the future. Everything happened fast. Lying on a resumé was the least of crimes committed in the name of expediency. The stock market was run like the personal fiefdom of its chairman. The property market was controlled like a cartel. To many Americans who landed there, Hong Kong's business affairs seemed clubby and lawless. But to me, another refugee from Communist China, Hong Kong felt secure and efficient.

Each morning, I rode the gleaming, noiseless subway to a rundown warehouse district called Lai Chi Kok. I walked through long, half-empty streets to the *Standard*'s office and took a seat at my desk. At first, my job as a reporter, bouncing from one topic to the next without time to look at anything seriously, seemed like a recipe for shallowness. To my surprise, I found being quick and shallow great fun. It was exciting to meet a new cast of characters on every story, with a license to ask probing questions, write it up, and then move on to something new the next day. It gave me many tales to tell when I retired to a bar with other reporters after work. I was exposed to the petty vanities, unrealistic ambitions, and quiet stoicism that ordinary people can carry. The pace was relentless—I wrote articles every day. It made me feel fully engaged, giving me a confidence I had lacked as a student in China. I was doing daily battle with the world, and sometimes winning. My newspaper clippings were physical proof, and I carefully saved each one in a scrapbook, watching it thicken.

I did not feel like a natural-born reporter, however. Beneath my newfound bravado, I worried what people thought of me. I wanted everyone I interviewed to like me. A better reporter, I felt, would be more belligerent, with an attack-dog mentality, never pausing to worry what other people thought. I did not have that and could not impersonate it. If an assignment involved confronting anyone, I usually wanted to shrink away and sneak back to the office unnoticed. Only the fear of facing an editor whose questions I heard in my mind—"Did you ask? What did they say?"—forced me onward, against my secret timidity. That first year, I made a lot of mistakes. I spelled people's names wrong, too shy to double-check. I was sloppy. Most times, nobody seemed to notice.

The assistant news editor at the *Standard,* Li Wing-on, was all smiles on my first day, welcoming me with a clap on the shoulder. He seemed a little overfriendly, taking care to praise my ability to speak Mandarin. The next day, he praised my Chinese again, this time adding that it was too bad Mandarin was useless in Hong Kong, where Cantonese was the primary dialect. That was not true. Many people in Hong Kong spoke Mandarin and appreciated a *gwei-lo* who could speak the mother tongue of China. But I said nothing.

During my first week at the *Standard,* I noticed that Li crossed my name off a political assignment in the desk editor's daybook, sending me instead to cover a conference of engineers, which was less newsworthy. I asked him why. He looked past me and said dismissively, "You'll catch up after a while." Another day I was assigned to cover Hong Kong's chief secretary, David Akers-Jones, as he toured the construction site of a new shipping terminal. It was just a ribbon-cutting event, and I followed fifteen other reporters, tromping on and off the media bus as we followed the chief secretary's limousine from site to site. Only at the end of the visit did Akers-Jones step up to the microphones and answer a few questions, dropping the bombshell that he would soon retire. It was big news for Hong Kong, and the other reporters buzzed with excitement as we headed back on the bus, playing back tape recorders and checking to make sure we had his exact words. I hurried back to the *Standard,* excited to be able to report a real piece of news to Li. He quickly took the story from me and gave it to another reporter, brushing me aside. "You just write about the tour," he said. "We'll take care of the real news." I sat down, steaming. There was nothing interesting to write about the tour. My story got spiked, not printed, while the story about Akers-Jones ran on the front page. Bitter, I mulled over something I had heard that day from a reporter for Hong Kong radio. When I told her I was new at the *Standard,* she raised her eyebrows. "Watch out for Li Wing-on," she said. "He hates *gwei-lo.*"

Li was a short man, with doughy cheeks and big, square plastic glasses. After fifteen years as a newspaper reporter and editor, he was very savvy about Hong Kong politics and society. He was a talented journalist, constantly pumping his friends in government for tips and information. Yet under British rule, where spoken English was a yardstick for social standing in Hong Kong, a man as capable as Li was marked by his accent, heavy with the staccato of Cantonese. It didn't matter that his English was grammatically excellent. He did not have the crisp aristocratic British accent that elite Hong Kong families sent their children to England to acquire. With that handicap, Li had difficulty getting promoted at the *Standard.* The newspaper was owned by a Chinese tycoon named Sally Aw, but she seemed to believe that an English-language newspaper needed a native English speaker as news editor. When that job became vacant a few months before I arrived, Li was passed over for a Canadian, Brian Power, who spoke no Chinese and knew little about Hong Kong.

Li acted like a politician. He smiled professionally, yet I could sense the way he resented the young Brits or Americans who landed in Hong Kong with no newspaper experience and gained an immediate edge over local reporters who could not write as well in English. Li was on a mission to shave away that advantage and to favor local reporters. He bristled under the racist mind-set of Hong Kong's colonial system. I bristled under the reverse racism I sensed that he was using against me.

I went to work on Sunday, when Li Wing-on was off. Brian Power was on duty, and he assigned me to cover a news conference with the British foreign minister, Geoffrey Howe, one of the architects of the deal with China on Hong Kong's future. Howe's appearance in Hong Kong was noteworthy, even though he simply reiterated Britain's existing policy to limit democratic elections. My story was splashed across the top of the *Standard*'s front page, a coup for a reporter who had been on the job only seven days. The next morning, Li frowned when I arrived in the office smiling. He picked up the paper and ticked off aspects of the story that I had missed. I nodded, listening patiently.

When Hong Kong's governor, Edward Youde, died in his sleep one night, it opened a political drama. A new governor would be chosen in London. Most reporters at the *Standard* were accustomed to getting by with a minimal amount of work on any particular story. I saw that this time, some extra effort might pay off. I chased down British diplomats, Hong Kong officials, and well-connected executives for tidbits of information about the men secretly being considered for governor. I eventually gathered enough material to name the four leading contenders and write thoroughly about each one. The day my profiles ran, the newspaper's editor-in-chief made a rare visit to the news desk to congratulate me. When a career diplomat named David Wilson was chosen, I wrote several articles about his arrival and first days in office, well displayed on the front page. It encouraged me to take more chances with my writing. I learned how to tweak an event to make it sound dramatic, to draw out the relevance and potential of a plain-sounding piece of news. I learned to write in a way that drew attention, hyping things without making them untrue. I was willing to bend the rules, without breaking them, in order to get noticed.

I also learned how to nudge the daily mechanics of the newsroom to my advantage. Schmoozing the morning editor who presided over the daybook of planned events sometimes got me a better assignment, if Li Wing-on did not interfere. Hanging around the newsroom at lunchtime, when most reporters were out eating, left me available if a big story broke unexpectedly. Writing a three-sentence "summary" of a story I was working on and teasing out a flashy element could grab the attention of the newspaper's top editors when they gathered at 5 P.M. for an editorial meeting to decide what would go on the front page.

A Sri Lankan man named Salya was the editor who actually laid out the front page. Although the editors decided as a group how to rank articles on any given day, Salya had final say over how the front page looked. I made a habit of strolling over to Salya's desk after he came out of the 5 P.M. meeting, looking over his shoulder and chatting with him as he took the list of top stories and decided how to arrange them on the front page. Salya mentioned one day that Li Wing-on had been finding fault with a story I had written, arguing against those who wanted to put it on the front page. It had not before occurred to me that personal bias could interfere with news judgment, but Salya told me that Li seemed to react negatively to almost any story that carried my byline.

Salya told me to go back to my desk, keep writing, and then come back around 7 P.M. When I did, Salya took a look around the newsroom for Li, who had just headed out the door for the day. "Is he gone?" He looked down at the piece of graph paper where his tentative layout for the front page was sketched. "Now," he said. "Where do you think your story should go?" I couldn't tell if he was joking. "Right here, I think," he said, crossing out an article by Danny Lo, one of Li's favorite reporters, and replacing it with mine. I felt like Salya was helping me outsmart the neighborhood bully. I was becoming a star at the *Standard,* in spite of Li Wing-on.

One condition of my employment visa in Hong Kong was passing a physical exam, which I put off until the six-month deadline was about to expire. The doctor recommended by the *Standard,* with an ill-lighted office in a run-down section of town, examined me in a cursory way. I didn't care. I assumed my visit was a formality. But a few days later, an X ray taken by that doctor came back with a scratch on it. The doctor sent a note to the *Standard,* asking me to return for a follow-up in case I had tuberculosis. I was out of the newsroom at the time, and an administrator at the *Standard,* Jenny Siu, misinterpreted the message. She charged into the newsroom waving the note over her head, yelling, "Seff Faysun unfit for work! Seff Faysun unfit for work!" Apparently, no one had explained the principle of confidentiality of medical records to her. Li Wing-on looked like he was trying to suppress his glee when I came back to the office, and he sat me down to break the news. "It looks like you have tuberculosis," he said gravely. Then he patted me on the back and said not to worry, that he would "try" to save my job while I took a few months off to recover. I walked out of the newsroom in shock. I knew nothing about tuberculosis and wondered if I would have to recover at a spa in upstate New York, as the novelist Walker

Percy had done. My adventure in China seemed to be over. I felt imaginary new pains in my lungs. Feeling terribly alone, I went home to my small apartment and fell into a deep sleep.

When my second X ray came back normal, and the doctor explained that it was only a scratch on the first one, I was elated. Li pretended to be happy at my return to the newsroom. Our daily jousting resumed.

Unknown to me, Li had bigger issues on his plate. He was gunning for Brian Power's job as news editor and was regularly complaining to the editor-in-chief about Power's mistakes. One day I came to work to hear from other reporters that Power had been fired, replaced by Li Wing-on. The change was announced in the newsroom at noon, and Li gave a speech to the assembled staff, breaking into tears to say how sad he was that Power was leaving. "I lost my best friend," Li wept. It made me sick. I exchanged glances with several other reporters, who apparently felt the same. My ally was gone, my enemy was in charge. It was time for me to look elsewhere for work.

I called the news editor at the *South China Morning Post,* the other English-language daily in Hong Kong, to ask for a job. The editor, Arthur Ingham, said he had been watching my byline. He invited me to meet for a beer in the evening. Before going, I called a reporter I knew at the *Morning Post,* who told me that Ingham looked kindly on job applicants who would drink with him. I was not much of a drinker, but I wanted the job. When I sat down with Ingham, I tried to keep up with him on each bottle of beer. By the time we got to our fourth beer, I was feeling tipsy. By the time we got to our tenth, I had trouble sitting up straight. "Just one more," Ingham kept saying. After thirteen beers, Ingham finally said it was time to call it a night. "You got the job," he said.

———

Not long after I joined the *South China Morning Post,* I met a reporter at a Chinese newspaper named Serena. She was my age, twenty-eight, though her compact body looked like it belonged to a teenager. She was spunky and funny and had a cutting sense of humor that I found appealing. She flirted gently with me. I flirted back. I could not tell if she really found me interesting, or if she was simply on the lookout for a man with an American passport. Or perhaps she was attracted to another race, as I was, for a taste of the exotic, the forbidden. Serena also intrigued me because, as with other Chinese women, I could easily imagine involvement without commitment. We exchanged numbers. She called me at home one evening. It was the first chilly night of the year, and I complained to her that I had no warm blankets in my apartment, not realizing that Hong Kong could get cold. Serena said her house was full of extra blankets and she volunteered to bring some over. I thought she was kidding, but an hour later she rang the bell.

Serena showed me a side of Hong Kong I did not know. She taught me about the cuisine of Chiu Chow, the area of southeastern China where her parents were born, taking me to restaurants with bright orange bird innards hanging in the window. She ordered us sautéed squid, chicken's feet, and fish soup. Serena taught me phrases of Cantonese and then laughed hysterically when I repeated them back to her in my best approximation of a local accent. I have a good ear and can repeat new sounds with reasonable accuracy, but I inevitably got one bit wrong that rendered a whole phrase funny to her.

Serena often called me at work in the evening when I was on deadline, writing a story, and demanded that I take a moment to read her my lead sentences over the phone. She made good suggestions about how to sharpen them. I grew to rely on her considerable knowledge of Hong Kong. When I was too timid to reveal my ignorance to a fellow reporter at the *Morning Post,* I could always ask Serena, even though she sometimes teased me about how little I knew. When we met after work for dinner, we compared stories about our days' adventures. Serena pointed out to me how Chinese tycoons kissed up to the British but seethed underneath at the racism inherent in a colonial society. She took me to Buddhist temples and pointed out how even bank executives and lawyers and other professionals went to pray for good fortune. We went on ferry rides to some of Hong Kong's many islands, where tiny villages served fresh seafood at outdoor cafés by the ocean.

Serena waited until she and I had been seeing each other for a few months before inviting me to her home. She lived with her mother and sister in a small apartment in a government-built highrise in an area called Sha Tin, which had been a small farming village a generation earlier. On the long subway ride, Serena seemed nervous and admitted that she was afraid I would think less of her once I knew how poor her family was. In her building, the elevator was broken, so we climbed eight flights in a stairwell that was dark and littered with small piles of garbage. *"Wai!"* Serena called out cheerfully as she unbolted three locks and pushed open the front door. It was one large room. A dining table sat next to an open kitchen area, where Serena's sister was already cooking, and a single bed was pushed into a corner. Serena and her sister slept on rollout mattresses they kept in a closet during the day. Serena introduced me to her mother, a sparrow of a woman who smiled softly, but then did not look at me again for the rest of the evening.

Serena's father left home when the girls were young, for reasons

Serena did not know. Serena's mother immersed herself in mah-jongg, the game of tiles, a sophisticated version of dominoes, and lost the family savings. Depressed and deeply in debt, Serena's mother fell deaf and dumb. A doctor told Serena he could find nothing wrong with her mother physically. Her soul had been broken. By the time I came for dinner, Serena's mother could no longer care for herself. Serena and her sister did all the housework, each working full-time, leaving their mother at home alone in front of the television during the day. At dinner, Serena's mother ate slowly once food was put on her plate. Halfway through the meal, she got up to pace, then opened the front door to look out on the balcony, a long hallway of other tenement housing. Serena told me she thought her mother was still waiting for her husband to come home, twenty years after he left.

It took courage for Serena to show me her home. But I did not have the same courage to introduce her to my American friends. I was afraid that they would question what I was doing with a Hong Kong woman. I was secretly ashamed to be with someone I knew I could not get really close to, someone who offered companionship without intimacy. I wanted to think I could immerse myself in the Chinese culture of Hong Kong, but that was more a wish than a reality.

The truth was that I kept one foot in the Chinese half of Hong Kong and the other in the Western half. Though I reveled in going to Chinese restaurants with Serena, I also enjoyed hanging out at the Foreign Correspondents' Club, a famous watering hole memorably described in John le Carré's book, *The Honourable Schoolboy*. I loved browsing at Cosmos Books on Hennessy Road, where books in Chinese and in English competed for shelf space. When I spent a Sunday alone, I often dined on steamed duck for seventy-five cents at my corner café, then treated myself to a ten-dollar coffee in the elegance of the Mandarin Hotel, where I could buy a Sunday edition of the *New York Times* for twenty dollars, even though it arrived a week late.

Things eventually soured with Serena. I found reasons to keep from getting too close. She could sense my reluctance, and she resented it. Serena felt me pulling away before I had the guts to say anything. She tried two different approaches to keep me. First she told me she was pregnant. (Not true.) Then she said she was being pursued by another Western newspaperman. (True.) Both tactics irritated me and pushed me further away. One day, she called and asked for her blankets back. We met at the entranceway to a department store, and I handed them over as stiffly as a clerk delivering a court document.

I had only been at the *South China Morning Post* four months when the editor, an Australian named John Dux, approached me. "How good is your Mandarin?" he asked. I told him I was fluent. Dux mumbled something about his wife wanting to learn, but I could sense something more was afoot. I asked around. Rupert Murdoch had recently bought the *Morning Post* and had apparently instructed Dux to expand coverage of China. A few weeks later, Dux called me into his office and asked if I wanted to open the newspaper's new bureau in Beijing.

The idea of going to Beijing as a correspondent both scared and intrigued me. The notion of writing about China, a Communist country with a highly secretive government, was intimidating. I was still learning the basics of reporting in Hong Kong, where I had been at it for only a year and a half. I knew little about Chinese politics or economics. Besides, I was thriving in the relative comfort of Hong Kong, and Beijing looked cold and forbidding in comparison.

My best friend, Larry Zuckerman, a journalist then working in New York, was impatient with my hesitation. "This is going to be the biggest break of your career," he assured me. He was right. Though I could not yet see it, political discontent was roiling under the surface in Beijing, waiting for a chance to burst forth.

chapter five

BEIJING SPRING

Near the entrance to the Forbidden City, on a path beside the immense rust-colored walls of that ancient palace, old men gathered in the late afternoon to play Chinese chess, hang their birdcages, and talk. Willow trees hung over green water in an old moat. An occasional car or bicycle ambled by, but it was quiet compared with the noisy streets that filled much of Beijing. The men playing chess sat on small bamboo stools, staring at the pieces, scratching their ears or chins as they pondered a move. Others stood watching in silence. Nearby, a man tied a small cylindrical whistle to the ankle of his gray homing pigeon. When the bird took off overhead, an eerie sound reverberated into the sky.

I came upon that spot by the Forbidden City one Sunday afternoon after riding on my bicycle through countless *hutong,* the mazelike back alleys that gave the city its character. I had recently moved to Beijing as a correspondent for the *South China Morning Post,* and it was my day off, a time to explore. I dismounted my bicycle and walked beside the moat. An old man twirling a pair of silver medicinal balls came up beside me. The man had gray stubble on his head and chin. He took out a match to light a cigarette, and I noticed that his forefingers were stained orange by nicotine. He lowered himself down to take a seat on the ground, folding a newspaper with a photograph of Deng Xiaoping and slipping it under his backside. "Excuse me, leader, I need you to keep my bottom warm," he said. The man told me his name was Old Wang. I asked him how much time was left for Deng, who was eighty-four and rumored to be ill. "How would I know?" replied Old Wang. Scratching his chin, he considered the question anyway. We talked about it. When Deng came to power, everyone hoped he would live long enough to outfox his conservative rivals. Now, after ten years in charge, Deng was holding back his liberal protégés, and everyone was asking when he would die. Old Wang took a long drag on his cigarette and uttered an old Chinese saying: "When the emperor nears death, the earth cracks open."

Politics seemed like the ultimate Chinese secret. The inner machinations of high-level government were completely inaccessible to outsiders. Chinese leaders selected themselves and generally behaved with arrogance and high-handedness, though they mouthed shibboleths about representing the people. Top leaders lived and worked inside a secluded compound called Zhongnanhai, located beside the Forbidden City, and as restrictive as that palace was in the days of emperors. Decisions were made at informal meetings and later officially approved by formal gatherings of the Politburo, which issued pronouncements so turgid they were nearly incomprehensible. A fierce code of loyalty among leaders and their staffs kept political secrets tightly bound. Outsiders guessed about competing factions among various leaders but could never be sure who was in what clique. In public, Chinese leaders were intent on preserving the appearance of consensus and kept their personal opinions and preferences well hidden.

In 1988, when I arrived, the mood in Beijing was quietly restive. People in the street, like Old Wang, believed that momentous events were coming. Chinese people have been conditioned by cycles of tragedy in Chinese history to expect the worst. Yet the rumors of turmoil inside the leadership turned out to be true. Over the following year, events would unfold in a way that allowed gigantic protests to emerge in Tiananmen Square and a massacre of civilians in the streets nearby.

The street protests and crackdown of 1989 were widely publicized and broadcast around the world. Yet they were intertwined with an intriguing drama, the political crisis inside China's secretive leadership, which was pried open for a short time. At first, snippets of information seeped out, as staff members began talking to a degree unknown before or since in Communist China. During the height of the protest movement, in what came to be known as the Beijing Spring, many secrets of China's political leaders spilled into the open. After the crackdown, the walls were sealed tight again.

My political education began slowly. At first, government operations looked opaque. Decisions were issued in articles in *People's Daily* or the Xinhua News Agency, long screeds that were turgid with Communist terminology. News conferences were dull, featuring expressionless officials reading a prepared text and answering questions only by referring to the text. I felt frustrated by the slow wheels of the bureaucracy, particularly the housing authorities, who demanded to be treated to expensive banquets in exchange for allotting me a place to work and took twelve months to do so anyway. In the meantime, my news bureau was a dark room at the end of a long musty hallway in the Friendship Hotel, where I relied on a single scratchy telephone line. I had one colleague, an American named Marlowe Hood, who had studied Chinese politics for years. He showed me how to parse official announcements for small markers of change. He encouraged me to befriend Chinese journalists, who could point me toward topics that they themselves were not permitted to write about. Once I got to know some of them well, they also passed on political gossip.

I gradually learned to read the rules and habits of the Communist Party. At the once-a-year gathering of China's legislature, journalists were allowed inside the Great Hall of the People, a massive building on one side of Tiananmen Square. I mingled with Chinese politicians in the red-carpeted area set aside for tea drinking, and they responded to my questions by repeating a government statement word for word. Inside the main hall, I watched as pending bills were read out loud and votes taken, prompting all the participants to raise their right hands in unison, like robots, while a chairman announced, *"Tong guo le!"* Passed! At one point the chairman, an undereducated man in his late eighties, yelled "Passed!" without looking up. An uncomfortable silence followed. A young aide came and whispered in the old man's ear. The chairman chuckled, embarrassed to realize that he had announced the bill's passing before a vote had been taken. Trickles of laughter echoed through the hall. Then the chairman took the vote. It passed, unanimously.

The old-fashioned brand of politics inside the Great Hall of the

People was falling out of step with a faster pace of change on the street. Beijing stores now offered television sets, refrigerators, washing machines, and videocassette players to any consumer who could pay, dropping the old rule that required a letter of permission from a *dan wei*. Many of the homes of new friends I visited had private telephones, virtually unknown in my days in Xi'an. Still, my Chinese friends all seemed to grumble about inflation and money-making scams, unsettling and new in a Communist country. Many people felt they were losing ground, even as their standard of living went up, and it caused broad resentment of Party members who used official connections to make money. People cursed Party leaders openly, in conversations at restaurants and in the street, something no one would venture in Xi'an. University students began holding meetings to talk about the need for democratic reform. Artists and playwrights and musicians displayed politically sensitive work.

In May 1988 a prominent astrophysicist named Fang Lizhi turned up at an outdoor meeting on the campus of Beijing University to call for political reform. Fang's high standing in his scientific field gave him a confidence to speak out on political affairs in a way that no one else dared, much like Andrei Sakharov had done in the Soviet Union. Fang calculated that the uncertain mood in Beijing made it possible to talk openly. Two years earlier, he had been fired from his job as vice president of a university in central China after saying publicly that socialism was outdated and encouraging his students to make more demands for democracy. Fang moved to Beijing to do research. He kept quiet for a time, but now he had decided to speak out again.

When Fang began welcoming reporters inside his apartment in northwest Beijing, I was one of the visitors who navigated a ghetto of ugly concrete buildings, traveling up a dilapidated elevator to Fang's simple home on the eleventh floor. In person, Fang was appealing. Relaxed and unpretentious, he had a placid expression and ordinary black plastic glasses. Fang liked to see the humor in politics, and he often let a full-throttled laugh bubble up from somewhere deep in his gut. Fang was the first heroic character I had interviewed. I was nervous about meeting him, afraid I might say the wrong thing. But Fang made my job easy. He was gracious and friendly, and he spoke Chinese in simple terms that I could always understand. He had a clear and compelling argument: freedom and democracy are universal desires, and there is no reason that Chinese people should not have the right to speak their minds and to elect their leaders. Obvious as that sounds, it was still an unpopular view in China in 1988. A large chunk of the population accepted the notion that China was not ready for democracy, that China's history had bred a culture of obeying authority that was unsuitable for voting, or that China's enormous population made it especially vulnerable to chaos. Rubbish, said Fang. Only through the exercise of democracy would China become a truly prosperous nation. Fang was not a political theorist and did not pretend to be one. He was a scientist with some firmly held beliefs, grasping a moment when he felt he could make a difference. To Fang, and many others, China's moves away from orthodox Communism—abandoning communes, easing price controls, allowing markets—were a step in the right direction. Free speech should be added to these reforms, Fang said. China was becoming more open every day. Why should people be stopped from criticizing corruption or voicing political opinions?

On January 6, 1989, Fang wrote a letter to Deng Xiaoping, China's highest leader. The letter was eight sentences long, in

Chinese characters written by hand. Its message was simple: China needed an amnesty for all its political prisoners. Letting them go, Fang wrote, would be a humanitarian gesture with broad consequences. Fang specifically called on Deng to free Wei Jingsheng, China's most prominent political prisoner. Normally, talking about political prisoners was forbidden. Writing directly to Deng was cocky and provocative.

To publicize his letter, Fang asked for help from Perry Link, an American scholar who was working in Beijing for a year. Link had met me a couple of times, and he called my office at the *Morning Post*. He told me about the letter, asking that I spread it around to other foreign journalists in Beijing. Intrigued, I sped across town in my old army jeep to Link's office to get a copy. As soon as I read it, I knew it was political dynamite.

As a young journalist eager to distinguish myself, I felt an illicit thrill to have an important letter in my hands before any of my colleagues did. It was a big scoop. I only planned to share it with other journalists after my own story was already in print. As I began to write, and read Fang's letter over and over, I saw the brilliance in its simplicity. In public, Chinese officials invariably lied about dissidents, insisting that China *had* no political prisoners. Dissidents themselves usually wrote long, pretentious tracts, bogged down by obscure history and convoluted language. Fang did not. The clarity of his letter was piercing. It said that any government with political prisoners is immoral. By making his letter public, Fang was challenging Deng to a debate. This was more than free speech. It was a daring political act.

As I wrote, I wondered how harshly the authorities might react to news of the letter, and whether they might blame the messenger. I decided to be cautious and to share the letter with two friends,

Andrew Higgins of London's *Independent* and John Pomfret of the Associated Press, so that I would not be singled out. Once our stories were out, the news spread fast, and it electrified Beijing.

The city's intelligentsia seemed inspired by Fang's example. Other professors and writers followed his example with similar letters. I and other journalists waited with apprehension to see if the authorities would imprison Fang. But the government was silent. Days and weeks went by, and Fang remained free. Beijing was bubbling with discontent, which seemed to portend big changes.

I knew that much depended on Deng Xiaoping, who had been China's leader for ten years. Deng fascinated me. A short, feisty chain-smoker, Deng was a pragmatic man who liked results. He was not a poet or a thinker, as Mao had been. Deng was a doer. He had been Mao's henchman in political campaigns of the 1950s, but he never fully embraced Mao's leftist vision. When Mao launched the Cultural Revolution in 1966, Deng was one of the first leaders to be persecuted, exiled to a tractor factory in Jiangxi Province, where he cleared trays in a cafeteria. Deng spent seven years in the political wilderness, returning to Beijing as Mao softened his policies a few years before his death in 1976. Deng wrestled with Mao's chosen successor, Hua Guofeng, for two years. Then all at once in late 1978, Deng outmaneuvered Hua, normalized relations with the United States, mobilized the army in a bloody war with Vietnam, and moved the government's focus from pure Communism to economic growth. It was quite a political feat, and it signaled a drastic shift in China's direction.

One piece of Deng's political strategy was the "Democracy Wall." At the time, Deng's pragmatism was popular with Beijing residents, and he reasoned that if free speech were allowed, most criticism would be directed at leftists, Maoists who remained in high positions. When handwritten essays were posted on an old brick wall outside a bus depot in Xidan, a central intersection in Beijing, crowds grew thick as people jostled one another to read. Exciting new journals of poetry and prose were eagerly passed out by hand. As Deng expected, most of the posters and discussion took aim at leftists. However, one poster attracted attention because it zeroed in on Deng himself. Written by an electrician from the Beijing Zoo named Wei Jingsheng, the poster argued that China's efforts to modernize could only succeed if the government embraced democracy. That was too much for Deng. Democracy Wall had served its purpose, as far as he was concerned, and he ordered it shut down. Wei was arrested and jailed after a show trial. Deng was hailed in the West for his open-minded economics and diplomacy, yet when it came to domestic politics, he was still a Communist.

Over the next ten years, Deng gradually delegated authority on day-to-day affairs to Zhao Ziyang, a glad-handing but shrewd politician who in 1987 took the title general-secretary of the Communist Party. Compared with other Chinese leaders, Zhao (pronounced Jao) seemed open-minded. He had a taste for well-tailored Western suits and he liked to play golf. In public, his face looked fixed in a permanent upside-down smile. In private, he did as he liked. When he sat for a rare interview with an American television correspondent, Zhao sipped a beer kept off-camera.

Ultimate power still lay with Deng Xiaoping and a collection of crusty Party elders, veterans of revolutionary war who were now in their eighties. Almost all of the *ba lao,* or eight elders, had retired from official positions and stayed out of daily government work. But the elders still wielded great influence through their personal networks of Party officials and army officers whom they had promoted over the years. Like mafia dons, they constantly demanded respect and patronage. Deng presided uneasily over the *ba lao,* usually leading but always listening to them. Several elders did not like Zhao, who favored reforms that undercut old habits of authority. They sniped that Zhao was becoming arrogant, that his attachment to golf was "bourgeois." When inflation flared up in late 1988, the elders blamed Zhao and arrayed themselves against him. Zhao's position became precarious. Yet some of my journalist friends warned that Zhao was crafty and that a power struggle could create unexpected opportunities. Zhao and his allies began voicing the need for "political reform," a code word for more democracy. Zhao knew that any public debate on democracy would favor him and hurt the elders, just as it had favored Deng at Democracy Wall ten years earlier. In a high-stakes political fight, even small matters can take on a big significance. When Fang Lizhi's letter to Deng appeared, Zhao disagreed with other leaders on how to handle it. That was why the government remained silent. They were deadlocked.

In late February 1989, an unexpected event gave Fang Lizhi a boost. A month after assuming office as president of the United States, George H. W. Bush visited Beijing, after attending the funeral of Emperor Hirohito in Japan. Bush had lived in Beijing as an unofficial ambassador in 1974 and wanted to showcase his diplomatic know-how by dropping in on his "old friend" Deng Xiaoping. Planning in a hurry, Bush's staff put the name of Fang Lizhi on an invitation list for a banquet to be hosted by President Bush on the second night of his visit. Chinese officials demanded that Fang's name be removed, arguing that their leaders could not sit in the same room with a dissident. Americans officials would not remove Fang's name, for fear they would be criticized by the U.S. media for buckling on a human rights issue. The Chinese called it an issue of national sovereignty. The Americans said it was about human rights. But it was really about a dinner invitation.

As the date of the dinner approached, Fang ignored advice from colleagues who told him that going to the banquet would embarrass China's leaders. For him, it was a matter of principle, something too few Chinese stood up for. Fang was suspicious when his research institute arranged a car to take him to the dinner. He feared it might be a ploy and take him out of town, effectively kidnapping him until the dinner was over. Not wanting to tip the authorities to his real plans, Fang agreed to take the official car. But as it idled outside his apartment block, Fang and his wife instead climbed into a taxi, already carrying Perry Link and his wife. As they neared the hotel where the banquet was held, however, they saw Chinese police stopping and checking every car. When the police saw Fang, they forced everyone out of his taxi. Fang pulled out his invitation, with the gold seal of the president of the United States, but the police, who were apparently under orders not to arrest Fang but to keep him away from the banquet, shooed him away. Fang and Link had to walk with their wives for miles on cold winter streets before a Canadian diplomat recognized Fang and escorted him inside a diplomatic compound. After some discussion, Fang decided to go public about what happened. He headed to the Shangri-La Hotel, where the White House press corps camped in the ballroom.

It was the first time I had seen the White House press corps, a curious breed of journalist, mostly overworked prima donnas trained to think only as far as the news of the day. Before Fang arrived, the White House reporters were undecided as to what made the story of the day. Bush's arrival in China on Saturday and his stop in Tiananmen Square to shake hands with ordinary people had been an engaging story in itself. But now it was Sunday, and no catchy angle presented itself. Bush's visit to a Chinese church on Sunday morning was charming but insubstantial. I was listening to two White House journalists despairing at the lack of a story when their solution walked in the door. Fang stepped onto a stage to speak, and I could sense the entire ballroom of White House reporters move toward him with palpable relief: a story of the day had arrived. Although Fang spoke halting English, his story was simple and irresistible: a leading Chinese physicist with liberal political views, invited for dinner with the president of the United States, had been blocked by his Communist leaders. Chinese and American officials energetically tried to downplay the event, fearing it would tarnish the visit. The reporters ignored them, and Fang's story dominated the news for a day, ruining Bush's trip and infuriating Chinese officials. For weeks afterward, several Chinese officials told me they were convinced that the Fang incident was part of an American conspiracy to embarrass China. They could not see the obvious. Keeping Fang from the banquet made him internationally famous and even harder to control. The mood in Beijing grew more restive.

In April, after finishing a day's work at the *Morning Post,* I went to dinner at the home of a friend who worked as an editor at a Chinese magazine. His name was Lin. He was one of Beijing's political cognoscenti, whose position at a media organization gave him access to the documents that communicated the day-to-day business of government. To the untrained eye, like mine, Party documents read like a company newsletter, a colorless recitation of decisions made by a unified team of wise leaders. But to the sophisticated reader, like Lin, what appeared and what did not appear pointed to trends and political battles within the leadership. Matched with the gossip traded among friends, these documents served as the daily basis of discussion for informed political watchers, much as the *New York Times* and the *Washington Post* are standard reading for insiders in Washington. The content of Lin's magazine was mostly garbage. But the Party documents that came across his desk contained everything he needed to know.

That night at dinner, Lin had a piece of inside information that he knew would interest me. He waited until we finished eating and were sipping tea before he told me that Hu Yaobang, the former leader, had suffered a heart attack in the middle of a Politburo meeting on April 8. Hu had survived but was in very serious condition. Lin assured me that his information was reliable because he got it directly from a member of Hu's staff. Secondhand information from the Politburo was rare in Beijing. Journalists like me mostly heard fourth- or fifth-hand accounts, inevitably garbled in the retelling. Here was a rare secret, spilling from the inner sanctum.

I knew about Hu Yaobang. A short man with a soft face, Hu had been dismissed as general secretary of the Communist Party two years earlier, in 1987. Hu was an old ally of Deng's, an effective backroom operator who fired many old leftists from the Central Committee after Deng came to power in 1978. By Communist Party standards, Hu was a relatively humane leader, presiding over broad economic reform, speaking out about the plight of Tibetans, and prodding the Chinese news media to more coverage about corruption within the Party. Among common people, Hu was best remembered for his impulsive remarks, like one encouraging Chinese people to give up chopsticks and communal eating in favor of knife and fork, to cut down on contagious disease. (He was ignored.) By

1986, after several years in power, Hu felt confident enough to try to ease out some of the elders. But he underestimated their tenacity, and the elders conspired against him, waiting for the right time to strike. When student demonstrations followed Fang Lizhi's calls for greater democracy in late 1986, the elders attacked Hu for being insufficiently Communist. Their assault was fierce enough that, rather than defending Hu as he had done before, Deng stepped to the side and let him fall. Hu was forced to resign in January 1987. Accepting a demotion, Hu was allowed to keep a seat on the Politburo. He attended meetings but did not often speak. He aged visibly.

Zhao Ziyang replaced Hu as general secretary of the Communist Party and as the leading candidate to succeed Deng as China's leader. Yet Zhao feared the elders, too, and it was not long before he clashed with them as well. In early 1989, my politically knowledgeable friends like Lin agreed that Zhao's days were numbered.

Now Lin told me that on April 8, Zhao was presiding over the Politburo meeting when Hu Yaobang collapsed on the floor from a heart attack. Space was made for Hu to breathe, and a doctor was called. A fellow Politburo member pulled a small vial from his pocket that contained pills for heart disease and forced two into Hu's mouth. Hu was taken to a nearby hospital and seemed to recover. As Lin told me the story, he speculated that Hu's illness could affect the dynamic of power within the Politburo. Although Hu had been sidelined for two years, he still represented the moderate wing of the Party. If Hu were to die, Lin said, it might provide students with a pretext for demonstrating. That sounded far-fetched to me.

Lin was right. A few days later, on April 15, Hu Yaobang suffered a second heart attack while attempting a bowel movement and died at 7:53 A.M., as a Chinese magazine later reported. Hu's death was announced at 3 P.M. At Beijing University, students soon gathered at the center of campus and began pasting handwritten tributes on signboards. Some put up white flowers, a traditional sign of respect for the dead. Others eulogized Hu in writing, calling him a hero among villains in the Communist Party. "A true man died, false men still live," wrote one student. Others followed, portraying Hu as a man who tried to save China. After Fang Lizhi's letter in January, students had been clamoring for ways to speak out about China's problems. Now Hu's death was a spark for the tinderbox that had been under construction for months. In one day, Beijing University was awash with big-character posters mourning Hu.

Making a martyr out of Hu Yaobang was a smart move. Hu had been only marginally more liberal than other Party leaders. It was a stretch to call Hu an ally of democracy, as many students did, since he had been a lifelong Communist. Yet Hu had been persecuted for open-mindedness and for the demonstrations that erupted on his watch in 1986, so students naturally had sympathy for him. Student politicians looking for a pretext to voice discontent also saw Hu's death as an excellent cover. A demonstration for Hu looked patriotic on the surface, even if it was really an indirect way to call for more democracy. Students guessed that Communist Party leaders would hesitate to stop a rally in honor of a former Communist Party leader. Hu's death was a rare opportunity.

On Monday, April 17, two days after Hu's death, about four hundred students from the University of Politics and Law gathered at Xidan, where Democracy Wall had appeared ten years earlier. Unfurling homemade banners that they had carried from campus by bicycle, the students grouped haphazardly and started marching toward Tiananmen Square. They wore white carnations and black armbands, more fit for a funeral than a protest. They looked nervous. Like the handful of other journalists who showed up to watch,

I followed the protesters breathlessly, eagerly scribbling in my note-book, fearful that they would be detained at any moment. Uni-formed police officers watched, and plainclothes officers videotaped the demonstration, but none interfered. (A government account of the protest published later denounced me and two other corre-spondents, Andrew Higgins of the *Independent* and Adi Ignatius of the *Wall Street Journal,* for being part of the conspiracy.) The stu-dents carried banners honoring Hu, and many of them wore red scarves signaling membership in the Communist Youth League, once led by Hu. The marchers proceeded to the center of Tianan-men Square, and thousands gathered to watch.

After laying flowered wreaths at the monument at the center of the square, the demonstrators extended their march up a nearby street. I followed them, curious where they were headed. The stu-dents stopped at a courtyard home marked by a pair of large red doors, the home of Hu Yaobang. As neighbors from surrounding al-leyways came out to watch, the students were met by Hu Yaobang's eldest son, who invited some inside to a reception room where other family friends and relatives had come to pay respects. I watched from the alleyway, surprised by the cooperation between student protesters and a prominent Communist Party family. Yet in show-ing mutual sympathy and respect, each side got something from the other. The students got cover for their protests by eulogizing Hu, and Hu's family welcomed the students to thumb their nose at Deng for having treated Hu shabbily. It made me wonder how many rank-and-file Party members were disillusioned with their leadership and would support more demonstrations.

A student watching beside me mentioned in a hushed tone that students from Beijing University, the nation's leading school, were also planning a protest that night. My friend Andy Higgins had heard the same thing. We went down to the square together at around 10 P.M. It was almost empty when we arrived, dark and windswept. A few students rode about aimlessly on bicycles, apparently looking for the protest themselves. As we stood near the center of the square, an old farmer came out of the darkness, hauling a sleighlike cart with a woman inside. A middle-aged peasant with a kerchief over her head, she spoke with the strong, hypnotic voice of an old village storyteller. Although it was dark and we could barely make out her face, we listened to her tale of aching hardship in China's countryside, of rapacious local officials who had robbed her family of their small plot of land, using some pretense that she told in a complexity that Andy and I could not decipher. Yet we sat mesmerized. She brought forth an age-old lament of Chinese people, who for centuries have trekked to the capital for the one-in-a-thousand chance that they could win an appeal over some injustice committed back home. Discontent always simmered in China, and it came to a boil at intervals throughout history, not necessarily when conditions became worse, but rather when there was hope that a protest might bring change. That woman's voice echoed in the back of my mind throughout the following weeks, as student protests grew to a scale never before seen in China. Parents of my Chinese friends sometimes grumbled that the student protests of 1989 were nothing new, that rebellions had occurred in China since history began. Yet even on that first day of protest, I had a feeling that we were watching a new version of the old story, with an ending that no one could predict.

That night, after waiting in the square for an hour, Andy and I drove randomly through the streets of Beijing in my old green army jeep, looking for the phantom student protesters from Beijing University. We reached the gate of another school, Beijing Teachers

University, at about midnight. The school's iron front gate was closed. Yet in the darkness we could see about two hundred students gathered inside the campus gates, stuck behind a padlock. "We want to march," one student said plaintively. "They won't let us out." They waited in the darkness, wishing the gate would open, not yet bold or desperate enough to climb it, still not willing to go back to their dormitories. Instead they stood immobile, waiting for the right time. It reminded me, when the student demonstrations later seemed inevitable, that they had begun tentatively.

Andy and I eventually gave up our hope of finding the Beijing University protesters. I dropped Andy at his apartment and went home. Unknown to us, they had waited until after midnight to leave campus, located on the outskirts of Beijing, in order to avoid alerting the authorities. I had been asleep about fifteen minutes when Andy called at 2:30 A.M. and told me to come back out. I got back in my jeep, picked up Andy, and off we went again to search the dark streets. It was another hour before we were driving through the musky darkness of a narrow street that runs alongside the Forbidden City. The first marchers emerged like an apparition, dimly illuminated by weak street lamps. Small bunches came into view, and then a large mass of marching students that numbered about 1,500, with another 500 or so riding on bicycles. At the heart of the group, a dozen marchers carried a long white sheet with the words THE SOUL OF CHINA writ large. In normal times, a lone demonstrator in Tiananmen Square would be swept away by security officers within moments. Here were more than 1,500 students, marching defiantly toward the square, chanting, "Down with autocracy! Down with corruption!" I recognized Hong, a law student friend, in the crowd. She was bubbling with excitement. "You never imagined, did you?" she asked. After many conversations at her dormitory room where I accused Chinese students of being timid and gutless, and her insistence that they were just waiting for the right time, it seemed that the moment had arrived.

The demonstrators reached Tiananmen Square about an hour before dawn, tying banners and laying wreaths of flowers on the Monument to the People's Heroes. After an hour of exultant chanting, some started to disperse. I expected everyone to stumble back to campus, and I was eager to sleep myself. Yet I noticed most of them gathering in an enormous circle, and I stayed to watch. As the sun began to rise over the horizon, two student leaders stood to conduct a meeting. One of them, with crooked glasses and disheveled hair, was Wang Dan, a history student from Beijing University who was emerging as the most thoughtful of the student leaders. On that morning, he meticulously led a negotiation of demands with nearly one thousand students. "Complete freedom of the press, with independent newspapers," Wang read out, to raucous applause. "Open accounting of personal finances for all leaders" was the second demand, which got equally loud applause. "And for their sons and daughters!" yelled one of the seated students, again to shouts of applause. A third demand was for an official rehabilitation of Hu Yaobang. A fourth was an increase in the nation's education budget. Some suggestions reflected the political immaturity of twenty-year-olds, mixing the vague ("an end to corruption") with the specific ("allow an independent student organization"). Yet those two demands were equally out of reach. Communist Party leaders would no sooner allow democracy on a college campus than in a city or a province. Watching the students in the dawn light, organized and disciplined, gave me hope that they would amount to something.

After that morning, it seemed unimaginable to me that student protests could grow larger. Yet that very afternoon, more than 20,000 students gathered in the center of Tiananmen Square. "Support the student demands" was one rallying cry, referring to the list of demands that had been drawn up at dawn and delivered to the National People's Congress, China's toothless legislature. Another clever stroke. By treating the legislature seriously, the students were encouraging an institution—set up to make the Communist Party look more democratic than it was—into actually functioning democratically.

One surprise followed another. Late that evening, I watched about five thousand protesters trying to force their way inside Zhongnanhai, the leadership compound a few hundred yards from the square. They were led by a charismatic student leader named Wuerkaixi, who held a bullhorn in his hand as he exhorted students to charge a stiff line of uniformed guards who had locked arms. The students did not get past the guards. Nor, however, were they beaten away with sticks or gunfire. As I stood watching, I mused about the soft response from the authorities so far. Since no protests were normally allowed in Beijing, and a second full day of protests had gone unpunished, I wondered if the leadership had some strategy I could not yet discern. Perhaps they were being lenient in hopes that the demonstrations would blow over or, more sinisterly, allowing student leaders to materialize so they could be identified and punished. It seemed more likely that the leadership was deadlocked, unable to agree on how to handle the protesters, the only reason their number was allowed to grow so large.

Hu Yaobang's memorial service was scheduled for Saturday, April 22, in the Great Hall of the People, adjacent to Tiananmen Square. The authorities announced that they would close off the square beginning at dawn on Saturday. That angered student leaders, who pledged to occupy the square on Friday evening. It seemed unlikely to me that the government would allow that. When Friday evening came, I headed out to the square around 9 P.M. to see what would happen. There were already a few thousand people milling about, abuzz with the excitement of people who sense the potential for violence. Word spread that students from Beijing University were already on their way. In an era before mobile phones, information was slow and unreliable, so I did not know what to believe. I stood with Andy Higgins at the northeast corner of the square, craning my neck for a view over the crowd that was starting to fill the Avenue of Eternal Peace. At about 10 P.M., Andy and I climbed up on the back of a flatbed truck as the first columns of marchers came into view. I was astounded. Student marchers stretched as far as my eyes could see. Marchers from several universities came in one cohesive group, striding in well-disciplined lines that held for miles. Andy observed that the paramilitary training that students had suffered through on campus was now paying off in an unexpected way, giving them the knowledge and resolve to march in an orderly fashion. We counted them as best we could and estimated that they numbered more than 100,000. They had lost all pretense of limiting their demonstration to commemorating Hu, and they were chanting, in unison, "Long live democracy! Long live freedom!" Since my newspaper in Hong Kong was going to press shortly, there was no time to get back to my office to write a proper story, and I rushed to the Telephone and Telegraph Office one hundred yards away. I dictated a few hastily composed paragraphs to an editor in Hong Kong, yelling so excitedly that he had to tell me to calm down.

By the time I got back to the square, the marchers were still patiently filing into the center area, carefully seating themselves in organized groups, separated by university and by department. I waded into the crowd and sat down with a group from Beijing Teachers University who were sitting in a clump and vigorously debating the merits and dangers of the demonstration. One predicted a violent clash with the authorities. Another argued that it was unlikely any action could be taken against so large a crowd. I spent that whole night circling through the square, talking to different groups of students, impressed by the commitment and self-control they had mustered, wondering if this might actually be the beginning of a revolution.

As dawn approached, many students grew afraid that the authorities would keep to their promise of shutting down the square by daylight. At around 5 A.M., street-cleaning trucks drove into one corner of the square, and word went out that water cannons inside the trucks would be unleashed. But as the trucks drew near I could see the drivers' faces, wide-eyed in amazement as they saw the crowds, and I could tell they were cleaning men, not officers. Shortly after dawn, a contingent of security officers emerged from the Great Hall of the People on one side of the square and assembled in a line, apparently to prevent the demonstrators from mounting the stairs of the Great Hall, where the nation's senior leaders soon arrived in limousines to attend Hu's memorial service. "Dialogue! Dialogue!" the students chanted as their leaders walked by.

The students negotiated with security guards to allow three representatives to climb the outdoor stairway of the Great Hall of the People and submit a list of demands. Kneeling before a grand doorway, three scruffy-looking young men rolled their list into a scroll and extended it in their arms overhead. Like supplicants before an ancient emperor, they were showing respect for authority, even as they flexed the collective muscle of 100,000 young souls watching behind them in the square. It was a striking sight. The three waited, on their knees, scroll overhead. Yet no one came out. Minutes ticked by. Eventually, the students' arms began to tremble. No one appeared. The students gave up. It seemed a bad miscalculation by the authorities, who could have defused an explosive situation by sending a junior official to hear the complaints. Instead, students went back to their campuses seething with anger and resentment. Unknown to the protesters, their demonstrations were bringing an ever greater sense of urgency to the struggle for power under way at the top of China's government. The main players—Zhao Ziyang, Deng Xiaoping, the Party elders—could not agree on whether to send anyone outside to defuse a momentous political demonstration on their doorstep. The real fight, I realized, was not between the students and the authorities. It was inside the leadership.

TIANANMEN

fter Hu Yaobang's memorial service concluded at noon on April 22, 1989, most of China's leaders went home to be with family members. It was a day for solemn quiet, and the culture of the Communist Party demanded that its upper crust, the top five hundred or so officials who had attended the service, act accordingly. Even those who had not cared for Hu personally kept up an appearance of mourning—except for Zhao Ziyang. Instead of going home, Zhao went to play golf. To his aides, who warned him that the elders would be offended by his sporting diversion, Zhao insisted that he needed the exercise. Zhao was leaving the following day for a weeklong visit to North Korea, where there were no golf courses. As general secretary of the Communist Party, Zhao felt he could do as he pleased. He had swallowed indignities for decades as he worked his way up the Party hierarchy. Let the elders criticize him. He was going to play.

Two days later, while Zhao toured moribund factories in North Korea, Deng Xiaoping convened an emergency meeting of the Central Committee. Angry that the rally in Tiananmen Square had disrupted Hu's memorial service, Deng called the student protests a conspiracy aimed at toppling the Communist Party. He accused a small handful of "bad elements" of manipulating the body of patriotic and well-intentioned students and labeled the student movement "turmoil," a politically loaded term that implied treason. Deng's message appeared as an editorial on the front page of *People's Daily* on April 26 and was read out loud on television and radio broadcasts. It was clearly intended to intimidate the students into silence and to suggest that Party officers at every level deal severely with future protests.

Student leaders were outraged, not cowed, by Deng's editorial. They had been scrupulously peaceful and had not incited anyone. In the face of real danger, they were brave and disciplined. Their demonstrations cried out for a conciliatory response from the government, yet Deng invoked clunky language to try to browbeat a popular movement. In response, student leaders staged an even larger demonstration on April 27, taking over the streets of Beijing with more than 100,000 marchers. It was a grave loss of face for Deng, whose personal appeal had been given the proverbial finger.

When Zhao returned to Beijing on April 29, he met quietly with several of his colleagues on the Politburo, suggesting that since Deng's tough approach had failed to cool the students, a softer tack might be in order. Deng was too old to be in charge anymore. At eighty-five, he was clearly out of touch with the mood on the street.

Other members of the Politburo watched carefully. No one would risk denouncing Deng. But many of them knew that if Zhao took a conciliatory approach and succeeded in defusing the crisis, he would emerge as a hero, while Deng and the elders would be disgraced.

Zhao waited for his moment. It came on May 4. Another protest of 100,000 marchers swelled in the streets of Beijing. At a meeting with leaders of the Asian Development Bank, Zhao said that he sympathized with the students. It was an open declaration of political rebellion. To speak publicly in favor of the students, directly opposing the line laid out by Deng's editorial, was a fierce insult to Deng. It enraged the elders but thrilled the students, who now hailed Zhao as a savior, having been indifferent to him the day before.

China's media was on Zhao's side. Following instructions from Zhao's aides, China's major newspapers and television stations reported extensively and accurately on the May 4 demonstrations, having been silent about the previous three weeks of protests. I could scarcely believe my eyes when I saw the next day's edition of *People's Daily*. The newspaper that had run Deng's editorial on the front page had now flipped to the other side, carrying banner headlines and large photographs portraying student protesters sympathetically. To readers across the country, it was a sign that Beijing's leadership was in chaos. Contents of Party meetings, normally considered top secret, now appeared in newspapers and in documents that would engage China scholars for years afterward.

Deng did not speak to Zhao, but he plotted his revenge, convening a secret meeting of the *ba lao,* the eight elders who wielded ultimate power in the Party. All were in their eighties. Only one, Yang Shangkun, was actually a member of the Politburo. The others were all veterans of China's civil war and decades of political infighting since then. The elders agreed that Zhao had to be dismissed. Some spoke angrily. Several were particularly irked by Zhao's insistence on playing golf at the wrong time. No one had to point out that it was Deng who had chosen and defended Zhao for years and was now disgraced by him. Now Deng's concern was the timing of Zhao's dismissal. A landmark visit by Mikhail Gorbachev, the Soviet leader, was scheduled to begin on May 15. It was a visit that Deng had intended as a major diplomatic event, repairing a twenty-year rift between China and the Soviet Union and cementing Deng's reputation as a pragmatist. Removing Zhao just before Gorbachev's arrival would tarnish the visit, the elders agreed. They would wait until after Gorbachev's departure on May 18.

Student organizers saw Gorbachev's arrival as a special opportunity. They knew that the world media would be focused on Beijing when the Soviet leader arrived, and that Chinese leaders would be reluctant to crack down on protesters at that time. Students came up with the idea of holding a hunger strike in Tiananmen Square. On the day they announced it, I thought a hunger strike sounded silly and melodramatic. It turned out to be a brilliant stroke. Chinese culture, after centuries of scarcity and famine, is so focused around eating that "Have you eaten?" is a common greeting. To many Chinese people, missing a single meal is considered a small tragedy. The notion that students were denying themselves food as a patriotic gesture was reported breathlessly on Chinese television, immediately drawing a wave of popular support from Beijing residents and people all over the country. Adults who had been cautious or skeptical about the protests, the kind of people who normally remained obedient, now felt safe coming out to help care for fasting students, and they rallied to Tiananmen Square to show support. Doctors and nurses set up volunteer clinics. Journalists for Chinese television carried long, sympathetic reports, broadcasting interview after interview about the students' desire for more democracy and political openness, with colorful footage from the square.

The demonstrations swelled to a gigantic level. More than a million people crowded into Tiananmen Square on May 17 and May 18. It emboldened student protesters, who now paraded posters of Li Peng, the unpopular prime minister, in a Nazi uniform. Others denounced Deng as a senile autocrat. Similar, if smaller, protests broke out in cities in every province of China. The scale of civil disobedience was growing so large that I wondered if the government might fall.

Gorbachev's visit, intended as a grand diplomatic moment, was overshadowed by turmoil in the streets. Gorbachev and Deng looked badly out of step with the times, their meeting meaningless when a million people were protesting outside. When Gorbachev met Zhao, technically equals as heads of their Communist Parties, Zhao said it was polite for the Soviet leader to refer to him as an equal, but that Deng was still the ultimate authority in China. Gorbachev visibly stiffened as he heard this comment, knowing instantly what Zhao was really saying: all the upheaval in the streets is Deng's responsibility, not mine. Another deeply disrespectful act, cloaked in polite language. Later, several elders accused Zhao of revealing state secrets when he acknowledged that Deng was really in charge. If so, it was the worst kept secret in China.

Zhao was losing ground, not gaining. For him, the hunger strike was a disaster. The students had not dispersed, as he had hoped. Instead, they had gathered in greater number. Moderate allies of Zhao had gone to the square repeatedly to try to persuade the students to leave, arguing that conciliation was critical to avoid bloodshed.

The students ignored them. As a result, Zhao's chances of rallying support within the Party dimmed. On May 18, the day Gorbachev left, Deng met with the elders again to decide to declare martial law, a step that had not been taken even in the darkest days of the Cultural Revolution. Zhao wrote a letter of resignation, saying he could not go along with martial law. Then he rescinded it. Zhao attended his final meeting of the Politburo that night, trying to see if he could obstruct or delay military action. He pleaded with his colleagues to listen to the people in the streets and to ignore instructions from Deng and the elders. Discussions went round and round for hours, but finally Zhao had to admit defeat. He emerged from Zhongnanhai shortly before 5 A.M. and went to Tiananmen Square. With tears in his eyes, using a bullhorn to make it look like he was addressing the nation, Zhao spoke to a small crowd of students camping inside an old school bus, making sure he faced a television camera. "We have come too late," he said. "You cannot go on like this. We were once young, too, and we all had such energy. We also staged demonstrations, and I remember the situation then. We also did not think of the consequences." Then he checked into a hospital, a politically neutral place that would temporarily delay the inevitable, house arrest. Zhao was no longer a free man. He was the highest-ranking political prisoner in the world.

With Zhao neutralized, Deng could take steps to remove the students occupying Tiananmen Square. On May 19, Prime Minister Li Peng officially declared martial law, to take effect the following morning. Many of the hunger strikers from universities in Beijing decided they had done enough and returned to campus. But by this time, the majority of students occupying the square had come from universities in other provinces, traveling long distances by train and bus to join the revolution in Beijing. They reveled in the excitement at the square and had no intention of going back home. They stayed put.

Chaotic and unkempt, Tiananmen Square was alive with protesters that night. Flags and posters adorned makeshift tents, and garbage from the weeklong occupation had accumulated in huge piles. Many students wore red bandanas around their heads like warriors and spoke of having the courage to die. I wandered through the square, expecting the armed forces to arrive at midnight, or perhaps at dawn. The prime minister had declared martial law. It would certainly be enforced by daybreak, I figured. Would the authorities use bullets or tear gas? Midnight came and went. The hours crept by, with no sign of police or military. When dawn crept into the edge of the eastern sky, and still there was no sign of any uniformed soldiers or police, a spontaneous cheer went up among the protesters, claiming another victory. They seemed intoxicated with the hope that a new and open-minded era was dawning in China. I was thrilled and perplexed, too. Did this mean the government would fall?

The previous day, Deng had ordered the army to mobilize several battalions around Beijing. But some army officers resisted the order, unhappy that the military was being asked to settle a political problem. The commander of one unit known as the 38th Army refused to move his troops to Beijing. Other commanders found ways to delay, citing logistical obstacles. The full extent of resistance among the military, and of the political maneuvering necessary to get army commanders in line, has remained secret. But several army battalions did arrive at the outskirts of Beijing, only to be surrounded by civilians, who cajoled and taunted the soldiers, trying to persuade them that the protesters were patriotic, not enemies of the state. The soldiers, mostly young recruits from the countryside, listened impassively. Deng and his allies decided that military action would not begin until they were confident that the army would follow orders effectively.

The gathering in Tiananmen Square evolved into a Woodstock-like atmosphere of counterculture. Young people sat together on random scraps of blankets or tarp, singing songs, playing cards, debating politics, hanging out in the sunshine. For many of them, Tiananmen became an exalted adventure of being away from the social and family pressures of home. Rock musicians played on a makeshift stage. Free love blossomed. Art students constructed a "Goddess of Democracy," a tall sculpture reminiscent of the Statue of Liberty. But political focus gradually faded. Student organizations that had been created in April, and were never really democratic, began to disintegrate. Student leaders with vision, like Wang Dan and Wuerkaixi, were booed away from the microphones when they spoke in favor of retreating from the square. Instead, an extremist named Chai Ling rose to power, taking the title Commander of Tiananmen Square. Funds that poured in from "patriotic" Chinese in Hong Kong disappeared into the pockets of the student leaders without accounting. Chai Ling, who replaced her grubby green army jacket with designer polo shirts and flashy sunglasses, later defended her right to take money by saying she needed it to fund her own escape from China and to have plastic surgery to make her eyes more round, which she said was for her own security. She later attended business school in the United States.

Tiananmen was like a small city, with its own autocratic rules. A security staff acted as enforcers at the command of student leaders, beating people for trespasses such as taking a photograph of a student leader without permission. A "Dare to Die" squad of motorcycle riders paraded up and down the Avenue of Eternal Peace, saying they would protect student demonstrators wherever necessary. The police disappeared. Students took control of major intersections, trying to direct traffic. A student with a red armband waved my army jeep to a stop at an intersection one evening and tried to pull me out of the driver's seat, saying he needed my jeep "for the good of the country." I resisted, unsure what to say, but my passenger, Andy Higgins, argued forcefully that, as journalists, we needed the jeep, and he instructed me to quickly drive away. It was evident that if the government broke down, people who normally felt disciplined by the presence of the authorities might run wild. The French Revolution came to my mind. I had fully sympathized with the students when their protests began, with talk of free speech and greater democracy. Their de-mands for dialogue with government leaders could easily have been defused. Yet protest politics can only go so far. By late May, the movement had lost its purpose.

In the political confusion, my attention span receded. For six weeks, I had been working around the clock. I had tried to answer a nearly limitless demand for stories by the *Morning Post*. My editors at the *Morning Post* wanted reams of raw information, and I often wrote as fast as I could. On top of that, I started writing articles for the *Boston Globe,* a newspaper without its own correspondent in China. I did not sleep much, ate on the run. As the political situa-tion grew murky, after weeks at this pace, I found it hard to keep go-ing and felt I was nearing nervous exhaustion. I called my editor at the *Morning Post* and told him it looked like the protests were dying down and that I needed a week off. He agreed. My friend Andrew Higgins warned me not to leave, arguing that a crackdown could come anytime. I could not wait indefinitely. On June 2, I took a flight to Hong Kong, where I went to a friend's house and slept.

That day, as I flew out of Beijing, Deng Xiaoping again met secretly with the elders to approve his decision to clear Tiananmen Square by dawn on June 4. By that time, only a few thousand students remained in the square, and they could easily be forced out with a few hundred police officers using tear gas or rubber bullets. But Deng's real goal was to silence all dissent, to cow everyone inside the Party who had begun to question his rule. Zhao's defiance had rattled Deng, as had the size of the demonstrations. It would not be enough to restore order to the streets of Beijing. Deng needed a brutal show of force. He needed to spill some blood.

On June 3, public announcements warned everyone to stay home. That drew hundreds of thousands of people into the streets. Small contingents of soldiers, sent to infiltrate the square and other crowded areas, suggested that a military move was imminent. After nightfall, army tanks and open-backed trucks full of soldiers began to enter Beijing, moving slowly down wide boulevards that were packed with people, many of whom threw debris and Molotov cocktails at the soldiers. Civilians yelled at them to side with the people, not the government. Although violence appeared to be coming, many people could not believe that China's soldiers would actually open fire on their own people.

On the west side of Beijing, thousands of people massed around a makeshift barricade of three city buses, reinforced by piles of carts and old furniture, to try to block the army's advance. The shooting began at 11:30 P.M. Dozens fell to the ground. Panic swept the crowd. *"Zhendan! Zhendan!"* yelled those who ran from the gunfire. Real bullets! Real bullets! The soldiers advanced slowly, and the tanks and trucks resumed their journey toward the center of Beijing. Soldiers in open-backed army trucks appeared to have orders to fire at anything that moved. Random victims fell in the street, on the sidewalks, and even in windows of apartment buildings facing the avenue. No tank ever fired. There was no military enemy, only civilians, running for their lives.

Hundreds were killed. Thousands more were injured, each survivor with a story to tell. A photographer named Yang positioned herself on the street near Xidan, where Democracy Wall had flourished a decade earlier, determined to take pictures as the army advanced. When the tanks approached at midnight, Yang stood to one side of the street to avoid the masses of terrified people running by. In the excitement, she said later, she lost sensation of the three heavy cameras hanging from her neck and shoulders. She knew the bright flash on her camera would attract attention and make her even more vulnerable, yet she could not resist taking pictures, flash included, as the soldiers advanced. She aimed and clicked continuously, even as a tank moved within twenty yards of her, and gunfire crackled out of the truck behind it. She finally turned to run into a side street. The gunfire grew louder. She felt a sting in her back but kept running, unsure whether a bullet had hit her. She looked down and saw blood on her shirtfront. She started to stumble, and one man grabbed her left arm as another grabbed her right, carrying her a few dozen more yards. One of the men screamed for help, and soon she was placed on the back of a flatbed trishaw. Dazed but conscious, she stared into the black sky as a stranger cycled her through several back alleys to take her to a hospital. It was dark and crowded when they brought her inside. A nurse cut through her shirt to get to the wound and discovered her black journalist's identification card in a pocket. "Are you a journalist?" the nurse asked. Yang answered yes, wondering momentarily if she would be left to die for admitting it. But the nurse soon reappeared with a doctor, and Yang was carried to a back room, where she received immediate attention, ahead of several other victims who were waiting. "We have to protect the witnesses," the doctor whispered.

That night, as I watched on TV in Hong Kong, I went numb. I could not believe that soldiers were firing indiscriminately at unarmed people and felt paralyzed at the thought that the hopes and dreams of so many were now evaporating in a crescendo of gunfire. I had lived in the thick of the movement for weeks, knowing it was the biggest political event I would ever witness. Now, at its horrific climax, I was sitting in a quiet room by the ocean in Hong Kong, a victim of my own bad judgment. After all my speculating with friends about how the protest movement would end, knowing all the while that it might be in violence, it was still hard to absorb this news. I also felt like a failure professionally. What kind of journalist misses an event like this? In my mind, I played over the seeds of my decision to leave Beijing, but now they all seemed hazy. I crawled into bed, feeling guilty and hopeless, powerless to affect an event I cared about, unable even to see it.

I called my editor at dawn and told him I was flying back to Beijing. I had missed the massacre, but I was determined to see what I could. My main fear was that the authorities might close Beijing airport and keep flights from landing. But China's leaders were occupied with securing downtown Beijing, not worried about air traffic. My flight, delayed repeatedly, landed at dusk. The Beijing airport was a madhouse. Ticket counters were jammed with people desperate to leave. Outside, the taxi queue was deserted. I spied a small crowd around a minivan, whose driver agreed to take me to the eastern corner of the city, free of gunfire so far, for ten times the normal fare. Stuffed into the van with five others, I listened to the driver say that tens of thousands of people had been killed and that the Chinese army was split into separate camps, one supporting the students and the other opposing them. A good battalion, the 38th Army, was trying to fight its way in to free the students, while a bad battalion, the 27th Army, had done almost all of the killing. I was skeptical, that story sounded too simplistic. Later, I learned that the 27th and the 38th and two other battalions took part in the massacre together, after reluctant commanders were all replaced. But on that first day, wild stories circulated, and no one knew what to believe.

It was dark by the time I rode on a bicycle to central Beijing. The streets were quiet. It was odd, knowing that a massacre had occurred, but seeing no sign of it in most of the city. The killing occurred primarily along the Avenue of Eternal Peace, the city's main thoroughfare, which bisects Tiananmen Square. After the army took over the square, dozens of tanks were positioned there, facing outward from each corner, as if some military threat remained. I walked through several back alleys to reach a side street near the square and was able to peek out and see the tanks and a line of sitting soldiers, aiming their weapons outward, ready to fire at anyone who came too close. Convoys of tanks and army trucks occasionally moved in and out of the square, up and down the avenue, periodically opening fire at civilians who tried to hide at the street corners.

Late that night, the tanks seemed to have stopped moving. I ventured out on the Avenue of Eternal Peace with a reporter for Reuters named James Kynge. It seemed suspiciously quiet, and

I didn't know if we were being brave or stupid. After walking two hundred yards, we heard the rumble of a truck and then the crack of gunfire about one hundred yards away. James and I darted to the sidewalk and scaled a brick wall on the far side, lying on the ground behind it. We heard the trucks go by, bits of automatic gunfire ripping the area. Once it was quiet again, we cautiously climbed back out. Random gunfire from a lone truck, a footnote compared with the terror of the previous night. But I had never been fired at before. My skin tingled with terror and excitement. The night air seemed to buzz.

Once the truck was out of sight, we emerged and saw a small crowd gathering at the corner where the gunfire had erupted. Like mice, men and boys came out of hiding and scurried about on the street, picking up spent gun shells, still warm from the shot. They put the shells to their lips and blew, producing an eerie whistle. In that setting, it was a haunting sound, full of yearning and sorrow. A man showed me a shell and wanted me to have it. Another man, drunk with outrage, noticed that two foreigners had arrived and ran at us, screaming, "You must tell the world! You must tell everyone what happened!" The man's eyes bulged wildly, and others held him back. The rest of them stood on that street corner, traumatized, able to do nothing but whistle on spent gun shells.

The following morning at 11 A.M., near the same spot, a young man walked out into the middle of the Avenue of Eternal Peace and stood in the path of an approaching tank. This time, no soldiers were shooting. The tank stopped and tried to turn, to go around the young man. But he moved in front of it again. He yelled at the tank, swinging a book bag. One man against the system, unafraid of being run over. One man defying an entire army. He did not reflect the tragic reality of Tiananmen, of soldiers shooting unarmed civilians to deliver a political message. But he embodied the hope and courage of the student movement preceding the massacre and became the lasting image of the event, reproduced on T-shirts and posters around the world. His identity remained unknown.

In a postmortem gathering of the elders on June 6, Deng sounded defensive and out of touch, surprised that the international media used the term *bloodbath*. Deng blamed foreigners for stirring up trouble. "Anybody who tries to interfere in our affairs or threaten us is going to come up empty," Deng said. "We Chinese have self-confidence. Inferiority complexes get you nowhere. For more than a century we were forced to feel inferior, but then under the leadership of the Communist Party, we stood up. No behemoth out there can scare us now." Deng's bravado and his attempt to deflect blame onto outsiders after ordering a massacre of his own people did not ring true when I read his statements later. Deng's reputation as a pragmatic reformer was ruined, permanently. After the massacre, the authorities released no information. Exactly how many people were killed in Beijing on June 4 remained a mystery.

The mood in Beijing went black. The authorities stuck to their gravity-defying argument that a few treasonous villains had engineered the entire student movement. Usual suspects were rounded up, and hundreds of executions were publicized to cow everyone else. Ordinary people did not fall for the propaganda. They simply learned to be quiet. A climate of fear reigned. All hope of constructive change in China seemed to evaporate.

My job as a reporter became difficult. After all the information spilling out of the leadership during the student movement, I now had almost no access. Many Chinese friends were afraid to see me. Those still willing had less access to information themselves, and little to pass on. My work stagnated. As the months wore on, I found it hard to marshal energy in such a dull, restrictive atmosphere. I felt burned out on China, where I had now spent seven years, and wanted a way out. Then I found one. I got a job back in New York City with the hometown newspaper.

chapter seven

A GOLDEN VENTURE

One night in June 1993, a rusty tramp steamer called the *Golden Venture* approached New York harbor after a weary journey halfway around the world. Below deck, nearly three hundred Chinese men and women were crammed together in a dark and smelly hold, physically exhausted and emotionally traumatized by an eighteen-month voyage that took them from the South China Sea to Africa and then across the Atlantic Ocean. Conditions on the ship were horrendous. Food and fresh water were scarce. A single toilet stopped working weeks before arrival, and passengers often relieved themselves in plastic bags or, toward the end of the trip, directly onto the oily floor of the ship's hold, where the passengers camped on plastic sheets and blankets. The captain was handcuffed to a sink in his cabin, victim of a mutiny a few weeks earlier. A primitive form of order reigned among the passengers, ruled by a handful of knife-wielding "enforcers" who hoarded food and took turns raping the eighteen women aboard. The passengers had agreed to pay $30,000 each for a chance to get to America, where they would be entitled to two to four years of hard labor in a Chinese take-out restaurant or a garment sweatshop, just to work off their debt.

In the mist and soft rain that fell before dawn, the freighter ran aground on a sandbar at Far Rockaway, a slim finger of land that runs along the southern edge of Queens, New York. When U.S. Coast Guard helicopters shined bright lights on the ship, panic erupted among the passengers. After such a long and treacherous journey, now within five hundred yards of American land, they feared getting caught and sent back to China. Touching American soil, passengers had been told, could mean the difference between winning asylum and being deported. About one hundred of them leapt off the deck into the cold seawater. Many of them reached the beach in their underwear, with a few papers taped to their sides in plastic bags. Ten passengers died from drowning or hypothermia. New York City police and federal agents patrolled the beach, wrapping the shivering young men in large orange blankets and herding them into groups to prevent escape. After serving hot drinks and sandwiches, the officers led their Chinese charges onto old school buses to take them to detention centers. The passengers proceeded in a quiet and orderly way, apparently surprised to be treated with civility by men and women in uniform, but unsure whether they had succeeded or failed in their quest to get to America.

When the *Golden Venture* ran aground, I was just finishing a shift on the overnight desk at the *New York Times*. I had been at the newspaper almost two years, and it had been a bumpy ride. I did not exactly distinguish myself. I had joined the *Times* with a swelled chest, having grown up in a home where my parents read it like the Bible. The newsroom was not as loud or boisterous as it once had been, as described in the books I had read by Russell Baker and Gay Talese. Reporters and editors worked quietly and intensely at their desks, staring at computer screens. They were friendly and conscientious and generally welcomed me like a new member of their club. I felt timid in their midst, not sure I deserved to join such an exalted league. New York City was fresh territory to me as a reporter. Even though I grew up there, after seven years in China I felt out of place.

At first, local news stories in New York seemed dull and inconsequential to me, compared with the political drama I had witnessed in Beijing. After a couple of months I liked the gritty, tragic feel of urban crime stories. Yet I soon was yanked off the crime beat and moved to covering Wall Street, then moved again to covering the transportation beat, and I had a hard time getting excited about it. I needed some nurturing but got none. The *Times* was a busy place, and editors did not have the patience to hold my hand. I got buffeted from assignment to assignment, unable to speak up for myself. I had a problem working with editors. Always eager to be seen as a nice guy, as Mr. Agreeable, I did not know how to hold my ground, usually giving in when conflict arose. Eventually, I ended up with the worst job in the newsroom, sitting on the desk for the overnight shift. When the office grew quiet at midnight, after everyone had gone home except a lone desk editor and me, I watched mice creep out of hiding to hunt for crumbs. I wondered if I had chosen the wrong profession.

The day the *Golden Venture* crash-landed, the Metro editor skipped over me as he made assignments, choosing a few veteran reporters to write articles, and sending two dozen other reporters out to look into various aspects of the story. I was sent to the detention center in downtown Manhattan where the Chinese passengers were transferred. As I waited outside for a chance to talk to these new immigrants, I began to grasp the scope of the story unfolding before me. The *Golden Venture* was not a one-day newspaper story. It was an opening into the secret world of people-smuggling. This would be a tale with many layers. My mind raced. The kinds of people who wanted to be smuggled, the identities of the smugglers, the number of other ships on the way, the factors behind this exodus: all needed exploring by an energetic reporter who was familiar with China. I could barely contain my excitement. After months of floundering at the *Times,* unable to get inspired by anything, here was a story I could fully report.

When I got back to the office and took a peek at the articles being prepared for the newspaper that night, my stomach fell. The stories lacked depth or perspective. Since the *Golden Venture* crashlanded a few years after the crackdown in Tiananmen Square, the editors jumped to the conclusion that immigrants from China must be fleeing political persecution. I was tempted to sit my editors down to give them a lecture: China was coming alive economically, allowing people with newly earned money to take chances, as old restrictions on travel loosened. Passengers on the *Golden Venture* were not political activists, they were working-class people whose families had gained access to new sums of money, enough for the large down payment required for a trip on a ship overseas, while setting their sights on earning much more. I knew it was a combination of access to money, relaxed restrictions, and the growth of a smuggling network in one specific part of China, Fujian, that created this new stream of immigrants.

My editors were in crisis mode, too busy to listen to lectures. The best way to make my point would be to write a forceful article myself. Next morning, I rose early and went to Chinatown, eager to find other Chinese immigrants who had already come to the U.S. illegally. On East Broadway, the busy street where immigrants from Fujian congregated, I searched the faces of young men I passed on the street, wondering how to strike up a conversation and persuade one to talk to me about his illegal passage, despite warnings from smugglers to keep quiet. I saw a side street where a crowd of Chinese men loitered outside a storefront with a sign in Chinese that said EMPLOYMENT CENTER. Bingo. An obvious gathering place for new arrivals. The first pack of young men I approached seemed happy to talk to a white guy who could speak Mandarin and readily revealed how they got to America illegally. Several seemed bewildered by New York. One asked me a question about taxes, another asked if there was a law against making him work sixteen hours a day. A third man told me how he traveled by boat to Central America, went by bus through Mexico, and sneaked on foot over the border into Texas, an incredible story of hardship and suffering. He had arrived in New York three days earlier and had a debt of $28,000 to work off, with no idea how he was going to do that. I immediately felt sympathy for these men. I also felt rejuvenated, interviewing in Chinese, parsing my way through a culture that was both foreign and familiar.

When I had enough information for a strong article, with gripping accounts of several immigrants who were fueled by economic mobility and not political desperation, I was ready to sit down and weave together the tales of these men and the broader issues of the day. I hoped it would earn me a byline on the front page. But when I checked in with a desk editor, he ordered me to "feed" my material to a more senior reporter, Sonny Kleinfield. As I dictated my information to Sonny on the phone, and realized that he did not even know if Chinese use a family name first or last (first is correct), I wanted to scream. Why was the China guy not writing the China story? Still, I knew it was time to be a good soldier. I did my part. Sonny's story appeared on the front page. He did a nice job, and it made my point. Yet it was painful to read an article based on my reporting that did not carry my name.

The next day, Tuesday, I started early again. This time I worked on a story about the Chinatown street gang called the Fuk Ching, which was believed to play a role in smuggling people. I already knew that most gangs in Chinatown, a lawless nook of lower Manhattan, acted as street muscle for businessmen who trafficked in drugs and gambling. The Fuk Ching often collected fees from newly smuggled arrivals, like the men I spoke with outside the employment center, and kidnapped or tortured those who could not pay. The Fuk Ching were feared by the more established residents of Chinatown, Cantonese people who looked down their noses at compatriots from Fujian, a neighboring province with a different dialect, cuisine, and customs. The Fuk Ching were young and violent. Every boatload of new immigrants contained potential recruits for the Fuk Ching, young men without family or community, unafraid of violence and looking for easy money. The leader of the Fuk Ching, a slithery twenty-seven-year-old known as Ah Kay, was a legend in Chinatown for his brutal style of command.

As I sought information from law enforcement officials and immigration experts, I could sense how little they knew. Until the *Golden Venture* landed, the FBI had focused attention on drug smuggling, closely following Italian-American and Central American gangs and virtually ignoring Asian organized crime. I scraped together bits of information from investigators, prosecutors, and people in Chinatown. The growing assumption, I learned, was that the Fuk Ching was branching out from its role as enforcers and that its leader, Ah Kay, had started to play a role in organizing groups of smuggled people. As I was gaining momentum on this story, the Metro editor assigned a more experienced reporter, Joe Treaster, to work together with me. Treaster and I cooperated well, but I had a long head start on him, and by the time our article was completed, ninety percent of it was my work. The story was printed at the top of the front page, but it carried Treaster's byline alone. When I saw the article in print, I felt proud of my work and bitter about losing credit for it. I worried that my big chance was slipping away. In the unwritten rules of the *Times,* a younger reporter like me was expected to selflessly hand over material to others. At the same time, I worried that the *Golden Venture* was a once-in-a-blue-moon opportunity for me to excel, and that if I missed it now, I might never succeed.

On Wednesday, I came to work early again. I focused my attention on Ah Kay, leader of the Fuk Ching, who was suspected to be the mastermind behind the *Golden Venture*. Law enforcement officials knew little about him, in part because of an unwillingness to share information between the FBI, the Drug Enforcement Agency, the New York Police Department, and the Immigration and Naturalization Service. Determined, dogged, unwilling to give up, I kept at it, pushing investigators and prosecutors with a belligerence that was new to me, eking out scraps of information from each one. After a lot of effort, the pieces finally started coming together.

Ah Kay, a wiry kid with poufed hair when he arrived in the United States at age fourteen, worked as an enforcer in the Fuk Ching, robbing Chinese stores, whose proprietors were reluctant to contact the police. Caught, jailed, and deported to China at age nineteen, he was sneaking back into the U.S. six months later, carrying a fake passport, when he was caught at the Mexican border near El Paso, Texas. He was released after twenty-four hours, as many illegal immigrants were, while the immigration bureaucracy processed his case. It took five years before his deportation hearing was held, and he used the time to take over as boss of the Fuk Ching, authorizing murder and kidnapping, and earning enough to hire a fancy mob lawyer. Facing deportation again, Ah Kay played a new card. He applied for political asylum. For arcane legal reasons, that automatically delayed his deportation indefinitely and gave him protection for gang work, earning him millions of dollars. It was hard to believe that a convicted felon and leader of a violent Chinatown gang could so easily manipulate the Immigration and Naturalization Service, but it was a hopelessly disorganized branch of government. A case officer at the INS who located Ah Kay's file at my request took one look at it and refused to reveal any of its contents. "He's a political asylum applicant," the officer said. "We have to protect his privacy."

Ah Kay disappeared from New York in January 1993, five months before the *Golden Venture* landed, after a rival within the Fuk Ching tried to kill him. I found out that he had gone into hiding in Fujian and chuckled at the thought. While boatloads of people were striving to get from China to America, a gang leader like Ah Kay was going in the reverse direction, finding it safer in China, where police could easily be paid off. Just like Italian or Colombian gangsters, Ah Kay was less afraid of the police than he was of his close associates. Holed up in China, Ah Kay had not organized the *Golden Venture*. But his own story stood out by itself. My article on Ah Kay ran at the top of the newspaper's front page. I felt a flush of relief. I could let go of the fears that I was inadequate as a reporter.

While my other colleagues at the *Times* became frustrated by the opaque nature of Chinese immigration and moved on to other topics, I kept at it. I was still curious about the exact circumstances of the *Golden Venture*'s voyage and the mystery of why ninety percent of China's immigrants to the U.S. came from one small area—just three counties—of Fujian. When I visited Chinese passengers in jails in New York and Pennsylvania, they gave short, muddled accounts, changing their answers as they guessed at what might improve their chances of winning the right to stay in America. I needed to find a passenger who already had asylum and who could speak at length.

After chasing a lot of bad leads, I finally found a good one. A friend in Chinatown introduced me to a teenager named Wang, who had been the youngest passenger on the *Golden Venture,* just fifteen when he set out. Most of the ship's passengers were held in prison as they waited for immigration hearings, but Wang and three others were released because they were minors. Six weeks after he was released, Wang agreed to talk with me, and we met at a restaurant in Chinatown that served Fujian cuisine. Wang was an appealing boy, wiry and handsome with a fresh-looking complexion. He did not look like he had just gotten off the boat ride from hell. He did seem quite hungry, though, leaning over his plate to shovel food into his mouth and pausing only to complain about the tofu and compliment the steamed fish. Once he had eaten his fill, he was ready to speak.

"I did not want to come to America," said Wang. His parents made the decision for him, yearning for the prestige of having a son in America, as well as the extra income. It was hard for me to imagine what kind of parents would take a fifteen-year-old out of school and entrust his life in the hands of a smuggler, no matter the potential payoff. Wang frowned at my question. "You don't understand," he said. "There's a lot of pressure. Every family wants a relative in America." In Wang's home county, called Chang Le, young men who did not try to go to America were considered cowards or incompetents. His parents were not greedy, Wang told me. They were trying to keep up with the neighbors.

Wang's father arranged his son's passage to America, negotiating a price of $28,000 with an illegal agent in Chang Le. Wang's father borrowed from a dozen relatives to come up with a $4,000 deposit. The remainder would be due the week Wang arrived in New York. When Wang set out on his journey, it was not particularly efficient. Wang did not board a ship on China's coast, near his home. Instead, he and about thirty others were taken on a long, meandering journey, traveling by train and bus across China, and on foot through the jungle of a thinly policed border into Burma. They were frequently stopped by Burmese soldiers, bribing them with U.S. dollars or small pieces of gold. Wang snorted heroin, ate rat meat, and lost his virginity to a Burmese woman in a straw hut. He saw three of the thirty in his group die from fever in Burma. After two months of slow, rambling travel, Wang finally reached Bangkok, the capital of Thailand. He was housed with sixty other people in a four-bedroom apartment for four months. "It was like a holding pen for animals," he said. "Waiting for the boat to America."

When he finally boarded a rusty freighter off the coast of southern Thailand, Wang was anxious about heading out to sea. He had never been on a large boat before and did not know how to swim. He liked relaxing on deck and looking out at the limitless ocean. But he and 150 other passengers were forced to spend most of the day belowdecks, where the stench of diesel fuel nauseated him. Wang had learned massage from his mother, and he ingratiated himself with the ship's "enforcers," a handful of men who carried knives to keep passengers in line, by giving them back massages. The enforcers got better food than the others, including bits of meat with their twice-daily bowls of rice, rather than just canned vegetables. Sometimes they shared with Wang. In the second week at sea, Wang saw two passengers fighting over a bowl of food. An enforcer pulled a knife on them, warning that a failure to obey would mean being tossed overboard. Wang befriended a pretty sixteen-year-old girl, who accepted his offer of massage. Three weeks into the journey, one of the enforcers dragged her to a crew room and raped her. After that, the girl was too ashamed to meet Wang's eye. Every one of the seventeen other women on board was raped as well, Wang said, an observation confirmed by U.S. prosecutors after they interviewed the victims.

Like other smuggling operations, the ship did not follow a well-planned route. It went first to Singapore, then to the Philippines, then back to Singapore, and finally headed west over the Indian Ocean. It docked at Mauritius, an island in the Indian Ocean with a sizable Chinese population, then again set down anchor at Mombasa, off the coast of Kenya. The ship's engine was practically inoperable. The passengers were told that they would have to wait in Mombasa for another ship to come get them. Wang stayed aboard the ship, buying fish from Kenyans who paddled up to the side. "We had little money. Sometimes we traded a piece of clothing or a watch for some fish, and then grilled it on deck," he said. Wang occasionally ventured into port. He had never seen a black person before and wandered through the city's market wide-eyed at the dress and habits of Kenyans. Wang and the others waited four months until another ship came. The enforcers ordered them aboard, even though it was already overflowing with its own passengers. Wang saw the ship's name, painted in white letters across the bow. It was called the *Golden Venture*.

There were already 120 Chinese people aboard the *Golden Venture* when Wang and his 180 fellow passengers moved in, prompting fights and arguments. The bunking area stank of human sweat and excrement, and the noise from the ship's aging engine was loud and constant. Back at sea, the *Golden Venture* headed south toward the tip of South Africa, where it encountered a storm. The ship was tossed so violently in the waves that Wang wondered if it might capsize. Many passengers vomited. The stench was nearly unbearable, but the enforcers would not let any passengers up on deck for fear of losing control of them. Wang heard later about a fight between the ship's captain and Lee Kin-sin, the head enforcer. The captain ended up handcuffed in his quarters as the ship chugged on toward America.

Weeks passed. One day the ship stopped, drifting at a spot eighty miles off the coast of North Carolina, waiting for small fishing boats to come ferry passengers to shore. The fishing boats never appeared. The head enforcer's attempts to radio his boss went unanswered. Following a back-up plan, the enforcer directed the first mate to steer the ship toward New York Harbor. A day later, the ship ran aground in Far Rockaway. When the Coast Guard's arrival prompted some passengers to jump overboard, Wang froze. He did not know how to swim but was terrified that he might be sent home after such a long trip. The police on a small motorboat eventually took him to the beach. "The police were friendly," Wang remembered. "They checked us each carefully. They gave us blankets and hot tea. They wanted to make sure we were okay.

I always expected the police to hit us, like they did in Burma and Thailand."

Once he arrived at a detention center in downtown Manhattan, Wang called a relative who lived outside New York City, a cousin who had left Fujian eight years before and now managed a Chinese restaurant on Long Island, outside New York City. The cousin came to see him two days later with an immigration lawyer, and Wang was released because he was under eighteen. The cousin took Wang to a house with bright electric lights, several television sets, and an immaculate bathroom. Wang gradually got used to his new surroundings, and by the time I met him he had already developed a taste for handheld computer games. Wang's family originally agreed to pay $24,000 upon his arrival in New York, and his cousin wondered if smugglers would track him down and demand payment. But none did. The *Golden Venture* had crashed. The arrangements between smugglers and enforcers had evidently fallen apart, as the failure of anyone to meet the ship off North Carolina suggested. Wang had made it.

Not all the passengers from the *Golden Venture* were so lucky; most of them were held in prison. After all the media attention around the ship's landing, INS officials did not dare release them, the usual practice. Almost all passengers from the *Golden Venture* applied for political asylum, most claiming to suffer persecution from China's one-child policy. It was impossible to know how many of those claims were genuine. Few, I figured. Yet it was hard not to feel compassion for these people, after all they had been through. Should they be denied entry to the United States? If Ah Kay had been allowed to manipulate the system, why should these young men be punished, guilty of nothing more than recklessness for getting on the *Golden Venture*? According to U.S. policy, immigrants who come to America for political reasons should be allowed entry, while those who come for economic reasons should not. As I considered the cases of these men from China, I wondered about my own ancestors, Huguenots who came to America from France and Holland by boat in the 1650s. Family lore has it that, as Protestants, they had been persecuted in France. But had they really come for political reasons or economic ones? Were the Irish who escaped the Potato Famine of the 1850s seeking a better life economically or politically? In the end, about half of the men from the *Golden Venture* won release through the efforts of relatives and human rights activists, in some cases after more than two years in jail. About 150 others, the unlucky ones, were deported back to China. After the *Golden Venture,* it was risky to try to organize many boatloads of immigrants, and smugglers retreated to older, safer, if less lucrative methods of using fake passports and circuitous air routes to move their human cargo. The smuggling did not stop.

By the end of the year, my standing in the newsroom turned around. I finally got off the night shift, moving to cover the court system in lower Manhattan, where I was able to write consistently about Asian organized crime. I gained confidence. My stories began landing on the front page regularly. After my earlier stumbling, I had learned how to work the system at the *Times,* when to cajole editors and when to stand my ground. More than that, I had learned to trust my own instincts and to bat away efforts by editors to distract me. The Metro editor submitted several of my stories with others about the *Golden Venture* in a nomination for the Pulitzer Prize. I began to dream about becoming a foreign correspondent, the pinnacle of reporting jobs at the newspaper. I knew that my background in China would make me a candidate for a posting there at some point. I wondered if it would take five years, or ten.

It only took a few months. One morning, the foreign editor, Bernard Gwertzman, called me to say that the newspaper was going to open a bureau in Shanghai, a city that was coming alive as China's economy took off. Gwertzman asked if I would be the new bureau chief. I was so stunned I remained silent on the phone. "If you are willing . . ." he said, waiting for an answer. "Yes," I said. Yes. I had been in New York for four years. Now I was headed back to China.

chapter eight

SHANGHAI COMES ALIVE

When I arrived in Shanghai, I spent my first days exploring the city on foot. The clanging of heavy machinery and wrecking balls vibrated through almost every neighborhood, the messiness of construction sites serving as evidence of a city on the move. In the old French Concession, half-demolished row houses were splayed open, revealing dilapidated interiors to anyone walking down the street. Elsewhere, new office blocks of frosted glass and shiny chrome reflected the morning sun. On Nanjing Road, a shopping thoroughfare, boutiques offered tasteful displays of expensive footwear and slinky garments behind plate-glass windows. Around a corner on a crowded side street, I saw residents stumbling out of tiny wooden homes to empty their chamber pots at a communal toilet. On the waterfront, stately old British bank buildings recalled the glory days of the 1920s, when Shanghai was one of the most cosmopolitan cities in the world. Now a new financial district lay across the river, sprouting a television tower of gaudy red glass that looked like a spaceship from a Star Wars movie. Old and new as close together, as the Chinese like to say, as lips and teeth. Shanghai was a visual cornucopia, a once great city in the throes of change, trying to recapture its place in the world.

I felt at home in Shanghai. It reminded me of New York, with the efficient bustle of its urban streets, its quicksilver dialect and air of imperturbability. Pedestrians walked with a knowing nonchalance, oblivious to traffic. Like New Yorkers, Shanghai natives are snobs about their city and don't mind being hated by the rest of the country for it. They think themselves savvier than people from anywhere else in China. I moved into a regal 1930s French apartment building with tall ceilings and wood floors and art nouveau trimmings. I found antique Chinese tables and chests at a warehouse at the city's edge, where migrant workers restored them for a few dollars each. In a smoky flea market, I bought old posters with advertisements for cigarettes and soap from the 1920s, adorned with attractive Chinese women in sexy gowns. The shops along my street offered almost everything a consumer could want, espresso machines and French wine and Irish butter.

Shanghai was riding a wave of excitement about its renaissance. A gleaming new subway opened, as did a world-class museum, and a grand opera house. Foreign investors were scouring the city for places to sink their cash. China's economy was booming, and Shanghai was being touted as the nation's financial capital. There was a political factor behind the economic boom. After Deng Xiaoping's reputation was stained by the 1989 massacre in Beijing, he wanted to make economic growth his true legacy. While his aides advised him to be cautious, Deng pushed through a broad liberalization of business operations. Deng chose Shanghai to be the model for growth in the 1990s, and a handful of government incentives were like matches to a pile of straw. Shanghai opened a stock market, once unimaginable in a Communist country, and it was greeted with a frenzy of trading that created a new class of speculators, as well as a string of financial scandals. Property could now be bought and sold, and real-estate prices quickly doubled and tripled. Old rules intended to protect workers were softened, construction companies were allowed to run long shifts for low pay, and migrant workers streamed in for those jobs at a terrific rate. The city's population, already fourteen million, swelled with four million more migrant workers.

Alongside Shanghai's economic liberalization came a relaxation in government restrictions on social life. The practice of assigning all jobs and housing for urban citizens was dropped, and graduating students were expected to find their own jobs and homes. To many young people, that prospect was scary; to others, it was liberating. My Chinese friends now drove their own cars. Mobile phones and computers were ubiquitous. The Party retained an iron grip over political matters but eased its chokehold over almost everything else in life. As the Internet caught on, the authorities were able to do little to stem the gush of information available to young Chinese hackers. Life was becoming remarkably free for ordinary urban residents. "The only thing I can't do is start my own newspaper, and I have no desire to do that anyway," said my friend Alex, who opened his own advertising company. Another friend told me that a big change in her life was being allowed to live with her boyfriend, without being married. "It's about time people were allowed to live the way they want," she said.

There was a wild, unstable side to the new freedom in Shanghai, too. Street crime was flourishing. Heroin and ecstasy were available at many of the discos with ear-splitting music that rocked until dawn. Rich Westerners opened expensive country clubs and private schools for their children. On the surface, it looked as though history were repeating itself, with Shanghai recovering its old cosmopolitan, anything-goes mentality. When I went to an afternoon lawn party featuring Westerners dressed up in tutus and sipping martinis as we played croquet on the sprawling lawn of an old British mansion, it occurred to me that we were replaying the rootless profligacy of Shanghai's heyday.

Easy money and changing rules created a permissive atmosphere. The old taboo of a sexual liaison between a Chinese woman and a Western man, so strong when I studied in Xi'an, had completely evaporated. I met women at parties or bars in Shanghai who flirted aggressively and openly. An attractive young woman who sold newspapers in my office building came home with me on the first invitation. A real-estate agent showed me apartments one afternoon and then seduced me at her own place in the evening. What surprised me most was the relaxed attitude of these women, who seemed to think nothing of taking off their clothes with me. I expected morning-after contretemps. Instead I got a peck on the cheek, a smile, and a good-bye.

Casual affairs had become almost the norm in China. Ten years earlier, when I studied in Xi'an, sex was virtually invisible, and lack of housing forced many young couples to dark corners of public parks. But in the 1990s, fading restrictions, a renewed emphasis on making money, and abundant real estate were conspiring to dilute the inbred conservatism of Chinese culture. Married, unmarried, engaged, retired—it made no difference. Almost anyone seemed ready to consider having an affair. As long as proper discretion was observed, everything was permitted.

I looked up from my desk one day and saw a tall, slender woman knocking on my office door. I had trained my assistant, Fang, to chase away door-to-door salespeople who came through the building every day, hawking life insurance or kitchenware. But this woman was lovely, her thick black hair combed to one side. She had such an engaging smile that I wondered if I already knew her. I invited her into my office and asked if we had met previously. She said we had not. But she knew who I was. Her job at a public relations company required that she read the pieces I wrote about China for the *New York Times*.

"You're very famous," she said. "I read all your articles, some of them twice."

I was used to hearing flattery from people trying to sell me something. But I was vulnerable to compliments about my writing, especially when they came from an attractive woman. Her name was Wen. We conversed easily, shifting back and forth between Chinese and English. Wen told me she had come to talk to me about one of her clients, but she never seemed to get to the point. I could tell she was more interested in talking about other things. She laughed frequently, and I laughed along with her, so loudly at one point that my assistant, Fang, peered curiously into my office, which reminded me that my encounters were watched. I invited Wen for lunch the following day, suggesting that it would give her ample time to tell me all she wanted about her client. She agreed.

The next day, Wen arrived at the restaurant in a red and blue floral-patterned dress that hugged the soft curves of her body. I could not take my eyes off her. Over lunch, she did not even mention her company. Instead, we talked about movies and books, about our families. Wen's father was a city official and her mother a paint-er, both of whom made Wen learn to play the piano and read liter-ature. Wen had studied in Europe. She acted independent and had a good sense of humor. When she squeezed my hand tightly as we said good-bye, I felt as though I would have done anything for her.

Wen was thirty-two, four years younger than I. She told me she had trouble finding a Chinese man because most of them wanted a submissive woman, and she was too strong-minded. I liked think-ing of myself as a guy who could handle a strong woman. It was not long before Wen was back in my apartment, unhooking her brassiere.

In contrast with the easy affairs I had enjoyed with women in Shanghai, my relationship with Wen felt serious, at least to me. Here was someone I could really connect with, I thought. Spending time with Wen was easy. She took me on long walks through private gar-dens that were hidden from the street. She took me to the movies, paying extra to sit in the puffy loveseats with a high back, so that we could make out unobserved. She held my hand as we walked along the city's waterfront at night, admiring the bright lights on either side of the river. Wen was proud of her Shanghai heritage, and her family history said as much about the city as any formal historical record.

Wen told me her great-grandfather was a farmer who came to Shanghai around 1900, drawn by the opportunity created by West-ern traders, or "red-haired barbarians," as they were called at the time. Shanghai was a young city by Chinese standards, transformed from a swampy fishing village into a thriving port in the 1800s, when British opium traders arrived. Other foreigners followed, grabbing land and declaring that Chinese laws and customs no longer applied. Under loose European rule, Shanghai bred capitalist traders, gangsters, writers, and beggars. Booming trade drew millions of poor farmers from the surrounding area, an endless supply of cheap labor. Westerners operated elegant country clubs and lived in aristocratic mansions with legions of white-gloved servants. Newly rich Chinese businessmen mixed elements of Western and Chinese culture in their speech and work and dress, adorning their wives in the body-hugging silk gown known as the *qipao.*

Wen's grandfather worked as a manager at a factory that employed hundreds of child laborers to weave textiles. He bought a house in the French section of town, decorated with carefully manicured gardens and steep-roofed houses. The French police were easily bought off by gangsters like Big-Eared Du and Pock-Marked Huang, who profited so grandly from the opium trade that they eventually founded their own banks. Shanghai also drew Chinese dissidents, including a young radical from Hunan called Mao Zedong. When Mao and twelve others convened the first meeting of the Communist Party of China in 1921, they chose as their site a redbrick house in the French district of Shanghai.

Wen's father joined the Communists as a student in 1949, the same year Shanghai was taken over. As a Party official, he joined the new rulers who closed the racetrack and the whorehouses, chasing away the gangsters and foreigners and taking over many of the largest factories and aristocratic homes. The Party took the city's most majestic buildings along the waterfront for themselves. Yet Mao and other leaders in Beijing were suspicious of Shanghai and remanded the bulk of the city's revenue, leaving little to spend on upkeep or infrastructure. The city deteriorated. For the next forty years, virtually no major building was erected, no major highway or bridge built. When I saw the city for the first time in 1985, Shanghai looked dark and dreary, like a crumbling museum piece.

With her father's connections, Wen easily found an office job at a trading company when she got out of school. She was polished and cultivated, a good catch for the international public relations firm that later hired her. She earned a high salary by Chinese standards, but I sensed that hidden family wealth supported Wen's indulgences in Italian shoes and European fashion magazines, and her shopping trips to Hong Kong and Bangkok. Relatives of Communist Party officials often had enormous sums of unexplained cash. To me, Wen seemed to epitomize Shanghai's new cosmopolitan sophistication.

One evening over a meal, Wen lectured me about how Americans do not care about family, how an American would never understand the sacred kind of bond that family holds in China. Chinese people often describe their family ties as virtuous, an almost holy kind of relationship. To me, a typical Chinese family's ties looked suffocating, a combination of obligation and forced closeness. I was taken aback to hear Wen voice an assumption that Americans were morally inferior to Chinese when it came to family relations. On most topics, she was refreshingly open-minded. The attitude she voiced about family sounded like a knee-jerk regurgitation of conventional wisdom. Besides, she knew nothing about my family in America.

As we spent more time together, I felt disappointed that Wen and I were not getting closer. She kept her distance, always holding something back. She referred to herself as my girlfriend when we were together, but she made me promise to tell no one. She refused to meet any of my friends, saying that would come later. She would not take me to her home, saying she did not want her neighbors to see her with a Western man. She was secretive about several aspects of her life. When she left my apartment after a night of lovemaking, I had no idea where she was going. She might have other men, for all I knew. She often disappeared for a few days at a time, without being in touch. "I have a thing," she would say. I had grown to like that phrase, using it frequently myself as a way to get out of unwanted social obligations. Yet when Wen told me she "had a thing," I felt frustrated. When I tried to talk about it with her, Wen changed the subject.

One evening as we lay together in the dark, I asked Wen if she ever wanted to have children. She was silent for a while. Then she said, "I already have a son." I thought I had misheard her and asked again. The answer was the same. She had a son. He was two years old. She was married, too, though her husband worked in Beijing and she saw him rarely. I couldn't believe it. I went back in my mind, trying to remember if she had told me she was single or if I had just assumed it. I reminded her that she had told me how hard it was for her to find a man who could handle an independent woman. It *is* hard, she insisted.

"And your son? How often do you see him?" I asked.

"Once a week," she said. Her mother cared for the child. Wen went to go see him most Sundays, but sometimes she was too busy. She talked about him as though he were an unnecessary appendage. "I have to work," she said defensively. "I have a lot of things to do."

Like go to bed with me, I thought. After her self-righteous talk about the sacred role of family, I now saw that she was essentially ignoring her infant son, leaving him with his grandmother. She was married to a man who saw their son even less than Wen did. It was a common arrangement in China. Many of my Chinese friends with young children placed them with their parents, the children's grandparents, or in state-run day care. It did not negate the intense closeness of many Chinese brothers and sisters, or the deep sense of obligation to serve one's parents. But the Chinese standard of family closeness, based on Wen's model, was not anything I wanted to emulate. Wen seemed to have no flicker of guilt about having an affair outside her marriage. She was only concerned with whether anyone found out. Appearances were all.

It took me a while to digest the fact that Wen and I had spoken for months about our lives and she had kept a major part of hers hidden. Had she been afraid that I would not be interested in her if I knew she already had a child? No, she said, adding that it simply wasn't any of my business until I got to know her well. Now she acted as though I should feel closer to her, privileged to be told about the existence of her husband and son, which she kept secret from her coworkers. But I was already retreating from her mentally.

I stopped calling Wen. Now it was her turn to grow irritated. As I was pulling away, she seemed more interested in me. She called repeatedly until I reluctantly agreed to meet her for dinner one night. As we ate, I told her I did not want to see her anymore. Tears welled in her eyes. She lamented that it was hard to find a man because she had a career and an independent mind.

"And a husband," I added.

She scowled at me. "You don't understand," she said dismissively. "It's very complicated." Yes, I thought, your life is complicated. But the truth was that I was cruel to Wen that night because I felt humiliated, having dated her for months without knowing that she was married.

Feeling helpless and hemmed in, I took my usual way out. I buried myself in work and began to travel more. My Chinese friends were fond of saying that the heart of China resided outside big cities like Beijing and Shanghai. I found that getting on an air-plane and landing in a new place was a good way to distract myself from wounded emotions. Every province in China seemed to offer its own particular drama, many of them hidden behind a veneer of orderly business.

chapter nine

IN A PIRATE'S LAIR

On a muddy street near the Pearl River, fish sellers hawked their offerings in a row of open-faced storefronts with spinach green canopies that sagged out toward the street. Short men in tall rubber boots tromped through puddles, chattering in the staccato of Cantonese, the dialect spoken in this city, Guangzhou. A pungent, briny smell of the sea infested the air. Inside white Styrofoam containers, red snapper and gray grouper cautiously trod water, facing life's final hours. In big straw baskets, hand-sized crabs tried to hide in clumps of seaweed. Bundles of shrimp languished in silver pails. The fish market, open since dawn, still pulsed with activity in the early evening when I showed up with a Chinese lawyer named Chu.

Chu led me inside a shop and pointed out

a corpulent red snapper. One of the fish sellers scooped it up in a plastic bag with enough water to keep it wriggling as we carried it to a restaurant a few blocks away. Chu handed it to the cook, with instructions to steam it with ginger. Cantonese people are particular about their cuisine, known for its delicate aromas. For side dishes, Chu asked for string beans sautéed in garlic, braised eggplant with bits of ground pork, and a plate of fried rice. We took our seats at a plain Formica table with plastic stools and shared a big bottle of local beer. Other tables were crowded with Chinese laborers and businessmen, older families and younger couples, yakking loudly in Cantonese. Before long, our fish arrived on a platter, adorned with green sprigs of parsley, steam rising off its plump body. With my chopsticks I picked at clumps of fish that slid easily from the bone. Chu frowned at the eggplant, saying it was too salty. It tasted fine to me.

Chu was a tall and chubby man. His wire-rimmed glasses dented the top end of his fleshy cheeks when he smiled. He laughed like a resonant drum. Chu was the friend of a friend, who recommended him as particularly well informed about the situation in Guangzhou, a lively city on China's southern coast, a hundred miles upriver from Hong Kong. Most of Chu's clients were Western companies. He kept close tabs on the machinery of local politics, in part for its fluctuating impact on the investment climate, in part for the gossipy titillation of political intrigue.

I came to Guangzhou after hearing rumors that an underworld was flourishing there. Gambling, smuggling, and other crimes were all on the rise. I had seen a news item on Chinese television trumpeting a crackdown on organized crime, showing police raids on hidden casinos with extravagant gaming tables staffed by young Chinese women wearing Playboy bunny outfits. I knew that when

China's media portrayed a successful police operation, it usually meant that the situation was veering out of control. Chinese gangsters operated in a secret world, not one I thought I could get close to. In a culture where ordinary people guard their privacy carefully, criminals are even more discreet. Still, if a Chinese underworld was getting unruly, I could not resist trying to get a peek inside it.

Chu filled me in on recent history. The economic boom of the 1990s bred payoffs and sweetheart deals for officers in Guangzhou's government, police, and military, who overlooked the growing prevalence of illegal activity and even took a hand in the more lucrative areas, like smuggling and prostitution. Word eventually reached leaders in Beijing about growing crime and complicity of local Party members. Deciding to act, Beijing replaced the Communist Party chief in Guangzhou with a tough-talking cadre from up north. He announced a "rectification campaign," aimed at curtailing excesses by firing or demoting suspect officials and replacing them with outsiders from Beijing. Now everyone was anxiously watching to see how far the new chief would go in his crackdown. Chu observed that in many parts of the world, people would applaud a move by the central government toward more law and order. But people from Guangzhou and Beijing have viewed each other with suspicion for centuries, and the latest move caused broad misgivings.

Beijing people generally look down on their southern compatriots as money-grubbing, cultureless elves. With its history as a center of commerce with Southeast Asia, Guangzhou breeds a trader's mentality, with people always on the lookout for a deal. In the south, northern Chinese are seen as too literal-minded and overly concerned with ideology. In the 1980s, Deng Xiaoping allowed

Guangzhou to experiment with elements of capitalism to draw investment from ethnic Chinese businessmen in places like Hong Kong, Malaysia, Indonesia, and Thailand. Hundreds of factories sprouted, making toys and shoes and plastic goods. Business flourished. Local officials took a flexible attitude toward favor-trading and bribery, sometimes taking positions as silent partners in a business. Business was temporarily reined in every time Beijing launched a political campaign, only to resume again once things blew over. When China's economy gained momentum in the 1990s, the pace of business quickened, over the table and under. Gangsters began to assert themselves, sharing the take with police and military officers as their grasp expanded from petty crimes into big business.

Chu said that whenever his clients started to make money, Chinese gangsters would quickly emerge to squeeze some cash out of them. The worst area was entertainment, where the pirating of movies and music was so lucrative that thugs had virtually taken it over. Chu said the volume of pirated movies was exploding, particularly those on video compact discs (a crude forerunner of DVD), mass-copied on special machines. Many pirates allied themselves with the police and the military, paying handsomely to protect their product and sabotage competitors. When gunfights erupted between drivers of competing delivery trucks, Chu said, some gangsters turned to friends in the army to arrange use of military trucks and soldiers to distribute the illegal goods. Chu knew a senior officer in the Guangzhou military garrison who spent all his time on pirating and trading, and none on military affairs.

Chu predicted that the new Party chief in Guangzhou would choose his targets carefully. A new boss often wants to assert authority and make it look as though he is genuinely cleaning up a dirty situation. But it would be hard to conduct a thorough housecleaning without making enemies with influential Party leaders, since so many of them and their relatives had a hand in the pirating business. In all likelihood, Chu said, a few scapegoats would be chosen and punished harshly.

Chu showed me a list of ten companies that were suspended for illegally copying music and movies. None had yet been prosecuted, but each company was undergoing a "review," which Chu described as a torturous bureaucratic procedure that gave officials time to decide what was politically feasible. I looked at the addresses. Three were located in the city of Guangzhou, the others were spread around the surrounding countryside. I was intrigued by the idea of showing up and asking to talk to the boss. Chu thought it might be risky. Since pirates often worked hand in hand with the military and the secret police, they might act irrationally toward someone asking pesky questions. Chu also warned me that the addresses might be bogus, since Chinese pirates often hid production sites behind dummy corporations and fake addresses.

I set out the next morning. At the first address, I found a clothing store. The second address was bogus as well. I became discouraged. But when I walked up to the third address, I was surprised to see that it was a military compound with a uniformed guard at the gate. Normally I had no business walking into such a place. Impulsively, I decided to try one of my old tricks, walking past a guard without looking at him, and when he yelled at me to stop, pretending I could not understand Chinese. It worked. Once I rounded a corner and was out of sight, I asked a cleaning woman for the office of the Cai Ling Video Company. She pointed me to the second floor of a nearby building, just inside a veranda that looked out at a grand auditorium used for military ceremonies. Inside the office, I told a secretary I was a reporter and wanted to see the manager. I gave her my card. She disappeared into an inner office. I felt apprehensive as I sat on a small sofa, expecting to be shown out any moment. Or would I be taken to a windowless room and beaten? Instead, the secretary came back smiling and took me to the inner office, where a genuine pirate sat at his desk.

His name was Wang Binyan. He had greased-back hair and the puffy face of a man who lived on cigarettes and alcohol. He wore a black jacket and a dark shirt, his gray long underwear peeking out at the collar and wrist. Wang did not get up from his high-backed swivel chair behind an ornate desk when I entered, and he nodded toward a black leather sofa. I sat down. A few New Year's cards were pinned to the wall behind him, and a Chinese watercolor of a dragonfly hung on a silk scroll. Wang smoked a 555 brand cigarette, drawing hard and exhaling out his nose. Wang looked at me cautiously, like a local chieftain who wonders if the barbarian at his gate has anything useful to offer. I could sense his pride as an operator, a boss, the ruler of a small kingdom, a man who was accustomed to getting his way.

I did my reporter thing, acting friendly, hoping I could persuade him to talk about his business. I presented myself as someone who understood China's needs, who knew that modern rules often clashed with an old culture like China's. I told him I wanted to understand how things really worked. I did my best to make Wang think I was on his side. Wang nodded and smiled as he listened. Then he gave me his philosophy, like a chief executive enchanted with his own vision. China needs access to American movies, he said, and they should be available to Chinese consumers at an affordable price, say, a dollar a disc. Rules about intellectual property were anti-Chinese. It was immoral for a rich country like America to demand royalties from a poor country like China. China's leaders were caving in when, in trade talks with Americans, they agreed to curtail pirating. "This isn't America!" he exclaimed. "Americans do not rule here!" Wang spoke with the bluster and bombast of someone who is used to intimidating people. I nodded sympathetically.

I gathered my courage to ask Wang whether it was true that he had been suspended for illegally copying movies. Wang frowned. It was just temporary, he assured me. "It's political," he said. "They have to make it look like they are doing something." That's a yes, I thought. Out loud, I suggested to Wang that he must be accustomed to seeing the cycles of political pressure, which build and then subside, based on the timing of political events. "Right," Wang said. It was the same in the movie studio where he had once worked as a director. Whenever a supervising official was about to come from Beijing, the studio head would restrict the free banquets and private use of company cars that were usually part of compensation for directors like Wang. I asked which studio Wang had worked at. He answered Xi'an Film Studio, a place I had visited several times when I lived in Xi'an, and where I had met several directors. I told him I knew Wu Tianming, a leading director whose movie *Old Well* was one of my favorites. Wang reached behind himself and pulled a New Year's card off the wall to show me that it was signed by Wu. "Wu Tianming is my *buddy,*" he said proudly. Wang stood and came over to clap me on the shoulder, like an old friend. Now it was his turn to ask me something. "How did you get past the gate?" he asked. "I played the dumb foreigner," I told him. We laughed together. We were pals.

Underneath the camaraderie, I knew Wang was not really my pal. He wanted to use me. He hoped that I would write a favorable newspaper article about an upstanding movie distributor who contributed to the health of Chinese society, the kind of "news" that regularly appeared in Chinese newspapers. If I mentioned him in an article, it might bolster his standing and hasten a lifting of his suspension. Most Chinese businessmen shy from publicity in the Western media, but Wang seemed to think he could win me over to his side, and that a positive story would help him.

The more Wang spoke, however, the more he fell into my hands. When Wang said that pirating was not a bad thing, he gave me the evidence I needed. I felt an illicit thrill grow inside me; I had a good newspaper story. I sat there, acting as if I were on his side, nodding sympathetically every three seconds or so, all the time knowing that his own words spelled his demise. Even though I had coaxed him to speak at length by acting friendly, I would report the spirit and content of his words accurately. Wang Binyan was being careless, opening up to an American reporter. I was glad he chose me. I left his office cheering inside.

My story was printed. It attracted attention in Washington and Beijing. In a trade meeting, an American negotiator held up a copy as evidence that China was all talk and no action when it came to cracking down on piracy. The result was inevitable. The call that I feared came to my office in Shanghai about a month later. It was Wang. "I'm in big trouble," he rasped. "You have to help me." I asked what I could do. "You have to write another article taking back everything you wrote about me." I told him I could not do that. "I wrote the truth," I said feebly. For a moment, I heard only silence. Then he said, "You know nothing of the truth."

Fair enough. A reporter rarely knows the full truth of a situation he or she reports on. The broad reality of the pirating business in Guangdong was certainly more complex and sordid than I had been able to describe in a newspaper article. Besides, Wang's crimes were similar to those of hundreds of other Chinese businessmen.

The main reason Wang was punished was that he made the mistake of talking to me. I felt bad. If I had more guts, I would have warned Wang during our interview that I disagreed with his assessment of pirating and that my article would reflect it. Face to face, I was afraid to be that direct. I preferred the Chinese way, to keep up the appearance of friendliness and to stick the knife in once I was out of sight.

I wondered if Wang might try to take revenge. For a few weeks, I felt flickers of fear every time a stranger showed up at the door of my office in Shanghai, wondering if they were sent by Wang, though they turned out to be deliverymen or salesmen. Nothing happened. My fear gradually subsided.

About two months later, I saw a small item in a Chinese newspaper about the government's efforts to curb pirating. It named Wang Binyan and said he was sentenced to eight years in jail. I was relieved that he was in custody, but I also felt guilty. Had I not written my story, would Wang be free that evening, eating dinner with his family, screwing a mistress, or drinking beer with his buddies? Instead, he was in jail, with a lot of time to think about how nice I had seemed that day in his office, how different things might have been.

I moved on to other stories, as I always did. One of the drawbacks of journalism was that the relentless pace, with a constant stream of new stories, often left me feeling unresolved about the old ones. In Wang's case, however, I was able to find out part of the back story, one that put my own role into perspective. About a year after Wang was jailed, I came across a man who had played a bigger role than I in his case.

His name was Cheng. He was an expert in copyright piracy. Cheng was nearing fifty, and he had the grizzled appearance of a man who had battled bureaucracies, from inside and out, for many years. He wore a dark suit and chain-smoked 555 brand cigarettes, just like Wang. He began a career in China's regulatory bureaucracy but was frustrated by government work, with its poor pay and endless score-settling. Cheng emigrated to Hong Kong in the 1980s and became a corporate detective. He often traveled to Shanghai and Guangzhou, where he cultivated friendships with people in the police and on regulatory commissions. With Hong Kong residency, he had partial legal protection when someone tried to intimidate him, as often happened. Hired by an organization of international music companies, Cheng focused his efforts on prodding the Chinese government to fight piracy of movies and music. He filed dozens of lawsuits against violators of intellectual property laws, trying to pressure the government into enforcing rules that were on the books but went ignored. Even though he lost more cases than he won, he felt progress was being made. "Only if we force the courts to look at real cases will the rule of law ever emerge in China," Cheng told me. "It won't happen soon, but it will happen someday."

When the piracy of video discs took off in the 1990s, Cheng concentrated his attention on Guangzhou, where he opened an office. Working with Chinese lawyers and investigators, he compiled a list of pirates who produced an unusually large number of fake copies. One of the names on his list was Wang Binyan.

Cheng contacted a friend of Wang's and asked him to set up a meeting. It took place about three months before I met Wang in his office. Wang seemed to assume that Cheng was like the other government regulators he often came across, who simply needed to be taken to a fancy meal or given a small stack of cash, to leave things alone. Wang arranged an elaborate banquet for Cheng at an upscale hotel in Guangzhou and talked about how he and Cheng could cooperate. Cheng had not told Wang what his real intentions

The sun sets on Mao: A peasant woman on the street in 1984, the year I arrived in Xi'an, when China was just beginning the transition away from fanatical leftism and poverty.

The timeless Chinese village: A woman outside her home in Anhui Province, in eastern China.

Winter in Beijing: Two old men sitting outside the Forbidden City in China's capital, where political gossip is a daily staple.

Tiananmen Square: At the height of the student movement in 1989, more than a million protesters filled the square at the heart of Beijing. A few weeks later, a massacre would clear Tiananmen of students and fill it with soldiers. DONG LI

Shanghai fashion: As China's old rules relaxed, Shanghai residents adopted the bourgeois practice of wearing pajamas, even during broad daylight, when going to market.

Children in Yunnan Province, in China's southwest.

Jin Xing, China's transgendered choreographer. COURTESY OF JIN XING

A fortune-teller on the sidewalk in Hai-k'ou, Hainan Island. He forecast to the author that he would find happiness when he let go of his ambition.

Tibet: Three monks relaxing on the grass outside their monastery.

Tibet: Two young novice monks at a center of Tibetan worship.

Tibet: Women farming barley in the mountains of eastern Tibet.

Sky burial: A Tibetan monk performing a sky burial.

were, though he told the truth by saying his aim was to learn as much as he could about the production of video and music discs in Guangdong. Wang did not hide his active piracy, and he dropped hints about his closeness to senior officers in the air force and secret police. Wang offered to introduce Cheng to his friends in the local government, and Cheng took him up on it. (Not, as Wang thought, to arrange favors or bribes, but rather to identify corrupt officials.) Feeling impervious to pressure, Wang told Cheng where his production lines were located. Wang made disparaging comments about a couple of his competitors, suggesting that Cheng look at them as the real offenders.

Cheng sent an investigator to visit Wang's factory surreptitiously. A detailed report was compiled, and Cheng submitted it with other evidence to the authorities in Guangzhou. He pressed hard for them to suspend Wang's operations. When Wang got wind of it, he went ballistic. "Those people are snakes!" he yelled to an acquaintance. "I help them, and what do they do? They sent people here undercover to see what we were making! They were spying!"

Precisely. Cheng expected Wang to be angry and to call his friends. He braced for a reaction. Soon enough, two officers from the Guangdong Security Bureau, the local branch of China's secret police, called on Cheng's office in Guangzhou. They invited themselves inside, sat down on a sofa, and suggested politely that Cheng call off all investigation into Wang's operations, or else "there might be trouble." Now Cheng was alarmed. He had expected Wang to try to interfere, but he was surprised that it was the secret police who came to threaten him in person. Still, Cheng decided to hold his ground, reasoning that his job as a representative of an international organization made it unlikely that anyone would go further than threatening him. If he had actually feared for his life, Cheng told me, he would have left Guangzhou. Besides, he had an important case in court the following week and did not want to miss it. He stayed.

A few days later, another knock came on Cheng's office door. This time it was the uniformed police. They told him to send his staff home and to close the office until further notice. Then they handcuffed him and took him to jail. Cheng asked what the charge was. *"Ni ziji hen qingchu"* came the reply. "You yourself are very clear." It was a line often used by Chinese authorities to intimidate a suspect while evading responsibility for making a charge.

The police put Cheng in a dark jail cell with ordinary criminals. He was never charged with a crime. Cheng calmly talked the guards into letting him make a phone call, and he contacted an influential lawyer who would make a public spectacle of his case if it were not resolved. The lawyer contacted a senior official in Beijing and showed him a secret file that Cheng had been holding for an emergency. It showed evidence that senior officers in the Guangdong Security Bureau controlled a factory that was mass-producing pornographic movies, a no-no even in China's relatively free business world. "When the people in Beijing saw evidence of that, they were really shocked," Cheng said. He was let out of jail after one week.

Wang Binyan's operations were investigated by Beijing, and he was ordered to suspend production temporarily. He was in that limbo on the day that I walked into his office. Had he been smart, he would have kept his mouth shut. But he was apparently used to being protected and acting as he pleased. Cheng was amused when my newspaper story appeared. Not long afterward, he heard that the authorities had decided to make an example of Wang.

I was relieved to learn that the circumstances of Wang's jailing went deeper than his meeting with me. Like many journalists, I sometimes fell for an inflated notion that my reports steered a course of history. In reality, they were usually one piece in a complex mosaic. Sometimes a bigger piece, sometimes a smaller one. But only a piece. In Wang's case, I was glad to know that someone else played a role, too.

"If Wang hadn't spoken to you, who knows where his case would be?" Cheng asked. He chuckled with a world-weariness I could not yet share. "He knew a lot of people, he was very well protected. But the timing went against him."

I asked Cheng if he ever had second thoughts about helping send people to jail. He smiled knowingly, sensing that I was really asking about my own role. "Not people like Wang," he said. "He's a criminal."

chapter ten

LEAVING FUJIAN

areering down a bumpy road in China's countryside, sitting in the backseat of a beat-up Volkswagen taxi, I enjoyed the warm, humid air streaming in the window. The sun was high, and white hibiscus grew in clumped bushes at the side of the road. The driver, a crusty man in his fifties, went fast. We zoomed through dusty villages of small wooden houses, with children playing in the dirt and old men sitting in straw chairs as they fanned themselves and read newspapers. We jostled unwieldy trucks overflowing with cheap wares, swerving in and out of traffic. We passed a town with an outdoor market where farmers sold vegetables and rudimentary kitchenware. We stopped at a roadside stand to buy bottled water from an old woman with heavy wrinkles and a toothless smile. This part of Fujian

Province looked like many out-of-the-way places on the southeast coast of China. Yet there was something to distinguish this area from the others around it. It was the spot in China where most illegal immigrants to the United States originated.

In New York, as I interviewed passengers from the *Golden Venture,* Fujian assumed a mythic role in my mind. A mysterious region of craggy mountains and rocky coast, Fujian sent millions of immigrants to America. For reasons no one could pin down, more than ninety percent of the smuggled men and women came from one small area of Fujian, three counties near the provincial capital of Fuzhou. Now I was finally journeying to the source to try to solve the mystery.

I began by looking for the family of a woman named Gao Liqin, who had been smuggled to America a year earlier. She was working off her debt as a seamstress in Brooklyn when she was kidnapped, tortured, and killed. Finding her family, and seeing where she came from and what her life was like before she set out, might help me understand why she had left.

Her family lived in Chang Le, a large town about fifty miles from the ocean. I called ahead and contacted the woman's brother, Gao Limin. He met me at a bus stop. Gao was an earnest-looking man of twenty-eight with oversized square glasses and a nervous tic that kept him scratching his left temple. He walked me to his home, passing a small market and a row of shiny new apartment blocks with blue-tinted windows, apparently a local fad. "Money from America," Gao said as he nodded at the buildings.

The Gao home was located down a narrow alley. Dark wooden beams and white plaster walls adorned the one-room ground floor. Gao's mother, a slight woman with soft gray hair, was crying on a stool in the corner. On another stool, a thirteen-year-old girl with a long ponytail wailed quietly. She and a ten-year-old boy nearby were now the orphans of the woman who had been killed in New York. There was something staged about the way they sat, as though they were intentionally showing their sadness for me.

I sat down, and Gao poured me a cup of jasmine tea. He refilled it several times over the next few hours as he told me his sister's story. Gao Liqin was smuggled to the United States at age thirty-four. Like other illegal immigrants, she and her family had borrowed more than $30,000 to get her to America, leaning on several relatives and a loan shark to scrape together the cash. Smugglers gave her a fake passport and a plane ticket that flew her to six cities around the world before she landed in Tegucigalpa, Honduras. With a half dozen other Chinese, she traveled by truck and bus through Mexico and finally on foot over a border into Texas. She ended up in New York City, where she got work as a seamstress in a Brooklyn sweatshop for a dollar an hour. It was backbreaking work. It would take years to pay off the family's debt unless she could get a better job. She called her brother once a month. Each time she said everything was going well, but he could hear the strain in her voice. "I think she was worried that we would be concerned about her. She said, 'Don't worry about me,' over and over," Gao said. "But we were not worried. She was in America."

From Fujian, America looked like paradise, overflowing with consumer goods. A country where even poor people have a car. No local Communist Party bosses to make one's life miserable. The reality, for Gao Liqin and most other illegal immigrants, was more prosaic.

One night as Gao left her shift at the garment factory in Brooklyn at 10 P.M., she was grabbed by three Chinese men who forced her into the backseat of a car, gagged her mouth, and tied her hands behind her back. They took her to a basement apartment in Sunset Park, a section of Brooklyn where many Chinese immigrants live. They shoved her in a dark closet with another victim, a Chinese woman who was also gagged and bound. At noon the next day, which was midnight in Fujian, one of the young men called the Gao home in Fujian. Gao Limin answered the phone and was told that his sister "had encountered a little danger." She would be released, the voice said, if the family paid an additional $38,000. Gao protested that since the family had not yet paid off their original $30,000, how could they possibly afford more? The kidnapper said if the family did not pay, their daughter would be killed. Gao listened as the kidnapper held the phone to the sister's mouth. In a hoarse voice, she pleaded with him to pay. The kidnapper came back on the line and said someone would knock on the door of the Gao home in China the next day and tell them where to make the payment. Sure enough, a young man came by the following afternoon and told Gao to go to the parking lot of a particular hotel in Fuzhou, fifty miles away.

Gao convened a meeting of four relatives who had lent money for the sister's voyage. They were businessmen with access to money. They all knew that reporting the kidnapping to the Chinese police would be pointless, since many police officers colluded with smugglers. The relatives, and two more loan sharks, pooled money. Gao carried the full amount in cash in a large envelope to the hotel in Fuzhou, where a man in dark glasses directed him to pass it through the slit of an open window of a black Mercedes in the parking lot. Gao could not see who was inside. He left quickly.

Two days later, the phone rang again in the middle of the night. This time it was a relative in America, with bad news. Gao's sister was dead. She was found in the basement apartment in Brooklyn where she had been held. The gang members had raped and beaten her. One of them hit her over the head with a television set, and though she evidently resisted, she was finally strangled to death with the television cord. Gao could not figure out whether the death occurred before or after he paid the ransom. Did the kidnappers kill her only after they knew they had the money? Was there some other reason? Would they have kept her alive longer had he not paid? Now, in addition to the shock of losing his sister, Gao was haunted with guilt that he had somehow caused her death.

It was a chilling story. But it was not over. Gao's family was deeply in debt. And now their main hope, a sister earning an hourly wage in New York, was gone. Gao and his parents were devastated. His sister's two children had lost their mother. Gao showed me photographs of his sister's coffin, sent from New York. To me, it looked unreasonably risky to put Gao Liqin's life in the hands of smugglers, who knew where her family lived in Fujian and could extort more money from them. The smugglers apparently knew that kidnapping in New York and demanding a ransom in Fujian split the crime in two and reduced the chances that the police in either place would pursue it. These smugglers had taken hundreds of thousands of Chinese to the U.S. each year, and only a handful were kidnapped and murdered. Why had bad luck befallen Gao Liqin? There was no answer.

I asked Gao why he and his family were now so willing to tell the story to me. Gao said he hoped that I would write a newspaper article about his sister's tragedy and that it might generate sympathy from readers. Gao's mother started to cry again. I was missing something. Sympathy from readers? He smiled awkwardly. "I hope you can help us," he said. "We need to get enough money to send them." He gestured at the young girl and boy who sat with us at the table, listening to a retelling of their mother's murder. Now I understood. Gao was angling to send his niece and nephew to America, too, even if it meant enduring the same risks that had killed his sister. From Gao's point of view, since his sister was dead, someone else was going to have to work off the debt. Like others in Chang Le, the Gao family had so deeply absorbed the belief in emigrating to America that they were pursuing it blindly. Beyond their grief over losing a daughter, they felt compelled to show me tears in case I could help earn them some money.

The hour grew late. Gao showed me out his front door and walked me down the alley toward the main road, so I could find a taxi to take me back to the city. I breathed in the cool night air, glad to be outside after hours of a draining, depressing interview. As Gao and I walked down to the end of the alleyway, I noticed a man standing in the shadow of the building on the corner. He stepped away almost as soon as I saw him, and for a moment I wondered if he was watching us. Then I wondered, was I *followed* to Gao's house? I mentally retraced my steps to figure out whether I had done something to tip off the police.

The man on the street corner retreated from view. I looked around once and did not see him. Maybe it was my imagination, I thought. There were no taxis on the street, so Gao suggested we ride a pedicab over to the town square, where I could get a car to take me back to Fuzhou. As we started off, I looked over my shoulder and saw the man from the shadows get into another pedicab and start to follow us. Now I was sure. Flushed with anger, feeling violated, I looked at Gao, sitting next to me, apparently oblivious to the pedicab tailing us.

I never knew how often I was followed during the years I lived in

China. I assumed the worst. Chinese authorities are inherently suspicious of foreigners, and anyone working for a large American newspaper was automatically suspected of being a government agent. The secret police in Shanghai did not need to follow me every day, since they bugged my home and office. When I walked around my apartment, I sometimes imagined an underpaid Chinese police officer sitting in a windowless room somewhere, listening through a pair of worn earphones as I flushed the toilet or made breakfast. But I became used to it, telling myself that I was not doing anything secret, that I had nothing to hide. Thinking about surveillance would drive me crazy. The police probably followed me more often than I knew. On a bad day, that suspicion made me paranoid, always glancing around and looking over my shoulder. Most of the time, I tried to ignore it. Being followed in itself was harmless. The real danger was to the Chinese person sitting next to me, who could get in trouble for disclosing improper information to a reporter. When I sat around over beers with other American reporters in China, we sometimes boasted about the precautions we took to protect our sources, recounting the good stories we had to abandon because to publish would endanger a friend. Most of the time we did not know if we were endangering people who spoke with us. That ignorance sometimes made it easier for me to push after a story. It was harder to ignore when I could actually see the man following me.

As we rode, I wondered whether the man in the pedicab behind us was following me or following Gao. Gao knew he was taking a risk by telling me his sister's story, since its publication would inevitably draw the attention of the authorities. Just meeting a foreign reporter was no longer considered a crime in China, as it once had been. When Fox Butterfield opened a bureau in Beijing for the *New York Times* in 1979, virtually everyone he befriended was later questioned by the police. But by the 1990s, the authorities could no longer keep track of every single contact between a Western journalist and a Chinese citizen. However, they could harass Gao if they wanted, creating a fresh page in his *dang an,* his police file, that might affect his prospects for work in the future. Still, it was unlikely he would be arrested for telling his tale of woe. Or so I told myself. I was only guessing at the consequences.

When we got to the town square, Gao paid the pedicab driver. I got out and looked up to see the other pedicab pulling up to the curb, about thirty yards behind us. Gao still seemed unaware of it. I grasped his hand and looked him in the eye. "Be careful," I said. He seemed to know what I meant. He laughed. "What can they do to me? My sister's already dead. What can they do?" I found myself laughing, too, for a bitter moment. The secret police did not seem like such a threat after what he had been through. It was unlikely that they would detain or jail him.

I got in a taxi, another old Volkswagen, and headed out of town. As the car pulled away, I turned to watch the man in the shadows. He was watching Gao, not me. I felt a flicker of relief, as though I had shaken the tail. But I still didn't know whether it spelled more trouble for Gao. I sank down in the backseat of the cab, repeating a mantra, the kind I often told myself when I hit morally ambiguous territory. Reporting and writing are not wrong. The system that opposes free speech, particularly about a murder, is immoral. A Communist system demanding secrecy would fall one day. Reporting a family's tragedy was a small step in the right direction if it shed light on the dangers of people-smuggling. I told myself these things to justify my role in China, to live with the doubt and the sense of guilt that I could never navigate the thickets of ignorance without making mistakes.

I called Gao the next day, hoping to find him at home, and not in jail. Gao answered the phone. He told me the police had not bothered him. He guessed he had been followed to intimidate him from speaking too freely with me. The tactic did not work. Gao was eager to show me around Fujian and help me learn about the emigration mania that had swept the area. He was willing to risk the consequences because he knew the authorities would probably leave him alone.

Over the following days, Gao introduced me to several families, each with their own emigration story. Virtually every family I met spoke proudly about their relative who had been smuggled to America. They seemed to believe that only those families who delivered a member to America could be considered successful. Several told me enthusiastically about the visits back to Fujian by immigrants who made good, carrying expensive gifts and wearing fancy jewelry. What better proof that city streets in America were paved with gold? If one of those returning sons or daughters spoke of hardship or disappointment, it would be disrespectful, deflating the dreams of family members who had borrowed so heavily to send them overseas. No wonder many of those immigrants never made it home, as they slaved away as seamstresses or busboys, making less than minimum wage. Fujian was infected with emigration mania, a mind-set that bought into an idea and ignored any evidence to the contrary. Families eyed each other carefully, neighbors competing to see who could send a family member to America first. As Wang the teenager had told me in New York, many immigrants acted on the keep-up-with-the-Joneses rivalry between families.

With emigration so much on their minds, Fujian residents were ripe for swindle. Local touts combed villages and towns, talking up the ease and convenience of getting to America, pledging swift travel and a guaranteed job on the other side, little of that promise being true. The real smugglers were ethnic Chinese businessmen and -women living in Taiwan, Fujian, New York—people who traveled back and forth across the Pacific, who could hire muscle on either side, who could move large amounts of cash. They often operated alliances among themselves, so that no one would be held accountable if things fell apart. The demand in Fujian fueled a network of smugglers to grow in their midst. The more customers, the easier for smugglers to pay off the police, customs officers, and ranking officials. The *Golden Venture*'s crash landing shined a light on the people-smuggling business, but it did not change it significantly.

I combed Fujian for intriguing tales, feeling drawn to the tragic ones. A particularly arresting one came from a woman I met in a small village outside Chang Le. It was a tiny place with one main street of wooden houses, a small vegetable market, and a single video shop. Li was a small, intense woman with fiery eyes and a bright smile. She welcomed me to her small two-story home with a strong, muscular handshake. Her eyes locked on mine. As she spoke to me, she frequently reached over and touched the top of my hand. She was agitated, bursting with a story she wanted to tell, and her eagerness to win my attention was tinged with sexual tension.

Li told me her husband, Rong, had joined the parade of men in Fujian who wanted to go to America to seek a fortune. He bought into the belief that he could go to America for two years and earn a pile of money. Everyone in this part of Fujian seemed to believe it, and Li had believed it, too. She had a cousin who went to America illegally in the mid-1980s, started as a dishwasher in Chinatown, and within ten years owned his own Chinese restaurant outside New York City.

Rong went to neighboring villages and counties, spending long hours talking to his uncles and cousins and persuading them that he would make it in America. Rong eventually borrowed enough money to pay the initial fee for his voyage. He departed for the U.S. about six months after the *Golden Venture* crashed in New York. Compared with those who suffered in the hold of a dilapidated freighter for months, his passage was relatively easy. His smugglers gave him a passport stolen from a Thai businessman, and he flew through several Central American cities before landing in New York. Rong moved to Seattle where he got a job cleaning in the kitchen of a Chinese restaurant. He called Li after he arrived, sounding excited and optimistic. He said he would call again when he could. The next call came two months later, and he sounded dispirited, though he insisted everything was okay. He would not talk about his job or living situation, and Li became worried. She did not have a mailing address or a phone number, no way to reach him. "I was going crazy," she recalled. "We were together almost every day for twenty years, and then suddenly he disappears and there is no contact at all. I could not stand it. I started wishing he had not gone."

It was four months before he called again. This time, Rong sounded terrible. There had been a crisis, he said, and he needed $50,000. Another man took the phone and yelled, "You better send the money!" Then Rong got back on and pleaded with his wife to send some money. He would not say what it was for but warned that he might die without it. He told her he would call back two days later to tell her where to send the money. After hanging up, Li wondered if Rong had been kidnapped. She did not see how she could possibly borrow that kind of money. She waited anxiously for the next phone call, planning to ask Rong where she should borrow. But the call never came. As each day passed, her concern grew. She wondered if Rong had been killed or if he was too ashamed to call her back. After weeks, she was desperate. After months, she was disconsolate.

When I met Li, it had been eight months since that last call from her husband. I was the first American she had ever spoken to. She seemed to hope that somehow I could tell her where Rong was or what had happened to him. "Is this common in your America?" she asked. I wondered if Rong had met the same fate as Gao Liqin, killed in a kidnapping gone wrong. But I also wondered if Rong, living alone in America, had found himself in a desperate situation that he could not bring himself to tell his wife about. There could be another woman, a gambling problem. The crux of Li's situation, like that of so many other families in Fujian whose relatives went illegally to the United States, was not knowing.

"I know he's still alive, I can feel it," Li said, her eyes brimming with tears. "Something is wrong, but I don't know what it is." Li wanted me to help. If I wrote an article about her, she suggested, maybe Rong or someone who knew him would see it. Maybe it would prompt him to contact her. I had little faith that mentioning her in an article would solve her mystery, but I promised to help if I could.

As Li spoke with me, her five children wandered in and out of the house. (Like many mothers in rural China, Li had ignored the one-child policy.) Her eldest daughter came and sat with us. She was an attractive, doe-eyed girl of nineteen. She wore a tight pastel pink cotton top, white platform shoes, and blushed whenever I looked at her. Though she said little, I had the feeling she was trying to get my attention. Maybe she thought that meeting an American man might get her a ticket to America, too. Li saw me notice her daughter. "We want to help her go to America, too," she said.

Even after what had gone wrong with her husband? Absolutely, Li said. I said good-bye.

About two months later, back in Shanghai, I got a call in my office. It was Li. "I need to talk to you," she said excitedly. She was in Shanghai and wanted to come by. She knocked on my door an hour later, accompanied by a younger man with sharp, chiseled features and the chest of a bodybuilder. He carried a leather briefcase with gold trim, holding it like a piece of treasure. We went to a nearby café for tea. I told her I had written about her and asked if she had heard from her husband. No, she said breezily, she had heard nothing. She seemed to have something else on her mind.

Li said her friend Zhang, the bodybuilder sitting beside her, wanted to go to America to look for Rong himself. Could I please help him get a visa? *Oy vey,* I thought. I had many requests from Chinese friends for help with an American visa, and there was little I could do without a compelling case of political persecution. I could not vouch for Li or her friend Zhang. I tried to explain that I had no power over anyone at the U.S. Consulate. Zhang eyed me carefully as I spoke, and said quietly, "All you have to do is introduce me to someone. I have money." He patted the briefcase knowingly, as though it were full of cash. So that's how it works in Fujian, I figured, where a passing acquaintance and a suitcase of cash solves any problem, including a visa to America. I looked at Li. She smiled sheepishly but said nothing. I had believed the heartrending story she had told me at her home in Fujian. Now I wondered if any of it was true.

chapter eleven

A DOG IN MY SOUP

o you like dog?"

My hand froze, chopsticks poised over a steaming bowl of stew. I looked across the table at Manager Wang, whose smile revealed a set of stained brown teeth. He and five other factory bosses in ill-fitting suits and V-necked sweaters sat waiting for my reaction. I looked down into the bowl and saw gray chunks of meat amid the green coriander leaves and red tomato slices. As I paused, a dog yowled in the distance, as if on cue. On my way to the factory, I remembered, I drove by an animal market where several mangy-looking dogs barked in their cages. With Wang's prompting, I now realized that these chunks of meat came from that market.

My hand retreated slowly. I rested my wrist on the plastic tablecloth. In the mid-winter chill of the unheated dining room, I could see my own breath. A dingy Chinese watercolor hung on the wall, and a faint smell of vinegar in the air. It was like dozens of other banquet rooms I had eaten in during my years in China. And once again, I was being tested. Wang and the others watched me carefully. I knew these men would regard me as a good American if I tasted their dog stew, a bad one if I did not. I had a choice. Refusing would draw an uncomfortable line between us. Partaking would signal our commonality.

Most times, I enjoyed tasting unusual kinds of food. In China, I had tried braised sea slug and sautéed scorpion and yak-butter tea. (I liked the sea slug and scorpions, the tea made me gag.) But I had not yet tried dog. I felt that eating dog would betray the memory of Terry, my family's old cocker spaniel. Dog is not a common menu item in China, at least to those who can afford pork or beef. But in a poor and remote area like this one, in the mountains of Hubei Province, dog was a treasured delicacy. I had come to this region with an American businessman to see a peanut butter factory, one of the odd places that American investors look for opportunities in China. On this trip, I had expected discomfort and inconvenience, bumpy roads and poor amenities. But I did not expect to find a dog in my soup.

Manager Wang was waiting. A sinking feeling invaded my stomach. I was not going to be able to disappoint a table of six men whose sense of national dignity was on the line. I would give in, as I always did. Picking a chunk of meat with my chopsticks, with a strand of coriander hanging on, I opened my mouth. I chewed. The meat tasted bland and tough. I swallowed. Wang waited for me to speak. *"Hao chi,"* I said. It's good. Wang smiled and nodded approvingly. I was worthy of joining his table. My face flushed. I tried to look nonchalant, like it was no big deal. At one time, I would have felt proud to bridge another border, to show I had the gumption to do whatever was necessary to become a citizen of the world. But this time, I felt as though I had violated an invisible line. Eating dog stew did not make me feel as though I belonged. I was trying so hard to fit in, but I still felt like an outsider.

It made me wonder what I was doing in this strange country. My determination to penetrate the hidden worlds of China, the curiosity that spurred me to travel to remote corners of Hubei, ran aground at moments like this. I felt worn down by the emotional dislocation of being an outsider. As a Westerner in China, I was constantly stared at, scrutinized, and discriminated against. Most of the time, I did not care, but there were days when it got to me. What bothered me now was the way Manager Wang, like many Chinese people, saw me as a symbol of the West, not as a human being. He judged me by how much I knew about China and how much I embraced Chinese culture. His demand that I taste dog was really a way to see if I accepted him and his way of life. He did not care if I was a decent person. If I respected the Chinese way, in his eyes, that was all that mattered.

In China, the sharp divide of insider and outsider dominates other distinctions. The insider, no matter how he fails, is accepted and welcomed in the fold. The outsider, regardless of character or achievement, is not to be trusted.

First-time visitors to China often come away excited about all the good friends they made. Chinese people are famous for being polite. Yet underneath the surface, people in China are deeply ambivalent about outsiders. Many say their trepidation is a legacy of the Opium Wars, when Western gunboats invaded and took advantage of China's weakness. But clinging to hundred-year-old incidents is a way to avoid facing present-day reality. China's hesitancy about outsiders is really a reflection of its uncertainty about itself. Chinese people will say they do not like or trust outsiders, yet they are obsessed with what outsiders think of them. They are proud of China's old culture and yet secretly worried that it now holds them back.

Of all the many strands in the Chinese psyche, two stand out: the self-satisfied attitude that comes from an insular belief that China has always been the center of the world, and the deep sense of inferiority that came with the modern discovery that China is actually far behind the West. These two conflicting mind-sets seem to mingle in the minds of most Chinese citizens. It is a cultural burden hard to grasp for Americans, whose nation is young and naïve in comparison. In the ancient world, Chinese emperors were accustomed to thinking they personified the center of the universe. That notion was reinforced by the cultural tradition of subservience, by Chinese courtiers and by the lesser, tributary states in the region like Japan, Korea, and Vietnam. The illusion of invincibility melted away in the twentieth century, when Chinese were forced to recognize that other parts of the world had far outpaced them. China's history over the past century is essentially a story of trying to come to terms with the West. While Chinese people argue passionately about the superiority of their culture to all others, in the twentieth century they adopted one new Western ideal after another and tried to make it their own. First it was Western science and technology. Then it was a Republican form of government. Then it was a socialist system run by the Communist Party. Then it was a capitalist system run by the Communist Party. Each incarnation was proclaimed to show the virtues of the Chinese way, even as they embraced an outsider's. Chinese people are confused about the role of Chinese culture in modern society, about how ancient habits of patriarchy and submission fit with modern demands of flexibility and openness.

Musing on this national sense of insecurity, I was reminded of a day during my first year in China, when I was still a student in Xi'an. I was out exploring, riding my bicycle down a dusty street with long rows of ugly gray buildings, when an unusual sight came into view. It was the Golden Flower Hotel, the first modern hotel in Xi'an. I had heard that it had recently opened and that its restaurant served a pretty good ice-cream sundae, something I had not tasted since leaving America nearly a year before. With shiny glass walls, an open courtyard, and a marble fountain, the Golden Flower gleamed like a jewel in a pile of dirty sand. I parked my bicycle on the sidewalk and headed inside. About one hundred people were gathered outside the front gate to gawk. As I walked by them, I overheard an old man in a Mao cap mutter derisively, *"Bu shi women zhong guo di dongxi."* This is not a Chinese thing. Several heads around him nodded in agreement. Nothing more needed to be said. They all knew what he meant, and so did I. If it came from outside China, it must be rotten.

I took a seat tentatively in the smoothly carpeted restaurant, which looked like a palace compared with the musty noodle shops I had been frequenting. I checked to see if my blue cotton peasant trousers were leaving dirt on the finely upholstered chair. Looking at the menu was jarring. A steak sandwich cost twenty-five dollars, roughly the monthly salary of one of my Chinese teachers at the university. I shifted uncomfortably on my cushioned seat. This is not a Chinese thing, I thought. My culture brought this hotel to China, and I felt guilty that my culture was charging so high a price for a steak sandwich. I worried what Chinese people would think. The sundae was good, though, a relative bargain at ten dollars (though still out of reach for most Chinese) and for a moment I escaped to home in the chocolate sauce, which smelled like the stuff at the Baskin-Robbins shop where I worked as a teenager in New York.

Back in the street, riding my bicycle amid the sea of Chinese cyclists in their blue or green Mao jackets, I played that phrase over in my mind. *This is not a Chinese thing.* Pedaling down the street, I felt like a Golden Flower myself, a symbol of the West and its money, tall and blond, even in my cheap Chinese clothes. I felt heads turning to watch me as I rode by, as I always did. Many people, like the old man in the Mao cap, doubtless felt the same way about me as they did about the hotel. I was a moral threat, a bad guy, maybe even a source of disease and ruin.

This is not a Chinese thing. It captured a mind-set that aimed to build a wall around an entire culture, as though it were too fragile to survive exposure to outsiders. It insisted on the superiority of Chinese medicine, Chinese philosophy, Chinese food, Chinese morality, but wanted to keep them separate from outsiders. I realized I would never be seen as an equal in this country. In the Chinese view of the world, the outsider was inferior, the outsider looked and smelled funny, the outsider was weird. My friends did not feel that way, but they were in the minority, those willing to befriend me. To most Chinese, the outsider was not welcome.

When I broached the topic with my Chinese friends, the knee-jerk response was that Chinese attitudes were a legacy of the Opium Wars and the feeling that the West had taken advantage of them. One friend said that Chinese people simultaneously admire and fear the West but cannot look on Westerners as equals. Another friend put it more simply. "Most Chinese think about it this way," he said. "They are Chinese, and you are not."

chapter twelve

A GAY WEDDING

One summer evening in Shanghai, as the heat of the day receded, a friend named Li came to my office to take me on an adventure. Li was a college professor who shared my interest in politics and changing social trends in China. We often got together to compare notes. Li grew up in Shanghai and went to the United States for graduate school before becoming a professor at an American college. Now he was living in Shanghai again on a sabbatical, researching a book. Li was a charming and very funny man, with a boyish face and an engaging giggle that he did not seem able to suppress. We became friends. In contrast to the occasional feeling of emotional dislocation I experienced as an outsider in China, when I spent time with Li I sensed a kindred soul, one with an insightful perspective on what was happening in China. His curiosity was contagious, and he always inspired me to push onward in my own investigations. We were both interested in whatever was hidden in Chinese society.

Li had promised to take me to what he called a "special place." He had not been more specific. But since his invitation followed a long conversation we had about gay life in China, I suspected that he was going to take me to a gay hangout. In China, where homosexuality was only tolerated when it remained out of sight, you needed to know someone who knew someone in order to get in. As our cab made its way through Shanghai's narrow downtown streets, Li giggled with excitement. I felt excited, too, venturing into forbidden territory. We stopped on a little street near the waterfront, where old British bank buildings built in the 1920s sagged with age and disrepair. Li led me toward a doorway that looked like a small oasis of color. Neat green awnings hung over two modest windows, and a small bouquet of violets adorned a straw basket on one side of the doorway. When we stepped inside, the slender entryway opened into a noisy room where a dozen round tables were packed with loud-talking diners, all of them men. To the unsuspecting, this dining room might have looked like any typical Shanghai restaurant. Yellow chintz curtains hung by the windows, and simple Chinese paintings of fish and vegetables hung on the wall. Yet to regulars, to those who came here on Friday nights, it was a special little corner of Shanghai.

Li recognized some friends at a table in the back. As he and I made our way across the room, I could feel many eyes follow me. We squeezed into seats at a back table, which was already crowded. Half-eaten dishes were already scattered over the table: salty chicken, sautéed snow peas, a clay pot of stewed tofu, spicy spareribs. Li introduced me to his friends around the table. I already knew Yin, who I suspected was Li's boyfriend. The others welcomed me casually with a nod or a *"ni hao."* No one stood or performed the kind of polite but insincere greeting that Chinese manners often demand. It helped me relax a little. I was the only white man in the restaurant and, for all I knew, the only heterosexual.

Li delved into conversation with his friends, and I looked around the room. The men at the other tables were dressed plainly, a few in business suits and ties, but mostly in white or blue button-down shirts, open at the neck. No one wore flamboyant clothing or body-piercing jewelry. Yet as I looked more carefully at the diners around the room, I could see subtle signs. One man held his hand to his face effeminately, another had a high, squeaky laugh. Everyone seemed to be smiling and laughing. It was Friday night, time to let go. Most of these men had to put on a false face at work all week, and now, gathering with their true comrades, they could finally relax and let down that heavy emotional armor. As soon as they walked back outside, they would again face a strongly conformist society that allowed little space for the atypical. For a few hours on Friday night, they knew they were not alone.

Li elbowed me in the ribs and nodded toward the other side of the room, where a singer in a black slinky dress and long curly black hair was climbing up to stand on a chair and sing into a microphone. A gently protruding Adam's apple gave away his gender. He sang a sickly sweet love song, apparently improvising lyrics in Shanghai dialect, making them gaudy and suggestive. It provoked peals of laughter from the crowd. The singer stepped down and walked between the tables as he continued to sing. As he approached our table, he eyed me and made a reference in his song to the "big foreigner," a joke about the large size of Caucasians, compared with Asians. I blushed, embarrassed, not knowing whether to acknowledge him. Li cupped a hand to one side of his mouth and said to the singer, *"Ta va zi."* He isn't. The singer leaned backward, exaggerating his surprise. *"Ta va zi?"* I wanted to hide under the table. *"Ta va zi!"* the singer yelled, repeating it over and over to the crowd, like a favorite new lyric. The laughter grew. Men at other tables turned to look at me. My face burned.

The singer moved on to another table, teasing other diners, and the color gradually left my face. Eventually, he climbed back up on the chair, his makeshift stage, singing ever more suggestive lyrics, using puns and double entendres that I could not follow. I asked Li to translate, but they came faster than he could handle, partly because he himself was laughing. The room's laughter grew even louder. It was almost thunderous. I could feel the collective release of tension, which had evidently been accumulating. I could not help getting swept along in it and laughing myself. Though I didn't understand the words, I shared a sense of frustration of being an outsider in China, of never feeling accepted or fitting in, of hating the conformity that reigned so unforgivingly. But my discomfort was mild compared with the pain these men suffered, ostracized in their own country, afraid to tell the truth to their own families, steadily suffering in secret.

Homosexuality was not officially tolerated in the stern days of Communist China. Gay men and women concealed their true lives, and their anguish remained unknown to many who lived around them. China had no law against homosexuality. None was needed. Those discovered coupling with the same sex were often arrested for "hooliganism," a catchall term that gave the police wide discretion. Schoolchildren were taught that homosexuality did not exist in China and that any sign of it was a remnant of "bourgeois" life that must be eradicated. Chinese doctors deemed homosexuality an illness and some hospitals administered electric shock treatment as a "cure." I had been surprised, during my first year in Xi'an, at how many people I spoke with seemed to believe that no one in China was gay. Perhaps some of them knew better yet felt compelled to stick to the official line when discussing it with a foreigner. But most argued that there really were no homosexuals in China and resisted my suggestion that gay people exist in every country of the world. I had a favorite question: More than one billion people in China, and not a single one was gay? That usually led to a grudging admission that maybe a few gays existed, inevitably opening the question of just how many. In 2000, Chinese researchers estimated that between 40 and 50 million people in China were homosexual.

I felt comfortable with many of the gay men I befriended in China. I have often been mistaken for being gay myself because of my tendency to downplay my own masculinity. In China, my ability to recognize and accept gay men, even when they were not yet "out," made me welcome among them. I felt as though I had X-ray vision, able to see gays even when they remained invisible to people around them. When I lived in Beijing in the 1980s, homosexuality was far less acceptable than it became a decade later, and I knew a pudgy but well-dressed clothing designer named Sai who often waved his arms wildly as he spoke. He asked my help getting American fashion magazines, which were hard to obtain in China in those days, and would explode with excitement when I handed him a copy of *Vogue* I had carried back from Hong Kong. I knew he was gay right off, and he could tell that I knew. We never discussed it. Many of his friends had no idea he was gay. But he evidently liked talking to someone who understood.

The gay hangout where Li took me that night in Shanghai was a telling sign of how open Chinese society was becoming. In the artistic world, gay painters and writers and actors began to speak openly about their sexuality. Magazines covering gay life in China began to emerge. Once the Internet arrived in the late 1990s, chat rooms and bulletin boards became a major meeting place for gays, a convenient and anonymous forum to discuss sensitive topics. Police raids on gay pick-up joints became less frequent, partly because the crime rate was growing fast and the police had more important things to do.

Though China is a strictly conformist society on the surface, conforming is above all a matter of appearances. Many people are willing to look the other way about a neighbor's personal life, as long as proper discretion is observed. Individuality is often considered less important than one's position within the family, as a son, a father, or a brother. As long as someone performs his or her family role, there is a wide latitude for other behavior. "Coming out" has not been a priority for many gays in China. As one Chinese scholar pointed out, few people were beaten to death in China for being gay, nor were any gays organizing public parades. There were exceptions, naturally. Yet by and large, discretion and privacy were the norm.

China's art world contains plenty of evidence of homosexuality through the ages. In ancient Chinese literature, poets wrote openly about love and eroticism between men. In *The Dream of the Red Chamber,* an elaborate novel of languid aristocratic life in the eighteenth century, sexual habits surface in almost every conceivable variety. Homosexuality was not uncommon in Chinese theater, where stage performances were often supported by aristocratic benefactors who sometimes indulged unusual sexual proclivities with actors after hours. In Chinese opera, gender lines were often crossed or toyed with by male actors who portrayed female characters, reflecting a slightly less rigid approach to gender roles in China than is known in the West.

A bizarre side story of Chinese gender roles appeared in imperial court life, where eunuchs were employed to guard an emperor's harem inside the Forbidden City. Politics in the palace were inevitably intricate and complex, and these castrated male attendants acted as aides and confidants who sometimes took over management of day-to-day government affairs. Under Emperor Wanli, who ruled the Ming Dynasty in the late 1500s, more than ten thousand eunuchs worked in Beijing as court administrators, guards, and messengers. The most senior eunuchs were able to control information and access to the emperor, giving themselves tremendous influence and wealth. Many Chinese families cut off the genitals of their young boys in hopes of winning them a chance at a coveted position in the palace, even though it did not guarantee a job and did promise a lifetime of incontinence and sexual frustration. Typically using only hot chili sauce as a local anesthetic, the specialists who performed this operation used a small, curved knife that would emasculate a boy in one swoop. Traditionally, a eunuch would preserve his "three precious" in a jar to make sure they would eventually be buried beside him, so that he could be reincarnated as a "full" man.

My friend Li, was himself slowly telling some of his friends that he was gay. China's relaxing attitude toward gays, Li felt, was long overdue. As a young man, Li had found it difficult to admit to himself that he was gay. When friends asked him why he did not marry, he would giggle and say he didn't know. Only after he lived away from family and friends in the United States was he able to think about it honestly. Now, back in China, he was starting to be more open with friends, no longer hiding his relationship with his boyfriend, Yin. Like me, Li is sensitive to what people think, and he was reluctant to tell anyone who might not approve, such as his parents, who were in their eighties. Yet his desire to be accepted for who he was, not to hide anymore, was the same for countless gay men across China.

One day not long after we visited the cross-dressing restaurant, Li met me for lunch. He said there was something he wanted to talk about. He was considering a marriage ceremony with his boyfriend, Yin, in Shanghai. Did I think it was a good idea? I had never heard of a gay wedding in China. But if it was what Li wanted, then yes, I thought it was a good idea. Restrictions on social behavior were getting looser all the time in China. Li did not think the authorities would object if they found out. They might not legally accept a gay marriage but would probably not interfere as long as it was discreet. Li was curious whether I had ever been to a gay wedding in the United States, hoping to learn about what kind of ceremony other men had used. I had not. Li was nervous, but I could tell he wanted to proceed, and I realized he had already made up his mind. He was checking to see if I approved before deciding whether to invite me to the ceremony.

A couple of weeks later, Li came over for a second talk. This time he told me that he and Yin had decided to go ahead with a marriage ceremony and that they wanted me to preside, in place of a minister. I was surprised, having no spiritual qualifications for the task. Li giggled and told me not to worry. He and Yin each felt comfortable with me, he said. It occurred to me that Li did not want to ask a Chinese citizen to play that role, in case there was any unexpected inquiry from the police. Since I was an American, the authorities would naturally see me as an outsider, and that would make the ceremony more acceptable, in their eyes.

Li asked me to write out the wording used in vows in a traditional Christian service in America, and then together we edited them to make a new set of vows that Li and Yin felt comfortable with. As a site for his ceremony, Li chose a private dining room in a fancy Western hotel, affording the elegance and discretion of a well-paid staff. Only twelve people were invited, and we sat with Li and Yin around a long and beautifully dressed table, six on a side. The meal was quite formal, and, as in many Chinese banquets, conversation was spare and awkward. We were a mix of friends, some gay, some not, two Westerners, and two relatives, a brother of Li and a brother of Yin. I felt the excitement of sharing a deep secret. No one there had attended a gay wedding before. I sat next to Mrs. Chen, the mother of a close childhood friend of Li, a woman who had watched him grow from a rambunctious boy to a medical doctor to a political scientist in the United States. She seemed quite proud. I asked her when she knew that Li was gay. "I knew from an early age," she confided. "Long before he himself knew." She told no one, not even her husband, who would have disapproved. She never spoke about it with Li.

After we finished dining, Li asked all the waiters to leave the room. Li thanked us all for coming and read a prepared speech. It was an important day, Li said. Not only was it a celebration of love for his partner, but it was also a vindication of a way of life. All the suffering, the misunderstanding, the secret anxiety that he and his fellow gay friends carried around with them for years in China, all were being countered here today. It was an act of independence, this marriage ceremony, a standing up for himself and all his fellows. I glanced at the other faces around the table. Everyone understood what Li meant. We all had some area of our lives we kept hidden. Yet I could not imagine that many of us knew the pain involved in keeping something as basic as sexuality a secret for decades, as Li had.

When the time came for the ceremony, Li and Yin stood next to each other, facing me. I faced the assembled diners. "Dearly beloved, we have gathered here today," I began. I led them in a set of vows. Li giggled all the way through, nervous and joyous. Yin beamed brightly. When I concluded with "And now you may kiss the groom," my two friends embraced. Everyone applauded.

Gay weddings were not the only unusual sort of matrimony surfacing in Shanghai. I was working in my office late one Saturday evening when the phone rang. It was my friend Li again. He giggled with excitement.

"You have to come see this," he said. "It's unbelievable." He would not tell me more on the phone but insisted that I come meet him at a fancy nightclub called Cash Box, known for its glitzy karaoke rooms.

"I hate karaoke," I protested.

"Trust me," he said.

When I arrived by cab, Li was waiting at the entrance. A bright red and green neon sign flashed overhead. Li giggled as he led me inside and down a plushly carpeted staircase, along a gold-wallpapered hallway, and into a dark room. A dozen people sat around a low table talking, and greeted us loudly, like drunken friends. Li sat me down and ordered me a drink. As my eyes adjusted to the darkness, I looked around. Two young women stood, microphones in hand, singing badly to the words of a music video that scrolled across an oversized TV screen. Several well-dressed Chinese men in their thirties lounged on the sofas. Li pointed out a small Japanese man with glasses and a corsage in his jacket lapel, sitting next to a dumpy Chinese woman in a pink frilly dress. He was the groom. She was the bride. A talkative man sitting beside them was the matchmaker who arranged their marriage, performed earlier that evening. This karaoke party was their wedding reception.

I had heard about the phenomenon of Japanese men buying

wives in Shanghai, a practice that the Communists had once banned. But as China's economy blossomed and government restrictions faded, brokered marriages between Japanese men and Chinese women were the kind of victimless crime that no one bothered trying to prevent anymore. Arranged marriages were once the norm in China, so perhaps it was not so odd to choose a financial transaction with a stranger as the way to find a mate. By the time I lived in Shanghai, dozens of agencies had emerged to broker Japan-China matches, despite the intense racial prejudice that flows in both directions between the nations.

Chinese people generally see other Asians as inferior. Historically, Chinese believe that, as the center of the ancient world, China was the leader of all surrounding countries, which generally acted as supplicants to the Chinese throne. Chinese writing was adopted as the basis of early written language in Japan, Korea, and Vietnam, and Chinese people often look at those languages as weak imitations of their own superior version. China reserves special hatred for Japan, which Chinese people say grows out of the atrocities committed by the Japanese army in China during World War II. It is a memory that Chinese people don't seem to want to let go of, sixty years after the end of the war. With them, it is more than a historical wrong. It has become a fierce prejudice, with the same characteristics of intolerance everywhere. The insecure and the shameful latch onto racial criteria to judge others. What really fuels Chinese prejudice toward Japan is the outrage among many Chinese that a small island nation had become so much richer and more powerful than China. It riles Chinese that they had been so easily overrun by Japan during the war and so dramatically outpaced by Japan in the years since.

If many people in China turned up their noses at Japanese, not everyone did. Sometimes they married for love, sometimes for convenience. Most often, it seems, for money.

The newlyweds sat together awkwardly. They took turns speaking to the matchmaker, Jian, but never addressed each other. They looked like a pair of mute sparrows, exchanging looks, searching for clues about each other, unable to speak the same language. It was odd to think that this might be the first day of a lifetime together. Their gregarious matchmaker, Jian, their only conduit for communication, seemed more interested in talking to others than in translating. At one point Jian went out of the room, and the newlyweds were left in silence, uncomfortably glancing at each other.

Li told me that Jian operated his marriage brokerage in Osaka, charging a man $20,000 to arrange a wife. Customers looked at a photo album of potential mates and, after choosing one, flew to Shanghai to meet and make a decision. Li giggled again as he told me another twist to this story. After this groom, Hitoro, had picked out a woman from the photo album and came to Shanghai to meet her, she had tried to negotiate a higher price for the transaction, demanding $25,000 instead of $20,000. Hitoro was offended and would not agree. Jian feared he was losing the deal and scrambled to find another Shanghainese woman who would agree to marry a stranger from Japan on one day's notice. He found one. Her name was Yu, and she was thirty-seven. The matchmaker told Hitoro that she was twenty-nine, but looking at her, I wondered whether he believed that. Once the papers were signed, Hitoro handed over half the amount in cash, the rest to be paid when Yu arrived in Japan a month later. Just like a commodity.

On the day of the agreement, Hitoro suddenly decided that he wanted a proper Chinese banquet to celebrate. He had come from

Japan alone, so he had no family to invite. But he suggested that Jian invite others to make it feel like a real wedding. So Jian scurried to invite a bunch of his own Shanghai friends, luring them with a promise of free dinner and drinks, all paid for by Hitoro. By the time I showed up at the karaoke room, several in the group were drinking cognac and getting boisterous. Li leaned toward me and giggled again. Shortly before I arrived, he said, Hitoro had asked Yu whether she spoke any English. Only two phrases, she told him: "I love you," and "I am a virgin." Neither true, in her case. Yu had recently retired from her profession of ten years, prostitution.

"Does he know?" I asked Li.

He giggled again, shaking his head. "No, he doesn't."

To my surprise, Hitoro sidled over to me and struck up a conversation. It turned out he could speak some English, so I was one of the few people in the room he could talk to. Hitoro told me he worked for a trading company in Osaka and, at thirty-four, was finding it difficult to find a wife in Japan. "I am not tall, and I am not good-looking, so it is hard," he said. He also complained that his parents, his mother in particular, were pressuring him to marry even though he felt ambivalent about it. He spoke in a mechanical kind of way, his face exhibiting no emotion at all. Maybe he was just uncomfortable speaking English. Maybe he was always emotionally at sea. Li told me later that the matchmaker sized up Hitoro as a mama's boy whose mother had rejected every woman he ever brought home. I wondered what she would think of Miss Yu.

I felt ghoulishly attracted to this spectacle and simultaneously repulsed by it. When the party migrated to a late-night restaurant called Shanghai Moon, well known for its dumplings and fried onion cakes, I took a seat beside Yu. I could not resist asking why she married a man she did not know. She gave me a long look. Then she

187

rambled about wanting to better herself, to take advantage of an opportunity. She spoke with all the conviction of a computer-illiterate
person signing for a new job in a high-tech industry. She would have
to learn some Japanese, she added. "Yes, that would be a good idea,"
I offered. A silence passed. Yu added that she had to do this for her
mother, who was apparently getting most of the money that Hitoro
coughed up. "Was this your mother's idea?" I asked. Yu shook her
head. But she had grown up poor, and her mother had worked hard
to get her through school. Yu felt indebted. Money had become an
obsession for many Shanghai residents, but Yu seemed to take that
obsession to a new level, willing to marry a stranger and follow him
to an alien culture for a few bundles of cash.

Talking to Yu, however, I was reminded for the hundredth time
that I, too, was still unmarried. Although I told my friends that I
wanted romance in my life more than anything else, I did not really
allow any room for it. I traveled constantly. I prized my ability to
devote myself to my job, frequently staying in my office well past
midnight. I met many available women, flirted with them, then
never saw them again. I was tired of easy affairs. I told myself I
simply preferred to spend evenings alone in my office, "achieving"
something by producing another news article. Each time I delved
into a new aspect of life in China, I felt I was getting one step
closer to the mystery at the heart of this country. It helped drive
me onward. I crammed my days full of interviews and meetings, as
though wasting a spare moment was a crime. I let my work become an addiction, all-consuming and unending. My work output
climbed steadily, but I gradually felt less and less energized. The
harder I worked, the more out of balance I felt. I knew it was unhealthy, driving myself so hard. But I did not know how to stop.

chapter thirteen

SAUNA MASSAGE

On a chilly afternoon in November, I took a flight from Shanghai to Changsha, a city in southern China known for its spicy cuisine and its favorite son, Mao Zedong, whose career began there as a young revolutionary. Changsha looked as gray and faceless as any middling Chinese city. It was overcrowded and run-down. As I cruised through the city in the backseat of a small taxi, the driver complained about how life was going to hell. A recent wave of factory layoffs had depressed the city, and business was bad for taxis and restaurants and hotels. I asked the driver about a demonstration that had occurred a week before, when three hundred men from a scissors factory staged a sit-in outside the front gate of city hall. I came to Changsha after hearing a rumor about the protest because I wanted to

write about some of the bumps in China's transition from socialism to capitalism and the trend of minor urban unrest that was
bubbling up in many cities. In Changsha, the manager of the scissors factory had taken advantage of a new policy encouraging
"privatization" to sell off all the factory equipment, promising to
pay workers nearly two years of back wages that had gone unmet as
the factory slowly went bankrupt. Once he had the cash, however,
the manager left town. The workers were angry. They knew that
getting their jobs back or their salaries paid was unlikely, but organizing a public protest might squeeze some money out of the local government. It was a pattern that repeated itself in cities all over
China. After two days of the sit-in, Changsha officials agreed to
pay a sum of money, about twenty percent of what was owed, in
exchange for a promise that the workers would go home.

I often came into a city where I knew no one and snooped for
information. I combed the streets on foot, striking up conversations
in shops and parks and offices. I asked anyone I could for help,
searching for people who knew someone who knew something
about a topic like the scissors-factory demonstration, then nudging
them to talk. It was always a challenge. I had to lose all my shyness.
I had to empathize and cajole. In Changsha, I found two witnesses
to the protest who filled me in on what had happened. It was satis-
fying to dig out the details and then write an article that weaved
them into a national context, with details that offered a flavor of
what life felt like on the ground. In my years in China, I went on
dozens of trips like that one to Changsha. But I never got to write
about my favorite part of each trip, a part I kept secret.

In Changsha, I chose a three-star hotel called the White Egret,
the kind Chinese businessmen stay in, half the price of the four-
star hotels where most foreigners stayed. As I checked in, my eye

scoured the reception desk for a leaflet advertising the hotel's "Sauna Massage," as they called the spa. Once I found it, I looked for a clue and saw one—the masseuses were all wearing miniskirts. It was subtle but distinct. They would have what I wanted. I left my bag in the room and went outside to explore, then came back to my room to type up my notes. I checked my watch frequently, counting the hours, then the minutes, until midnight.

It was a ritual I fell into when I was on the road. Explore, eat, write, and then at midnight, head for the Sauna Massage. My stomach tickled with anticipation as I got in the elevator to head downstairs. On the second floor of the hotel, I pushed open a frosted-glass door and entered. A petite woman with dark eyes stood primly behind a counter. She gestured toward the men's changing room as she greeted me in a sickly sweet voice, "Welcome, Honored Guest." An assistant manager stood and smiled obsequiously as he too gestured the way inside. I felt their eyes follow me.

A boy in the changing room jumped to attention as I stepped inside. He tried to help me undress, but I waved him off. I enjoyed the sound of my belt buckle unclicking, one step of the ritual, releasing me from the pressure of a long day. I was entering the pleasure zone, once a forbidden zone in China, now available to those who knew how to ask. Naked, I stepped into the men's bathing area. Hot and cold tubs, each large enough for ten men, were built into a wall of white marble. Four middle-aged Chinese men, three of them with the big bellies of sudden wealth, lounged in the hot bath. I showered, then slipped into the hot tub beside the men, who looked slightly alarmed that a "big nose" was allowed in this place, sharing their bath water. I tried to ignore them. I let the warm water swallow my body and looked away, glancing up at the wall overhead, where a white marble carving portrayed a woman with fulsome, bare breasts. Another clue. Not that I needed one.

I moved to the steam room, my body enveloped by the moist heat. The boy came in, offering a cold washcloth. It felt cool and soothing on my brow. Sweat streamed down my chest and back. I relaxed more deeply with each long steamy breath I exhaled, feeling cleansed and calmed. But my mind tingled with quiet excitement. I stepped into the shower once more to rinse off, and as I stepped out, the boy stood waiting with a tall pile of towels, a pair of loose cotton shorts, a terrycloth robe, and slippers. I shuffled through the swinging doors to a darkened lounge with two long rows of puffy chairs, each with a puffy footstool. Three young women in hotel uniforms echoed another "Welcome, Honored Guest," a phrase that sounded like sweet candy. It was a Chinese way to make a guest feel special, like offering sweets at every turn. One woman brought me a cup of tea and a glass of water, another woman carried two open boxes for me to pick from, Q-tips in one and cigarettes in the other. I used to feel uncomfortable at all the service. But it was part of the package and now, part of the ritual I savored. The manager, in white shirt and tie, took a seat beside me. After small talk about my nationality and my job—I always bent the truth and said I was in publishing—he asked me what kind of masseuse I wanted. I knew the lingo. "A pure one" meant young and virginal-looking. An "abundant one" meant busty and fulsome. For me, the answer was always the same. A talkative one. I was going to spend two or three hours alone in a room with a woman, and I wanted someone who liked to talk.

My first visit to a Sauna Massage came by accident, a few years earlier. I had been looking for a way to relax after a long day's work on a trip to Sichuan, in western China. I noticed on a flyer in my hotel room that massage was offered until 2 A.M. That seemed unusually late for any kind of service in a state-run hotel in Communist China, where restaurants often closed at 8 P.M. When I went to the spa, it was plush and tastefully lighted. In the past, the only massages I got in China had been from men, and there was never a hint of anything illicit. So I was pleasantly surprised when a woman came to the room where I lay waiting on a massage table. I always preferred to be touched by a woman. I chatted easily with the masseuse as she worked on my back. She was well informed about local political gossip, since government cadres and police officers frequented the spa. Chinese people are usually careful discussing anything political with a stranger, but we were in a private room. Besides, the masseuse knew it was unlikely she would ever see me again. She told me an intriguing tale of her own, about her odyssey from small town to big city, with a litany of broken dreams, abusive bosses, and bizarre customers. Talking seemed to soften her defenses, and her hands began to linger on my body. She asked me what kind of "other services" I wanted. I didn't know what she was talking about. She saw my confusion and laughed at me. Embarrassed, I left in a hurry.

My shame subsided. Later it occurred to me that in my busy routine as a reporter I rarely had two hours alone with anyone to talk so extensively. I learned more from this plain-speaking woman than I did from any of my regular interviews of factory managers and party secretaries. On subsequent trips outside Shanghai, I found myself keeping an eye out for the Sauna Massage. I told myself it was a useful way to round out my reporting, to listen to gossip and the working-class view of things. But the truth was that I was looking for a personal, and physical, connection. I had little intimacy in my life at the time, and the touch of a woman slowly and thoroughly kneading my back was rejuvenating. I relished the intimacy of a dark room and a locked door. In a country where I was constantly followed and spied on, I felt safe in a Sauna Massage. When I entered the massage room, I knew I would be undisturbed. And after a few visits, I gradually lost my shyness about "other services."

At the White Egret, one of the uniformed girls led me down a twisting maze of hallways and left me alone inside a darkened room. A massage table was covered with soft towels, and a single lamp had a silk scarf thrown over it, muting the light to a soft maroon hue. I took off my robe and lay down on the table, blanketing myself with towels. I lay silently, eyes closed, nose tickled by the jasmine flower on a side table. I envisioned a light-stepping Chinese lovely as she tiptoed down the hallway toward me. Soon enough, I heard a light knock on the door and felt it open and close. "Good evening," said the young woman standing before me. I opened my eyes. She had long hair parted down the middle and wore a tight-fitting peach cotton top and a white miniskirt. She had soft brown eyes.

"Knock your back?" she asked. I nodded and rolled over onto my front. She spread towels over my back and climbed to stand on me, holding onto a bar on the ceiling as she used the balls of her feet to massage my spine. "Hard or soft?" she asked gently. Hard, I told her. She methodically dug her toes into each vertebra, and each one seemed to release more tension from deep within me. We talked softly as she worked, and after a while she let herself giggle flirtatiously. Her name was Chen. Soon she sat down, straddling my rump and kneading my back with the palms of her hands. It was a soothing rhythm. She lowered my cotton shorts a little, enabling her to rub my entire back in one long, slow motion. My body was warming to her touch. I asked where she was from, why she had left, how the manager treated her. She told a common story, of boredom in a small city in northern China, of hearing from her girlfriends that there was money to be made down south. She said she was seventeen, but I knew most masseuses lie, since Chinese men are obsessed with virginal women. I teased her until she admitted she was really twenty-three. I asked how the system worked at the White Egret, and she told me that the manager demanded a $500 deposit when she arrived, just for the right to work there. She knew the work was lucrative, so she did not object. A masseuse was often vulnerable to abuse by a manager, sexual or financial. Few young women from out of town would get anywhere complaining to the local police, many of whom were well paid to not interfere with the business of a Sauna Massage.

Chen's voice became coquettish as she asked me her question. "Sir, what do you like?" I let it hang in the air for a moment. "If you are willing, I'd like you to push the oil," I said. "Push the oil," she said in assent. She slowly finished massaging my lower back, then gently tugged on my shorts until they were off. I lay fully naked, facedown on the table, warmly bathing in the smell of the almond oil she spread on her hands and then started rubbing evenly on my rump. Her fingers spread down to my inner thigh. She expertly gripped and caressed each of my thighs, finding every muscle and tendon in my upper legs and lower torso. It seemed to relax all the tension from my body.

"Turn over," Chen whispered. She glanced down as I revealed myself to her. Her eyes widened, but she said nothing. She placed a towel over my lower body and climbed on top, straddling my hips with hers. She reached for her bottle of almond oil and put a small puddle in the palm of her hand. She looked me in the eye as she spread the oil over her hands and then massaged my chest, rocking gently back and forth. We were silent now. Her fingers moved slowly, firmly, thoroughly. I kept looking her in the eye, and she met my gaze with a tenderness I did not expect. She smiled, vulnerable and knowing. Then she leaned back and lifted her shirt. She undid her brassiere in the back and tossed it gently to the floor. Her breasts looked like full pears, light brown and firm. She reached for the oil again and put some in my hand. I gently rubbed my hands together and reached up to touch her, coating her flesh with a silky layer of oil. I explored the contour of her skin with my palms and felt her softness with the tips of my fingers. Her skin seemed warm and giving. The muted maroon light, the almond scent, the slow assurance of her rocking hips, the luscious feel of her body. The utter quiet, the padded distance from the rough-edged life outside. The comfort of a woman who touched me. It was all I wanted in the world. We lay in our two-backed embrace, and I was enveloped in a momentary illusion of equality and closeness.

Once my eyes were opened, I discovered that Sauna Massage was available in some form in most hotels in China. Those who did not know might never see it, hidden behind the legal decoy of a health club or a hair salon. But once I knew about those concealed, scented rooms, I always tried to find my way there. I knew how to sweet-talk a masseuse, and I invariably coaxed a compelling tale from her, about getting away from overbearing parents, about squandered savings, about supporting a boyfriend's heroin habit, about plans to work "just one more year" and then go home and open a clothing store. More than anything, I reveled in the pampering and the intimacy that I so badly lacked in my daily life. My trips to the Sauna Massage helped keep my inner equilibrium, part of my emotional survival in China. I needed them.

I was too ashamed to tell my friends about this piece of my life. I knew it was immoral to pay a woman to touch me and let me touch her. I told myself lies to dodge my own sense of guilt. I would say to myself that I wanted to deepen my reporting in a given city by collecting nighttime gossip. I never had intercourse with a masseuse, and I let myself rationalize extensive touching as little more than a thorough two-way massage. (Most women seemed relieved when I turned down the "complete package," though some were disappointed to lose a higher fee.) I could not quite face the reality that I was misusing these women, most of them from poor familes, simply because I had the money they wanted. My soft conversation and gentle interaction with a woman behind a closed door gave me an illusion of intimacy. I paid well for that illusion.

I did not want to look at the inherent inequality in this kind of commercial transaction. The women who nurtured my fantasies came from unhappy circumstances. Perhaps some were forced into it by their parents, but most seemed to be running away from their families, chasing the national obsession with money, desperate enough to sacrifice their dignity. For some, it was probably an extra disgrace to bare themselves before a Westerner. For me, the reverse was true. In China, on the far side of the world, I could act in ways I would not feel comfortable trying in my native country. I felt a special freedom, exploring a secret side of a foreign land, without any responsibility to act in a humane way. At the time, I fancied myself an enlightened man who treated human beings with respect everywhere. My visits to Sauna Massage suggest that was not completely true.

Customers at Sauna Massage places were mostly Chinese government officials and businessmen. Foreigners like me were rare. The managers did not care about a customer's passport, only his wallet. Sauna Massage was for men who could afford more than the tawdry options available on the street, like the "taxi girls" in dance halls (only paid when taken for a ride) or ladies in short skirts who stood by roadside restaurants to lure customers in for a meal and a quickie in a shack out back. For men in officialdom, the relative luxury of a massage and more in a discreet setting was often paid for with government money, since the cashiers at checkout handed over an official-looking receipt, conveniently marked *can-fei,* or "meal cost." I wondered what portion of China's official spending went to "entertainment." (I did not have the gumption to submit a bill from Sauna Massage in my own expense accounts.)

When I traveled in China, in a quiet moment on a train or in a car, my mind often wandered back to a visit to a Sauna Massage. Even in memory, I could savor the ecstasy of prolonged sensual contact, with the added thrill of the hidden and the illicit. Those memories lived in my shadow, a part of myself that I could not ignore. I knew something in me was broken, needing to search for sustenance in a dark corner. I knew my visits to Sauna Massage fit in a particular time and place, not to be repeated in another stage of my life. They were my guilty pleasure. They made me feel emotionally whole, physically cleansed, yet spiritually incomplete.

chapter fourteen

JIN XING

At a glitzy party one evening in Beijing, Chinese artists and musicians mingled easily with foreign diplomats and businessmen and journalists. A jazz trio played in the corner. I was talking with a fashion photographer about the anything-goes mentality that was spreading in China. An attractive woman sauntered by in a body-hugging gown of mauve silk. "Just look at her," I said. The photographer raised his eyebrows. "That is no ordinary woman," he said. I turned to look again and recognized her. It was Jin Xing. She was a dancer and choreographer, and I had seen her photograph in newspaper stories after she created China's first independent dance company. That was a notable achievement. But she was famous for something else: shifting her gender from male to female. Jin Xing was China's first transsexual to go public.

I was surprised that a transgender operation was permitted in a Chinese hospital. The real surprise was that Jin Xing (pronounced Gin Shing) was living openly and honestly in a society where most people guard their privacy fiercely. She voluntarily discarded the shield of secrecy that many celebrities in China wear and spoke freely about what it meant to her to become a woman. It made me very curious about her. My photographer friend offered to introduce me, but Jin Xing was surrounded by others at that moment. Later, I said.

When Jin Xing's dance troupe performed at a theater in Shanghai later that year, I bought a seat in the orchestra section. I had studied modern dance as a young man and normally loved attending dance performances. However, most of the dance I saw in China was mediocre, state-run troupes moving sloppily and without enthusiasm. This time was different. From the moment Jin Xing and her dancers took the stage in a daring, energetic piece called "Red & Black," I was captivated by the stunning visual effect and technical excellence. In pieces that followed, Jin Xing and her dancers expressed desire and frustration, hope and despair, in movement that was innovative and quite beautiful. My favorite piece was a duet called "502," a bittersweet depiction of the emotional ties between two lovers (and named after a brand of glue, 502, that Chinese schoolchildren use). Jin Xing danced that piece herself with a muscular young man, moving as though they were bound together by an invisible paste. Each attempt to get free by one dancer provoked a physical reaction in the other. It was as though they were both striving to breathe alone and yet afraid to let the other be free. It was sensual and emotionally true. All of her dances were. I sat at the edge of my seat.

I wanted to meet Jin Xing. From watching her choreography, I could tell she was an unusual thinker. I was curious about how she had navigated China's bureaucracy to win permission to perform such artistically daring work. My journalist antennae zeroed in on her as a powerful symbol of burgeoning free expression in China. But beyond that, I was most curious about her personal life. It must have taken considerable courage to take her path. How did she evaluate the feminine and masculine impulses inside her? What did she think of Westerners? If she agreed to an interview, I would have professional license to ask her all kinds of questions I was personally interested in. The following week I called her and left several messages. She was traveling in Europe and did not call back.

Months later, I attended a performance at Shanghai's new opera house when I noticed Jin Xing in a black and violet gown sitting a dozen seats to my left. She looked poised and regal. At intermission, I introduced myself. We walked to the lobby together. She was funny and perceptive, not arrogant, as I had feared. We shared a drink and compared thoughts on the first act of the opera, agreeing that it had been awful. I noticed that my heart was beating rapidly. I felt oddly attracted to her. I asked if we could meet again, and she gave me a penetrating look. We set a time for the following day at a café called Park 97.

When I arrived, Jin Xing was sitting in a banquette by the wall. Her long hair was pulled back in a ponytail, her eyes looked soft. She seemed serene and quietly aware of her surroundings. I had the feeling she saw everything. She noticed my black cashmere jacket, my ringless fingers, my cheap watch. She had asked around about me and said I had a reputation as a sensitive writer with a good feel for life in China. I was usually on guard against flattery from someone I was interviewing, but this time, I felt glad she was taking me seriously.

Our conversation, flipping from Chinese to English and back, glided easily. She asked about my personal life, told me snippets about her own, and I felt an intoxicating sense of connection. I sensed that she could quickly become a good friend or a soul mate of some kind. Beneath her confidence, I sensed a vulnerability. She was lonely. I guessed that meeting a potential mate, someone unafraid of her, must be difficult. I was not afraid of her; I wanted to know everything about her, and she seemed ready to tell. After about thirty minutes, I reminded myself that I was supposed to be pretending to write about her. I reached for my notebook. She made a face. "You're not going to *interview* me, are you?" We were already speaking the same language, emotionally. Reaching for a pen was like inviting others into our conversation. I put it down.

I had to remind myself that she had once been a man. Her face looked feminine. Her shoulders and jawline hinted at something else. Yet she felt like a woman. There was a softness and a gentleness to her that made me relax. I commented on it. "My whole being is female," she said, adding that she had known since the age of six that she was born into the wrong body. She echoed what I soon read about others who had taken this journey, like the English writer Jan Morris who told her own story in a remarkable book, *Conundrum,* in which she described knowing herself as female from an early age. It was a feeling so deep, Morris wrote, that to determine whether its origins were biological or psychological was impossible.

Part of me could relate to the abstract notion of not wanting to be male. I felt a vague discomfort with my own masculinity. I was always more comfortable around women than men. I had plenty of male friends but considered them exceptions, special men. I disliked strong displays of the masculine, recoiled from macho exploits. On some level, I was uncomfortable with maleness. Yet I felt quite secure in my own body as it was. I could not imagine ever wanting to change my gender. My uneasiness with the masculine was vague, an overlay on my personality that preferred the feminine, nonconfrontational way. The Chinese way.

It was odd to listen to Jin Xing describing her childhood as a boy. Jin Xing learned discipline growing up in a military dance troupe where one endured pain in order to achieve. As a young man, Jin Xing traveled widely and enjoyed better food and clothing than children in ordinary families. He had to undergo the training required of everyone in a military school, learning how to take apart and reassemble a rifle in the dark. Jin Xing was ethnically Korean, a descendent of immigrants from the Korean peninsula who had settled in China's northeast. In dance competitions, he sometimes suffered discrimination from Chinese judges, who often felt that a "minority" dancer should always finish behind an ethnically Chinese one. Energetic and determined, Jin Xing worked harder than anyone in his troupe and beat long odds to win a national dance competition at age nineteen, a distinction that earned him a military rank of colonel. He began to dream about studying in America. When he heard about a dance workshop with American teachers, he was desperate to attend. His school leaders tried to bar him from the workshop. Jin Xing went on a weeklong hunger strike. It worked, he was allowed to go. Once there, Jin Xing impressed his teachers so much that they awarded him a scholarship to study dance in New York.

Jin Xing thrived in New York's go-it-alone ethos, where dancers were judged on ability and no one seemed to care about background or connections. He got an apartment in the Chelsea section of Manhattan. He loved the pace and the noise of a sleepless city. Jin Xing started experimenting with choreography. Several of his dances were performed in New York. I was intrigued, when I later looked in the *New York Times* database, to find reviews of his work. One critic, Anna Kisselgoff, wrote, "Mr. Jin choreographs with astounding confidence." Another critic, Jennifer Dunning, praised a separate performance but complained about Jin's "distracting androgyny."

In New York, Jin Xing explored the possibility of undergoing transgender surgery. He was daunted by the high price and the extensive psychotherapy and hormone treatments that were required, since he was still a penniless dancer. Yet a seed had been planted. When Jin Xing moved back to China after seven years abroad, it was time. He interviewed surgeons carefully at a hospital in Beijing. In early 1995, at age twenty-seven, he became she.

I found out later that the first sex-change operation in China was performed in Beijing in 1983, the year before I arrived in Xi'an. At the time, it was a secret, known only to a small number of doctors and hospital officials. Yet by 1999, gender-changing operations in China had become numerous enough—in the hundreds, each year—that Beijing Medical University brought their guidelines for the procedure out into the open. It required a five-year waiting period, extensive psychological counseling, and a year of hormone treatment before the operation. It seemed incongruous to me that a government as conservative as China's—with its puritanical attitude, frowning on anything out of the norm—was openly allowing sex-change operations. As with so much in China, however, behind the stern face of officialdom was a more pragmatic approach that made many things possible.

As Jin Xing pointed out to me, Chinese society is highly homogeneous, and individual expression is often snuffed out at an early age. Putting the group first and the individual last is the age-old Chinese way. The authorities like to portray it as a noble concern, a way to keep members of Chinese society on equal footing, although more often it is a way to mask intolerance and control by those in power.

At the same time, overcrowding and a lack of privacy in China have often put a premium on discretion. As long as no one felt threatened, Jin Xing's sex change was regarded with acquiescent respect. "I don't feel any discrimination," she told me. "Many people do not understand, but no one is saying, 'You can't do this.' " After speaking publicly about her operation, Jin Xing got hundreds of letters from Chinese men and women who praised and thanked her for giving them hope and inspiration.

For Jin Xing, the scariest part of her decision was telling her father, an army intelligence officer. Politically, he was deeply conservative, but he surprised her and promised his support. He used his influence to help switch the gender on her national identity card from male to female. Jin Xing felt no need to change her given name, which means "gold star" and is not gender specific. Her father's reaction seemed to me to reflect the Chinese way, carefully keeping to orthodoxy most of the time, and then shedding it when necessary. I wondered how many American military men would accept a child's change in gender.

By the end of our long conversation that day, I felt enraptured by Jin Xing. She had faced and beaten enormous obstacles, and it seemed to have made her quite clear about what she could control and what she could not. She spoke with certainty, as if she had struggled long and hard to become self-aware. Talking about herself, she was remarkably unguarded, especially for someone with so much to be guarded about. She looked at me with an incisive gaze as she spoke. I wondered what she thought of me and guessed that, with her perspective, she could intuitively understand an outsider like me in a way that few of my Chinese friends could. Her views on gender also tickled my imagination, and I felt she might hold answers to questions about myself that I had not yet formulated in my mind.

For the next two days, I could not stop thinking about her. I heard her voice in my mind, I envisioned her face. I had often interviewed people who fascinated me, and felt an urge to befriend them. But in most cases, I left an interview promising to be in touch, only to get distracted by a new assignment. This time felt different. I told myself to wait at least forty-eight hours before calling her, as I did with other women I wanted to seduce. I surprised myself with that thought. Did I actually want to seduce her? I felt drawn to her emotionally more than anything—a desire to get close. When I reached her on the phone she seemed pleased, saying she did not expect to hear from me again, since many people were intrigued by her but never asked for a second date. I felt an urge to prove myself different.

Three days later we met for dinner. I took her to an elegant French restaurant. The waiters all recognized her and acted with obsequious respect. I felt a flush of pride to sit with a celebrity, since everyone glanced at me, too. That sensation lasted about three minutes, then it became uncomfortable. I wished we could blend into a crowd and talk without feeling observed. I said so and apologized for my choice of restaurant. She smiled softly and touched my hand. "I forgive you," she said. My fingertips tingled.

Jin Xing called me late that night to say goodnight before she went to sleep. We fell into another long conversation. Her take on Chinese society—its old-fashioned racism, its stubborn unwillingness to accept outsiders, its tendency toward closed-mindedness—was refreshing. I felt kinship with her. She seemed able to speak insightfully about her own contradictory impulses for closeness and distance, for fame and anonymity, for responsibility and freedom. She seemed to understand me, too. I felt she could see me as a person, not as an American or as a reporter. I felt accepted by her. She laughed with a squeak that was endearing, and I had the urge to reach through the phone and embrace her.

We spoke by phone late the following night, and the one after that, and then every night. It became my favorite ritual of the day, my just-before-bed telephone call with Jin Xing. In the weeks that followed, my work took me traveling to several Chinese cities. Jin Xing was traveling as well. Yet we always had time for a long late-night phone conversation. Jin Xing was always soothing, always curious about my adventures of the day and always understanding about my emotional aches and pains. I sometimes wondered what the state security thugs, who presumably eavesdropped on our calls, thought about this courtship. I didn't care. I needed her.

I felt an inner pride, knowing it took a special man to look past her unusual circumstances and find our common ground. I understood her obsession with work, her fear of, and desire for, closeness. Her relationships sounded like my own: drawn to someone who desires an intense intimacy, only to feel hemmed in and to push away. She and I could be different, I thought. I knew how to be close without suffocating her. She could trust me.

Still, as we grew close, I found it hard to think about our future. At times, I asked myself what I was doing, becoming emotionally involved with a transgendered celebrity. On paper, it did not make any sense. Yet when I did not analyze our bond, it felt right. I had become somewhat desperate emotionally. Earlier that year, I had a stormy relationship with an American woman in Beijing, and she had dumped me, leaving me depressed. Jin Xing nurtured and soothed me in a way that I needed, and in a way I had not found anywhere else.

I shivered with excitement the day Jin Xing came to Shanghai and accepted my invitation to stay at my apartment. Going to bed with her felt like a natural next step. I was afraid, but she made it easy. She was very tender. She asked me to promise, no matter what happened between us, never to tell what it was like in bed with her. I promised.

We had an easy intimacy in my home. We listened to a favorite recording of *La Bohème* over and over. I loved watching her dress and teased her about how much time she took. She defended herself. "People look very carefully at me," she said. "I have it much harder than ordinary women. They can dress sloppily, but I feel like I have to be perfect every day."

I was curious about her ambition. As a young dancer, her dream was to study overseas, which at the time looked like a nearly impossible goal. But she achieved it. Then she decided to start the first independent dance troupe in China, another impossible-looking task. Again, she had done it, by the time she turned thirty. Now, as she neared her thirty-second birthday, Jin Xing said her next goal was to be a movie star or a television talk-show host. I chuckled to myself, knowing what a longshot that was. But she seemed fearless. And China was changing fast, so there might be no limit to what Jin Xing could do. At the same time, I wondered what spurred her to work so hard, to be in perpetual motion, to demand perfection of herself constantly. Getting hooked on an idea and pursuing it doggedly, though it made her enormously productive, seemed to me like a sign of her deeper unhappiness. I recognized that tendency because I had it myself.

What I did not share was her gigantic appetite for attention. "I am most comfortable on stage," she told me. "That is the real me. That is when I feel completely alive, completely whole. There is no hiding. The lights are on. Everyone is watching." Offstage, she did not seem like a prima donna. She acted as though she had faced and tackled such serious problems that the normal strains of every-day life could not rattle her. Yet I wondered about that craving for attention on stage. It suggested that, despite her evident equanim-ity, the hole inside her heart had not yet been filled.

Jin Xing had carefully staged her coming out as a transsexual, clearing it with officials in the Ministry of Culture and then ar-ranging a series of interviews with Chinese newspapers timed to co-incide with the opening of the new dance troupe she had founded. She knew that talking openly about her operation would attract at-tention and draw people to her dance performances. Chinese audi-ences seemed more intrigued than repulsed by the idea of a dancer who changed gender. Once they had paid for their seats, many peo-ple forgot why they came and simply watched the dance.

Jin Xing was politically savvy, too. She knew how to identify people in power and how to sweet-talk them, how to lobby or of-fer the right gift at the right time. Planning her independent dance company, she had to overcome the immediate suspicion that Chi-nese officials have of anything outside their control. Jin Xing per-suaded officials in the Ministry of Culture that she was politically reliable and that her dance troupe would never threaten anyone. She also proposed to share income with the ministry, on the condition that there would be no artistic interference. It was an unusual arrangement at the time. As long as she kept officials happy with praise, gifts, and a small stream of revenue, they left her alone. Her dance company thrived.

After two years, however, the ensemble fell apart. A male dancer led a mutiny, accusing Jin Xing of being an imperious and exploitative leader. The feud was reported by Chinese newspapers and attracted attention because of Jin Xing's fame. In her view, the male dancer had led a vendetta against her because she had demoted him. I only heard her side of the story and wondered what she had really been like as the director of a dance troupe. Regardless, she felt deeply wounded that other dancers sided with him. They were too young to appreciate the independence she gave them in a company operating outside the normal rules of Chinese bureaucracy. She abandoned the company. Part of her was relieved, freeing herself from its tremendous demands. But she also felt she had lost her baby, her creation.

The same year, Jin Xing won an award from the Ministry of Culture. Like many awards in Communist countries, it had less to do with talent than with connections. But it bestowed a formal star of approval that made it permissible for government organizations, who looked to Beijing for signals, to hire Jin Xing as a choreographer or a director. Jin Xing had gone from being a bizarre celebrity to a part of China's cultural establishment. Now offers poured in from government art troupes that wanted Jin Xing's expertise in staging.

When I met Jin Xing, she had just been invited to direct a performance of Buddhist monks at the Shaolin Temple, a famous monastery in a province of central China called Henan. Legend has it that monks at the temple learned martial arts centuries ago to fend off bandits, and Shaolin eventually became known as the top school for kung fu, helped in the 1980s by popular Hong Kong movies that glorified its monks as virtuous heroes. Now the temple's leaders were trying to capitalize on its fame by fielding a troupe of monks to perform an act of acrobatic martial arts and take it on tour overseas. Someone advised them that they needed help with staging and costumes and music and lighting, and they hired Jin Xing to direct the show. It was something of a lark for her, spending a few weeks at a monastery in rural China to work with martial arts experts.

She invited me to visit, and I went for a weekend. I was amused to see Jin Xing prancing about in shorts and a peasant blouse as she directed a crew of bald Chinese monks in brown monastic robes. The administrators, who seemed to me like typical Chinese bureaucrats, all were entranced by her. They acted comfortably with her but were more distant with me, probably assuming I was some kind of sexual deviant. When they hosted a lunch banquet for her, none of the officials wanted to sit next to me. But Jin Xing didn't care, so neither did I.

I didn't know what to tell my friends about Jin Xing. I did not hide my relationship with her, but I did not talk about it. My connection to her was so unusual that I did not feel able to define it. Although I considered myself a writer, a professional communicator, at that time I did not have words to explain what I was going through. I wanted to explore new emotional territory with Jin Xing and sensed that I could learn something from her. I told no one in my family about her. I did not know how.

Over dinner in Shanghai one night, Jin Xing told me that she was not attracted to Chinese men. "They are not strong enough, too feminine," she said. I told her about my sense of Chinese culture as feminine. In my mind, the masculine ideal in the West was of brute strength and independence, of conquering and dominating. In China, the masculine ideal was of a peaceful scholar, in tune with nature and poetry, coexisting peacefully. Jin Xing asked if that was why I was attracted to Asian women, so I could feel like more of a man. I realized that it was true. I was attracted to the delicate manner of Asian women, to their gentle femininity that let me feel more clearly masculine. I thought I wanted women to see me as a human being, but I had frequently warmed to women who I sensed were drawn to my Western appearance.

The twist was, I had been unable to ever have a serious relationship with a Chinese woman. Although I easily began affairs, exhilarated by physical attraction, they never lasted more than a few months. Now, I realized, the Chinese person I was most seriously involved with was a woman who had once been a man. Although I was not aware of it consciously, I was evidently intrigued by what it meant to be a man and how to balance the feminine and masculine sides of myself. And yet, for all my ideas about culture and gender, what I really wanted underneath it all was a strong bond with a partner, an emotional attachment that felt equal and mutual.

In the days after that dinner, I mulled over what so attracted me to Jin Xing. I was drawn to the exoticism of her circumstance and the inherently forbidden flavor of knowing a transsexual. Yet what I found utterly magnetic was her confidence, her self-knowledge, and her compassion. She had a firm sense of who she was and what she wanted, even as she grew and changed. Jin Xing so strongly believed in her inner sense of femininity that she was willing to take a physically and socially treacherous path to be true to her spirit.

I did not have an equally firm sense of myself. When I took a cold look at my life, I saw that I worked relentlessly and was addicted to telephones and e-mail, making sure that I was busy all day long. As a foreign correspondent, I was ready to drop everything when news broke. It was easy to say to myself that my commitment was what the job demanded. But the truth was that I was constantly distracting myself so that I would not have to think about deeper questions, like why I had a gnawing sense of emptiness at my core.

When Jin Xing asked what I wanted, I did not know how to answer. For years, my goals had revolved entirely around work, wanting to succeed as a foreign correspondent. I had steadily put my career ahead of all other considerations, like family or relationship, and had worked hard to earn notice from my editors and other correspondents. Yet I had recently begun to feel the bittersweet sensation of having reached my professional goal. I had established myself as one of the premier Western correspondents in China, but found my work less and less fulfilling. I recognized that I had no real personal life. Jin Xing could tell that my devotion to my job was a way to hold intimacy at bay, just as it was for her. Yet she could also tell from the way I spoke that intimacy was what I wanted.

As I looked at myself in Jin Xing's eyes, I could see a romantic and thoughtful man, an adventurer, an emotionally vulnerable man. Jin Xing seemed to look past the ways I usually identified myself, as a *New York Times* correspondent or as a China expert. Underneath, I had a masculine soul that wanted to protect her. With other Chinese women, in my affairs and my interactions with women at Sauna Massage, I had seen myself as they did, as a Western man who knew how to talk to them but never showed any of himself. Normally, I was afraid of letting anyone look beneath my outer shell. Yet Jin Xing did that, in a gentle and loving way that did not threaten or scare me.

Jin Xing showed me that my search for the feminine in China had been a search inside my own mind. I had been looking for a sense of masculinity, an elusive notion that had nothing to do with China but with my sense of self. My long journey through China had sated a youthful desire for adventure and had given me thick notebooks tracking my progress as I probed the hidden realms of China. But ultimately I wanted something deeper: I wanted a soul mate. My attempts with women had always failed, and I always found fault with my partner. But the truth was that I was the bad partner, afraid to let anyone get too close. When I looked at Jin Xing, I wanted to be like her. Not to change my gender, but to have as firm a sense of myself.

I felt a tenderness for Jin Xing that was as wonderful as it was surprising. By providing me with a mirror to see myself clearly, however, she unintentionally spelled the end of our romance. As much as our relationship had taught me, it was not the long-term bond I wanted. Looking back later, I could identify my familiar pattern of pursuing a woman who was not ultimately suitable for me. That way, I always had an exit, leaving our bond emotionally risk-free. That gave me an invisible sense of leverage over her, not related to my role as the man and the Westerner in the relationship, but simply because I had the power to say no. Perhaps she knew that all along. Perhaps that was part of her attraction to me, too.

When Jin Xing flew to Shanghai to see me a few days later, I picked her up at the airport and drove her to my home. We sat down on the living-room couch, and I gave her a gift and told her it was over. She knew why. We went for dinner at an Italian restaurant nearby. It was raining outside. I tried hard to make her laugh. "I look fine on the outside, but inside I am crumbling," she said finally.

A tear rolled down her cheek, and she tried to hide it, leaving for the ladies' room. When she came back, composed, she asked if she could stay over one last time. We held hands in the taxi. We had coffee in bed the next morning, laughing again, savoring our closeness.

Two months later, she invited me to Shenyang, in northeast China, where she was staging a show at the air force dance troupe where she had trained as a child. As part of the military, it would once have been impossible for administrators there to hire an openly transsexual dancer. But rules in China were becoming ever more relaxed, and Jin Xing's fame and good relations with the Ministry of Culture gave her great flexibility and opportunity. It was her birthday that weekend, and I knew she would appreciate it if I went. As I sat at her dinner table with army officers in uniform telling old stories about a dancer who was now a transsexual choreographer, I marveled that it was something I never expected to hear in Communist China. But Jin Xing was an anomaly, a special person in any country.

I could not resist writing a profile about Jin Xing for my newspaper. I ought to have warned my editors about my relationship with her. Had I done so, they would have nixed the article. I would have done so, too, had I worn an editor's shoes. Journalistic ethics frown on writing about friends or lovers, for good reason. But I decided to sneak this one through. Like any journalist, I cannot resist telling a good story, and Jin Xing's lifestyle spoke volumes about the flourishing of social freedom in contemporary China. I think I also had a lingering impulse to show off, to get attention for netting a China story in a way that few other journalists could. As I wrote, I checked my article carefully to make sure I was not being unduly friendly or unfair to her. The bare facts of Jin Xing's story were powerful enough by themselves, and when the article was printed, it brought me a chorus of compliments. But like so many newspaper stories, that article did not touch a more significant truth, of what I knew about her and what knowing her did for me.

chapter fifteen

SOUTH OF THE CLOUDS

One of my favorite places in China was a province of rolling green hills and bamboo forests known as Yunnan, which means South of the Clouds. That pastoral-sounding name captured the sense of romance I felt about China in my first year there, when my notion of exploring a foreign culture involved long walks in an inviting countryside. Yunnan, located in China's southwest, was named by northern Chinese for its sunny and temperate year-round weather, like that of southern California. I loved exploring the stone villages that dotted the landscape, talking with friendly townspeople, and taking solitary strolls through the woods.

As my fortieth birthday neared, I found myself drawn to this region more frequently to escape the noise and impatient pace of my work life. I craved moments of calm and spent more and more time searching for places where I could spend a meditative morning by taking a quiet walk. As a foreign correspondent, I was tired of always dipping into other people's lives and leaving quickly, constantly hurrying from one news event to the next, and juggling multiple demands on my time. I craved a deeper sense of connection with others, but after my experience with Jin Xing, I had a nagging sense that I needed to find peace within myself before I would be ready.

One warm sunny morning, on a break from reporting, I wandered through a bamboo forest in Yunnan, following a dirt trail. The sunlight flickered down between the thickets of green leaves and shafts of bamboo. The air was humid. The forest was quiet except for a gentle clackety-clack of bamboo shafts hitting each other. Damp underbrush smelled musty. I savored the sense of serenity that seemed to hang from the trees.

A small path presented itself off to one side of the trail, meandering deeper into the wood. I took it without thinking. Over a hill, I heard the sound of a drumbeat in the distance, a thumping that reverberated softly through the bamboo trees. As I walked farther, it slowly grew louder and more distinct, drawing me onward. Eventually I could hear banging cymbals and the simple melody of a flute. I grew more and more curious.

At a clearing, I saw one hundred people involved in some kind of a mystical assembly. Dozens of middle-aged women, along with a sprinkling of men and younger people, sat cross-legged in meditation while others performed a set of exercises in unison. Several others stood, arching their backs, with arms open and eyes closed, as if yielding to a greater power. Two or three women leaped about in ecstatic dance, ungainly and graceless but charmingly uninhibited. Off to one side, a three-man band of drummer and cymbal percussionist and wooden flute player, each wearing a red bandanna wrapped around the forehead, offered up a primitive rhythm.

I stood and stared. With the beat of the drum and the swaying of the dancers, I could feel a collective sense of peace and letting go. These people looked like they were journeying within, trying to touch a moment of the eternal.

A young man with a gleeful smile came over to talk to me. "We are followers of Falun Gong," he said. These were new words to me, and I asked him to repeat them several times. He explained that Falun Gong was a branch of *qi gong,* the ancient Chinese practice of marshaling inner energy. The smile on this young man, whose name was Han, seemed to take over his narrow face, his wispy beard, his lively eyes. He exuded warmth and patience. He told me that the worshipers sitting in meditation were "spinning the wheel." He pointed to his abdomen and spun his finger around like an electric fan. Feeling the wheel and hearing its hum, Han said, let worshipers find inner peace and communicate with the messiah. And who was this messiah? A teacher named Li Hongzhi. "Which one is he?" I asked, looking around to see if someone was leading the group. Han smiled and gently shook his head. "Li Hongzhi is not here," Han said. "He is everywhere."

Almost everyone raised in China believes in *qi,* pronounced "chee," which means inner life force, or vital energy. Chinese medicine is based on the principle that the free flow of *qi* through the body brings physical and mental health. Blocking one's *qi,* it is believed, can cause disease. Curing disease, with acupuncture or herbs, improves the flow of *qi* through an afflicted area of the body. In Chinese culture, *qi* is as widely accepted and as hard to pin down as a soul in Christianity. It cannot be measured, but its existence is not in doubt.

Qi gong is an effort to nurture and harness one's *qi,* from simple breathing exercises to elaborate spiritual healing. Like prayer, *qi gong* can help followers find a connection to the divine. Some followers are drawn to *qi gong* masters who develop intuitive power and charisma. Others practice alone. For many, *qi gong* is a way to bring a touch of the spiritual into daily life, a way to find peace through exercise or meditation.

I looked at *qi gong* skeptically, suspicious of anything spiritual-sounding. It was easy to poke holes in the fantastical claims of *qi gong* masters, who professed the ability to spark a fire, fly across great distances, or move objects without touching them. When Chinese friends tried to persuade me to go see a well-known *qi gong* master, I laughingly dismissed the entire field as bunkum. Yet in doing so, I saw later, I let the odd extremist distract me from a broad scope of moderates and a whole layer of Chinese life I had not penetrated.

That day in the forest, I could not help recognizing the deep sense of calm and generosity that emanated from Han and the other worshipers. Whether it was from harnessing their *qi* or from deepening awareness through meditation, they were achieving a sense of spiritual peace that I could feel. I was curious about it. I myself had no religion. I grew up with parents who attended a Unitarian Church a half dozen times a year. The closest I came to anything spiritual was listening to music of my personal guru, John Coltrane. Yet I felt a distinct yearning for the kind of peace that these people were experiencing. My days as a reporter were often consumed with fighting the system, intruding on people's lives, pushing my nose where it did not always belong. It was often unsettling and exhausting. I wore the exterior shell of a tough guy, a swaggering correspondent who would let no one stand in the way of getting to the news. But inside, it was wearing me down. In the forest that day, I wondered if the followers of Falun Gong understood something that I did not.

Religion in China is often hard for outsiders to understand. Spiritual worship in China does not fall easily under one religion, like Christianity or Islam or Judaism. In Chinese culture, Confucianism and Buddhism and Taoism all mingle together. Each school of thought has its adherents, yet none really acts as a national religion. Confucianism and Buddhism and Taoism each have a prominent role in China, but none has quite carved out its own separate corner. Chinese culture incorporates elements of each and fully worships none.

The main religion of China is being Chinese. Chinese culture itself forms the structure of belief that addresses the principal mysteries of life and gives meaning to daily existence. Chinese culture is rooted in Confucian principles, such as obedience before authority and honoring one's parents and ancestors. Yet standard Chinese culture also includes visits to a Buddhist temple on particular holidays, to light incense and bow, and it includes belief in the eternal power of the *tao,* the Way, which is the basis of Taoism. A typical Chinese person considers all those practices part of being Chinese, rather than part of a particular religion. When asked, most Chinese people will say they have no religion. For them, the words *I am Chinese* carry all the meaning in the world.

The mythology of Chinese people is that their nation is the center of the world, their civilization the oldest and grandest on earth, dating to the Yellow Emperor, who set up the first lunar calendar in about 2600 B.C.E. The early invention of paper and gunpowder reinforced the Chinese belief that their people were superior to others. They viewed neighbors like Japan, Korea, and Vietnam as insignificant, vassal states. They pointed to the enduring strength of the Chinese state, which has survived for two millennia, while the Roman, Ottoman, and British Empires all rose and fell. The state relied on a sophisticated code of Confucian principles, stressing ethical behavior by leaders and obedience by followers. Yet moral teaching was built into China's language, with the common use of *cheng yu,* or colloquial sayings, based on old stories that offered a lesson for every situation, like an encyclopedic collection of fables that were commonly sprinkled into daily conversation. Chinese medicine, based on a theory of energy pathways through the body, offered an omniscient system with answers for every ailment. As a whole, Chinese culture became a cohesive belief system, self-satisfied and complete.

Traditional forms of worship in China were largely destroyed after Mao came to power in 1949. Mao proffered Communism as a new religion and offered himself as a messiah. Common people were given no choice but to worship him. After his death, pure Communism was exposed as a sham. Deng Xiaoping tried to replace it with the ideal of modernization, a poor spiritual substitute that could not really captivate the popular imagination. Instead, during the years I lived there, the most powerful trend became an obsession with money, which fascinated many and satisfied few. It was no wonder that Chinese people were looking for something deeper to believe in at the turn of the century. *Qi gong* appealed to many Chinese people as a way to get to their cultural roots, to find a spiritual element in their lives, something more meaningful than money and modern appliances. By the 1990s, hundreds of schools of *qi gong* flourished in China. Falun Gong became the largest, with tens of millions of followers.

Falun Gong was devised by Li Hongzhi, a simple man who evidently came up with a formula that resonated with common people.

Li based Falun Gong on the Buddhist principles of patience, benevolence, and nonattachment. He taught followers that in Falun Gong, which literally means law of the wheel, one can learn to spin a wheel of energy inside the abdomen as a way to find the truth and to cure illness. The wheel, a microcosm of the universe, could spin without stopping once a worshiper enabled it to begin, and with access to cosmic energy, one could lead a clean and moral life and nurture an inner sense of goodness. Li promised his followers that conscientious practice of Falun Gong would eliminate the need for doctors or medicine, could cure AIDS and cancer. As his movement grew, influence and money went to Li's head, and he seemed to develop a messiah complex, placing himself on the same plane with Jesus and Buddha. Facing possible arrest, Li moved to New York City in 1998.

Falun Gong drew countless middle-aged women with its promise of a homegrown system for preserving health, particularly in northeast China, a depressed industrial area where many had lost factory work and health coverage. Other people who were dispirited by the chaotic and money-minded trends of contemporary China also found solace in the mind-calming benefits of meditation. Participating in Falun Gong was free. Those who organized group exercise and meditation did so without pay. The goal was to spread the word and to help others improve their physical and spiritual health. Many followers began to hope that Falun Gong could solve China's modern ills. As word spread, Falun Gong was practiced in public parks and in homes in every province of China, and even in bamboo forests like the one I stumbled on in the southwest. By 1999 Li and his supporters claimed they had 100 million followers. That number was probably too high, but it was impossible to measure accurately, since many followers practiced secretly in their own homes.

China's leaders paid little attention to Falun Gong until one day in April 1999. I was in Beijing that day, working in a newspaper office. I saw an item on the news wire about a protest outside Zhongnanhai, the Party's leadership compound, located a stone's throw from Tiananmen Square. I called my friend John Pomfret, then the bureau chief for the *Washington Post*. He answered his cell phone, already at the site. "You'd better get out here," he said. "It's pretty weird."

It was eerily quiet in the center of Beijing, slightly after noon. More than ten thousand men and women and children sat in long rows, surrounding Zhongnanhai, the most politically sensitive building in China. They had managed to gather despite the watchfulness of the police, who had been permanently on alert to prevent any unauthorized protest in central Beijing since the student movement of 1989. I could tell by their plain, threadbare clothing that the protesters had come from outside Beijing. They did not chant slogans or carry banners. Instead, they sat silently. I tried to speak to a few, but they all declined, some smiling and softly shaking their heads in apology. They acted with the discipline of soldiers and the equanimity of true believers. It felt quite strange. They were clearly there in protest, but they were not saying anything. What did they want?

A handful of leaders negotiated with China's prime minister, asking for formal recognition from the government. Promises were made. Yet the sit-in had alarmed China's leaders. China has a long history of political uprisings led by peasants with mystical beliefs, and Falun Gong was immediately seen as a threat to the Communist Party's authority and legitimacy. Party leaders were always suspicious of any organization they could not control. They particularly feared a movement that people truly believed in, because no one believed in

Communism anymore. True believers take risks and resist compromise in a way that nonbelievers will not. Even scarier to Communist leaders was the discovery that Falun Gong had spread among senior members in the government and the People's Liberation Army. To the authorities, an ability to mobilize peasants made the movement look like a dangerous flame that could ignite even greater numbers if it was not snuffed out.

Despite the steady growth of personal freedom in China, there were limits. When it came to threatening the government, the policy was still zero tolerance. A fierce crackdown was unleashed. The police arrested tens of thousands of ordinary believers in Falun Gong. Those who resisted or had the bad luck to fall under a jailor who wanted to impress his superiors with his toughness were beaten and sometimes killed. The government formally outlawed Falun Gong, calling it the greatest political threat to Communist Party authority since the student movement of 1989. Government organizations were instructed to denounce Falun Gong publicly and to hold political study sessions to recite Marxist theory, even though no one, not even China's leaders, believed in that anymore.

The crackdown had mixed results. China's legal officers had been taking steps toward making the system more rational and based on law. China's police and courts could no longer use old methods of enforcement and intimidation. Taking part in a peaceful demonstration no longer ranked as a serious crime. Most Falun Gong protesters were held for a few days and then sent home. Once released, few suffered the social stigma that once accompanied anyone arrested for opposing the Communist Party, since most ordinary people no longer cared what the Party thought. In some towns, however, the police reverted to old measures, torturing and even killing some Falun Gong worshipers. In 2004, two years after the initial crackdown, Falun Gong organizers claimed they had confirmed nearly one thousand followers who had been killed in custody.

The crackdown elicited broad sympathy from people in the United States, who saw it as a suppressing of religious freedom. Yet Falun Gong was more of a movement than a religion. As I read the teachings of Falun Gong, it was hard for me to take them seriously. I found the movement's bible, *Zhuan Falun,* a confusing mishmash of Buddhist principles and superstitious nonsense. I was a little put off by the movement's emblem, a *swastika* with four yin-yang emblems revolving around it. I also had trouble swallowing Li's insistence that a practitioner had to cultivate the ability to see through a "celestial eye" in the middle of one's forehead.

Yet I remembered how, back in the woods of southwest China, I had been mesmerized by the gathering in the woods that I stumbled on. I watched the ecstatic dancers and meditators for hours. Why was I so drawn by these worshipers? No part of me wanted to join them. Yet I felt envious of that devotion, wishing that I could taste something spiritual and not be blocked by my constant skepticism.

Han, the man with the wispy beard, had told me how Falun Gong had changed his life. He used to work nights at a bar, a heavy smoker and drinker who spent his free time chasing women. He felt no yearning for anything more in life, but he had noticed a group of young men meditating and practicing Falun Gong outside his home when he stumbled home, bleary-eyed, each day at dawn. "Friend," one of the men addressed him one day, "why don't you come sit with us?" So began his conversion, which was not ecstatic or colored by lightning bolts but took place gradually, over the course of a few months. He found spiritual peace by meditating, and his life grew immeasurably richer. He married and reconnected with old friends. He became more considerate and less self-absorbed. He felt a duty to perform good deeds, and he began training to become a schoolteacher. In the meantime, he practiced Falun Gong with a group at dawn each morning, reversing the times he rose and went to bed each day. "My life felt empty," he said. "Now it feels full."

Han seemed to have a message for me. "Find the goodness in your heart," he said. "Everyone has a different way of finding it, and no way is better than another. You must find your own way."

I did find my own way, in Tibet.

chapter sixteen

PILGRIMS IN TIBET

In the cool silence of dawn, hundreds of worshipers marched on a long path that circled the holy city of Lhasa, the capital of Tibet. It was early winter, and the walking faithful wore thick coats and dark robes, twirling prayer wheels, murmuring religious tributes, stepping with grace. Their faces were bronze and russet-colored. An old woman's eyes danced in greeting to me as I passed, though she did not break the prayer humming on her lips. A young man smiled and nodded slightly without stopping his own devotions. I followed them alongside a gold-roofed temple, where the scent of smoldering juniper rose from a blackened stupa. Continuing on, past a Chinese factory, down an ill-paved street, and across a grassy field, many of the worshipers stopped at a stone courtyard. They flattened their hands together and then touched forehead, throat, and heart before prostrating themselves facedown on the smooth stone, only to stand and resume their walking meditation. It was a holy procession, a daily prayer that seemed to keep them awake to the mystery of life. Nurturing their spiritual devotions, they had plenty of leftover goodwill to share with random visitors like me.

A toothless man and his wife sitting at the side of the road were sharing a piece of flatbread and a cup of tea as I walked with the worshipers. The man smiled at me and offered a traditional Tibetan greeting by sticking out his tongue. I returned the gesture. With a hand motion, he invited me to stop and partake. The man, Dawa, had deep wrinkles in his dark skin. He wore a yellow silk hat with rabbit-fur lining and enormous earflaps that looked endearingly clownish. His wife's gray hair was long and braided. She handed me a piece of their flatbread, hard and chewy. They had only one cup for tea and passed it to me for a sip before taking it back. Speaking Chinese, Dawa told me they came to Lhasa from their home in Amdo, a region of northern Tibet, a three-day trip in a truck. At least once in his life, Dawa said, he wanted to worship at the Jokhang Temple, the holiest place in Tibet. He exuded contentment, sitting there, sharing his meager breakfast and soaking in the morning sun that was just rising over the rooftops. As he spoke, he looked me in the eye with a penetrating gaze. I felt as if he could see all the way to my core. Nothing seemed to block his vision. He was an animal herder, and we had little in common. Yet I felt as though he knew me.

Two men approached on the path. They were filthy, their faces and cloaks black with dirt. They prostrated themselves at every step, flattening their hands together in prayer, touching forehead, throat, and heart and then lying facedown in the dirt with arms stretched overhead, only to stand up and step forward one body length. They

230

were on a pilgrimage, like Dawa and his wife. But these two chose the devout method, traveling the entire distance like human inchworms, moving a body length at a time, facedown. Some Tibetans traveled hundreds of miles this way, begging for food along the route and spending years on a single pilgrimage. We watched in silence as the two men approached. I glanced at Dawa. He raised his eyebrow in appreciation. The men passed by slowly. I wondered what kind of mental state a traditional pilgrim needed, or attained, prostrating his way across Tibet.

Tibet is a land of majestic mountains, clear, clear sky, and intense spirituality. With Himalayan peaks on one side and desert on another, Tibet carries an age-old mystique as a secret, forbidden land. Access has been made worse by China's Communist rulers, who restricted entry to a region they invaded, colonized, and pillaged, murdering and torturing uncounted thousands in five decades of occupation. I went to Tibet eager for a peek at this most secret of places under Chinese rule. After reading about the horrors committed by the Communists, I expected to find it sullen and depressing. Although there was indeed plenty of resentment toward the Chinese, the degree of goodwill and resilience Tibetans had preserved was eye-opening. At first, I watched dumbfounded at the religious fervor of ordinary people. Yet each day I spent in Tibet, I felt more and more absorbed by the palpable humanity of the Tibetan spirit. With my inchoate hunger for something spiritual, Tibet was the right place to go.

The Jokhang Temple looked majestic as I approached, its golden spires gleaming in the morning sun. Massive red pillars adorned the central doorway, covered with multicolored prayer flags. Outside the main gate, dozens of worshipers faced the temple to pray in a cycle of prostration. Inside, the blood-red walls and garish ornaments conspired with a smell of sweet incense and rancid yak butter to make me feel I was entering a new realm. Two dozen monks in vermilion robes sat in ceremony, chanting a rhythmic prayer, hoisting elaborate drums overhead and beating them in unison. Two monks blew long brass horns, emitting a deep *moo*.

An undercurrent of whispering by Tibetan pilgrims reverberated like a steady hum. In their wrinkled faces, I could read the hardship and poverty they had endured to stay alive in the desert mountains of their homeland. Many wore black wool robes crusted with dirt, slung open at one shoulder, at once noble and filthy. An old woman with countless long braids like dreadlocks clutched at her prayer beads as she murmured, stopping to knock her head against a wooden sideboard beneath a ceramic Buddha who gazed down at her. A smooth-skinned young woman in a lavender turtleneck and stonewashed jeans carried a gold chalice of yak butter, pouring a few drops into each of the grand candles that lined one wall.

In the main hall of the Jokhang, a central prayer area was lined with musty round cushions on long benches. In the center, twin monuments of the Buddha faced outward, heavily adorned with turquoise and coral jewelry. On each side lay rows of giant prayer wheels, elaborately painted cylinders with holy sutras stuffed inside. The pilgrims paraded down row after row, twirling a worn wooden handle on each one. Each twirl was believed to be the equivalent of reciting a sheaf of sutras, contributing to one's karma. I followed along, twirling the prayer wheels as well.

In a rear hall, a dozen pilgrims lined up next to a small window. Inside, one monk took money and requests while another used a worn feather quill to write out couplets on a slender sheet of red paper, carried away like a treasure by the pilgrims. Inside a narrow doorway nearby, the pilgrims crushed their way into a small chamber where an ancient Buddha figure reclined. The walls of the chamber were blackened stone, coated with the oil of long-burning candles. In here, the murmur of prayer dropped to a whisper. The pilgrims stepped forward slowly, some of their mouths hanging open in awe as they circled the reclining Buddha, a gift to the first king of Tibet in the eighth century as a dowry from his Nepali wife. The central monument in Tibet's central temple, a direct connection to the divine. Pilgrims presented their red sheets of paper to another monk to be burned in front of the Buddha statue, blessing the message. Some handed the monk sacks of yak butter, to be spooned into the central candle. The pilgrims jostled for a chance to lean in and touch their foreheads on a bed of silk before the statue. A tall monk stood by, knocking each pilgrim firmly on the back to make sure they did not dally. I watched, mesmerized.

In the Jokhang, in the long pilgrimages, and in the daily processions, the Tibetan spirit lived on vigorously. Tibet was not yet free from the Chinese, but Chinese efforts to conquer Tibet had clearly failed.

Chinese people often lectured me, in the years I lived in Beijing and Shanghai, about how Tibet had always been part of China and how Tibetans were uncivilized. China had done plenty for those ungrateful natives, this argument went, building new roads and hospitals and bringing modern culture to Tibet. No matter what extremes of oppression the Chinese authorities had committed, most of my Chinese friends believed in the racial and cultural superiority of China over Tibet. To me, Tibet looked like a land of rich spirituality. Chinese tended to see Tibet as a land of ignorance and backwardness. Over the years, I took part in countless arguments about whether Tibet was part of China, and those disputes spurred me to read a fair amount of history about Tibet.

For centuries, forbidding mountains and harsh climate kept Tibet isolated from the rest of the world. Most Tibetans were nomadic herdsman or barley farmers, scattered thinly across a vast mountainous plateau the size of Europe, practicing an animist worship of rocks, rivers, wind, and mountains. Buddhism arrived from India in the eighth century, and a belief in cycles of karma and reincarnation blended with old Tibetan oracles. With a mystical appreciation for the power of the unseen, Tibetan Buddhists believed that acting with compassion and cultivating a high state of awareness through meditation and prayer would lead toward enlightenment. For most Tibetans, daily life was plagued by poverty and malnourishment and the cold of winter at high altitude. Few things survived in the highlands of the Himalayas beyond barley, yaks, and Buddhist temples. Yet by respecting every life, from ant to antelope, one could find deliverance from eternal suffering and reach nirvana.

In Lhasa, Tibet was ruled by a tiny elite of aristocrats and lamas in competing sects of Tibetan Buddhism. Starting in the 1600s, a "Yellow Hat" sect came to dominate Tibetan politics, presided over by a Dalai Lama, revered as the ultimate spiritual leader. Each Dalai Lama was believed to be a reincarnation of a predecessor's spirit and was chosen in a secretive blend of mystical divination and backroom politicking. Tibetan elders scoured the country to look for a boy born with identifying marks or behavior suggesting he was a reincarnation of the lama's spirit. But recognizing signs in a small boy was an inexact process, vulnerable to interference from politics of the day in Lhasa. The elders often claimed they took direction from a vision or a dream, only to redefine the criteria after they found a candidate. Several Dalai Lamas were weak and ineffective, dominated by powerful regents, dying in mysterious circumstances.

The thirteenth Dalai Lama, born in 1888, was a powerful exception. A broad-minded and strong leader, he battled incursions from the Chinese and from the British while rejuvenating Buddhist learning at major monasteries in Lhasa. Still, the thirteenth Dalai Lama feared that outside information would undermine the ruling theocratic system, and under his leadership Tibet continued to keep out virtually all visitors. A sophisticated culture of elites thrived in Lhasa, but the great majority of Tibetan people remained poor and uneducated, battling fierce natural elements to stay alive. In 1950 the life expectancy of a baby born in Tibet was just thirty-six years.

Among Westerners, Tibet gained a special mystery and allure for its inaccessibility. Those who spent months trekking through the Himalayas inevitably ran into vigilant Tibetan guards at the border. Sven Hedin, a legendary Swedish explorer who traversed central Asia many times, darkened his skin with soot and sheep fat as he posed as a Mongolian pilgrim to try to sneak into Lhasa in 1900, traveling with a caravan of camels and donkeys. He was discovered and turned away. Heinrich Harrer, an Austrian mountain climber, did sneak into Tibet in 1944 by climbing successive Himalayan peaks and forging fake documents of invitation. Treated as a curiosity in Lhasa, Harrer eventually became tutor to the fourteenth Dalai Lama and later recounted his adventures in the remarkable book *Seven Years in Tibet.*

Through the centuries, Tibet and China entertained an uneasy relationship. Historically, a strong emperor in China demanded submission from Tibet, as he did from other neighboring areas, such as Mongolia, Korea, and Vietnam. A healthy degree of autonomy was allowed as long as respect and tribute flowed toward the emperor. In periods when China's emperor was weak, however, Tibet and other neighboring areas were ignored and allowed to act independently.

In the first half of the 1900s, China was politically unstable and Tibet was essentially independent. That ended when the People's Liberation Army invaded Tibet in 1950, trumpeting claims that that it had always been a part of China. Tibet's monastic government was paralyzed with indecision, its ragtag army carrying outdated muskets easily overrun. The fourteenth Dalai Lama, then just sixteen years old, was no military leader. In 1951 he went to Beijing to meet Mao, who promised autonomy for Tibet and its religious culture as long as Tibetans accepted that they were part of China and Communist Party rule. The Dalai Lama agreed.

As Chinese authorities gradually exerted more control over Tibet, armed clashes broke out. In 1959 the Dalai Lama feared he was about to be kidnapped and fled to India, crossing the mountains with an entourage of aides and aristocrats. The Chinese fully took over in Lhasa, executing those who resisted, confiscating property, defrocking monks, and closing temples. There was little outcry from the West, whose leaders saw the invasion as a *fait accompli*. Beijing redrew the map of Tibet, assigning huge chunks of its eastern territory to the Chinese provinces of Qinghai, Sichuan, and Yunnan. Over the next twenty years, fueled by a sense of cultural and racial superiority, Chinese forces killed uncounted thousands of Tibetans and wrecked more than ten thousand temples and monasteries. Extremist politics reigned in Beijing, and Tibetan culture was deemed outdated. Religious worship was banned altogether. News of the devastation reached the outside world in bits and pieces, and the Chinese authorities obscured it by arranging show tours for selected guests, like the sycophantic Eurasian writer Han Suyin, whose book *Lhasa: the Open City,* described Tibetan peasants happily singing the praises of Communism.

In 1980 Deng Xiaoping shifted direction, authorizing a modest reopening of temples and permitting religious worship. A delegation of Tibetan exiles, including the Dalai Lama's brother, visited from India. After a generation without religious worship, Chinese officials believed that ordinary Tibetans now supported Chinese rule and would behave in a restrained way. To their surprise, the Dalai Lama's brother was met by a riotous outpouring of thousands of Tibetans trying to touch him, crying for an end to Chinese rule. Chinese officials in Tibet were badly humiliated. The new Party chief in Beijing, Hu Yaobang, ordered a housecleaning of the old Maoists in Tibet and promised a raft of reforms. Few materialized. In the years that followed, despite modest improvements, Chinese officials and soldiers continued to occupy Tibet like a colonial force. They governed harshly, cracking down on monks who staged large protests in 1987 and 1989.

In the 1990s, Tibet remained virtually closed to journalists. Some correspondents applied again and again, only to be turned down every time. A few were allowed to visit in well-supervised groups. My colleague in Beijing, Patrick Tyler, was denied permission for four years and ended up trying to drive through the mountains to get there. (He got as far as Qinghai, a neighboring province, before he was stopped by the police and forced to return to Beijing.)

After years of fruitless applications myself, it occurred to me to approach Tibet in a Chinese way. Not directly, but in a roundabout fashion, telling the authorities what they wanted to hear. I wrote a letter of application saying that I wanted to write about economic development in Tibet, to show how China's efforts to spur private enterprise were raising the standard of living. I guessed that Chinese authorities would be eager to draw attention to recent growth in Tibetan income. My roundabout letter implied to the authorities that I would not be the obnoxious bulldozer many journalists were and that I would try to be reasonable. I got no response to my letter for months. Then one afternoon the phone rang in my office in Shanghai. I heard a woman's voice tell me over a crackling telephone line that my application for Tibet had been accepted and that she would be my guide when I was scheduled to arrive, two weeks hence. The woman's name was Basang, and she sounded friendly. I was thrilled. I knew I might be accompanied at all times by an official, that genuine reporting would not be easy. But at least I would get a peek at this secret region.

The day before my flight to Tibet, I went to get my certificate of permission in a small government office in Sichuan Province, where my flight originated. Basang had faxed the necessary forms to this office, where a polite Tibetan man sat behind a simple desk. Once he finished filling out my document, he asked a favor: could I carry a small carton with me to Tibet? A colleague there needed a delivery, he said. I hate to carry things when I travel and had become such an expert at traveling light that I was heading to wintry Tibet with a single shoulder bag. In China I had learned to rely on favors and to do favors in return, even the ones I silently hated, like carrying things. I said yes. The Tibetan man handed me a heavy cardboard box with the word MANGOES printed in Chinese on each side. I lugged it back to my hotel room. I wondered if I might be walking in to some kind of trap, carrying contraband that would be "exposed" on my arrival as a pretense to jailing or expelling me. As the hours passed, my curiosity grew. In the privacy of my hotel room, I opened the box. I found six glass jars of sliced mango.

The flight from Sichuan was bewitching. Snowcapped mountain peaks stretched as far as I could see, partly hidden by wedding-cake cloud formations. I looked down at the earth below, trying to discern some sign of a road winding its way through the mountain passes. I had heard that traveling by road from Sichuan to Lhasa would take six days, covering a distance I was flying in two and a half hours. On the horizon, the steep peaks eventually started to soften and then fall off. When the airport outside Lhasa came into view, the hills on one side looked like steep sand dunes, with tawny and vermilion rock faces on another. The air was clear, the sun blindingly bright. As soon as I stepped from the plane, I could smell the strong scent of burning juniper, a sign of Tibetan worship.

Basang was waiting for me. She had dark skin and a long nose that was slightly too big for her narrow face. Her hair was parted in the middle and held back in a matronly bun. She greeted me formally and said she would be my guide and translator. In theory, that meant that she would accompany me at all times, "facilitating" my contact with Tibetans. In practice, my relationship with Basang would be a blend of professional obligation, human kinship, and adversarial tension. On that first day, I was surprised that my official guide was a Tibetan woman. I had expected a faceless Chinese agent without a drop of humor or flexibility. Instead, Basang seemed quite human. The mangoes were for Basang herself. She told me she wanted them for her parents, who loved fruit and could buy little of it in Tibet. She was grateful.

Basang took me to lunch at a Tibetan restaurant at the edge of the Barkor, the market square at the center of the Tibetan section of Lhasa. I felt a sense of disbelief that is common to travelers on a first day in a truly foreign land. Nothing looked quite real. Maybe it was my nausea from the high altitude, since Lhasa is twelve thousand feet above sea level. The yak meat Basang ordered us in the restaurant made me queasy, too. As we talked, however, I became curious about her. I gently asked her personal questions. Basang told me her parents were well-connected Tibetans who taught her how to get along under Chinese rule by never directly challenging a person in authority and by keeping feelings well hidden. Basang went to high school in Beijing, a privilege reserved for Tibetans with good connections in Chinese officialdom. She mastered Chinese and learned English as well. After four years, she was accepted at Foreign Affairs University, which I knew as a training ground for Chinese diplomats and spies. I asked how she was treated there. She looked outside for a moment before answering. "They were patronizing," she said. It was a relief for her, after graduation, to move back to Tibet. She married and had a daughter, now nine years old, although she had separated from her husband. I asked if she was Buddhist. She smiled sheepishly. "I am a Communist Party member, so I am not allowed to believe. But you can't live in Tibet without living in Buddhism." To fellow Party members, she was atheist. To her Tibetan friends, she was Buddhist. With me, she was both.

Basang admitted that it was hard to balance the demands of Chinese officialdom and Tibetan humanity. Working for the government, she had to accept the superiority of Chinese officials who knew little about Tibet, not bothering to learn a word of the local language. In return, she enjoyed free housing and a steady salary, while many of her relatives were jobless. At work, she had to sign assurances that she believed in the invincibility of the Party, and attend political classes with those mind-numbing theories about the superiority of Communism, all evidence to the contrary. "Why am I telling you all this?" Basang asked, as if surprised at herself. Then she gave me a firm speech about following the rules, staying within proscribed boundaries. I figured that her partial opening up with me was calculated, to build an emotional connection, so that I would "behave" while I was under her supervision. As I listened to her talk, I wondered how much Basang informed on her guests like me, or on her own colleagues. The fact that Basang had worked in the Foreign Affairs Office for thirteen years—a period during which many in her office were purged—suggested that she had learned to play the game well enough. At the same time, she had never been promoted from her position as a junior officer, so maybe she was telling the truth when she said the Chinese did not trust her.

By now I had plenty of experience working with an official guide in the Chinese system. A guide could be an ally or an enemy, but not a friend. With a good rapport, a guide could be flexible and an invaluable source of information. If things went sour between us, a guide could throw up all kinds of obstacles. I preferred the friendly approach. But I knew that if Basang succeeded in factoring herself into my considerations, if I worried too much about hurting her feelings, it could compromise what I wrote.

Basang outlined the schedule she had prepared for me. To my relief, she had included visits to Lhasa's main religious sites and had sprinkled meetings with Tibetan businesspeople in between. Although I rode the economic angle to win permission to visit, Basang was evidently accustomed to taking visitors to the big temples and monasteries. Like any good bureaucrat, she did not like to vary the routine too much.

As we finished lunch, I told Basang I needed a day to rest and acclimate myself to the thin air. She warned me not to go by myself to the Tibetan part of town. I nodded gravely. I went to my hotel room and, after waiting ten minutes, found a way out through the laundry room in the back of the hotel, since I figured security officers would be watching the front door. I walked down some side streets toward the central square of Lhasa, looking over my shoulder now and then to see if any plainclothes officers were following me. I saw none.

I headed toward the center of town, finding my way by glancing up at the Potala Palace, which presided magnificently over the city from its position atop a steep hill. Once the residence of the Dalai Lama and his court, the Potala Palace was now an empty fortress, open for a few hours each day as a museum. I made my way toward it and approached from behind. At its base, a parade of Tibetan pilgrims rounded the palace on a long, circular path. I followed them, twirling a long row of prayer wheels. On one side of the palace, a number of Tibetan women sold trinkets and jewelry laid out on blankets, necklaces and rings and bracelets with heavy turquoise stones. One of the sellers was particularly friendly. She was strikingly handsome, nearly six feet tall, with an oval face and smooth dark skin. Her eyes were lively and warm. She picked out a Tibetan ring and put it on my finger. "A present," she said. "Because I like you." As I sat and spoke with her, a few of her friends gathered round. The women asked direct questions and answered mine. They consistently expressed two thoughts: a love of the Dalai Lama and a hatred of the Chinese. "It is our land, it is our sky," said the tall trinket seller, to eager nods from her friends.

In the days that followed, I spoke with countless other small merchants as I wandered alone through the streets of Lhasa, in between my engagements with Basang. (I was often followed by one or more stone-faced men when I left my hotel by the front door. But when I emerged before dawn, as I did on the day I shared a cup of tea with the pilgrim named Dawa, no one came along.) My passing conversations with Tibetans suggested that modest economic growth in

Tibet was indeed bringing a modest degree of flexibility to their lives. The more that money moved around, the more choices people had. The trinket seller had said she was earning enough to go back to her home in Kham, eastern Tibet, to spend several months of the year living with relatives and worshiping at her local temple. In the following days, other traders echoed the same message. A successful cashmere trader told me she was giving about forty percent of her profits to rebuild a Buddhist temple in her hometown, two hundred miles from Lhasa. I asked if improving business conditions made her feel more friendly toward the Chinese. She looked at me sharply. "I'm Tibetan. How do you think I feel?"

Since the 1990s, the conventional wisdom in the West has been that the influx of Chinese businessmen was swamping and diluting Tibetan culture, posing an even bigger threat than Chinese politics. Once I was in Tibet, I could see how naïve that wisdom was. The destruction caused by Chinese politics in the 1960s and '70s, when so many Tibetans were murdered, was horrendous. By the 1990s, though China's presence in Tibet was still oppressive, living conditions were clearly better. More food was available in stores. Restrictions on travel within Tibet had been dropped. Access to money made it easier to worship. Many foreign visitors to Lhasa were distracted by the ugly neon signs at Chinese stores and massage parlors, reflecting an influx of Chinese traders. But those were surface changes, not relevant to most Tibetans. It seemed ironic to me that oppression in Tibet became a fashionable cause in the West in the 1990s, attracting movie stars and rock groups and college students, just as conditions in Tibet began to improve modestly. After all, Tibet has been tormented by Chinese rule for fifty years, most of that time ignored by the entire world.

In Tibet, the question everyone was asking was whether the

Dalai Lama would ever be able to visit. Tashi, an attractive twenty-four-year-old man with shoulder-length hair who ran a clothing stall in the central market, told me that he would give back all the money he had earned in the past year if the Dalai Lama would return for one day. "I think everyone here would," he said, gesturing at the other stalls and merchants nearby. Tashi echoed the message I got in conversations all over: We hate the Chinese. We love the Dalai Lama. We would trade all the roads and hospitals built by the Chinese, all the money we have, in exchange for a chance to see the Dalai Lama, if only for a moment.

One day I met an elderly woman as she navigated her way down the old stone stairway from the Potala Palace. She said she went there every month to pray for the Dalai Lama's return. She was seventy-six, though the deep wrinkles blanketing her face made her look older. "I always come carrying the hope that I will live long enough to see the Dalai Lama here again," she said. "But I am getting old, and now I am afraid I may never get the chance." She began to cry. "People tell me that good things will come in the future. But I wait and wait and never see it. It never comes."

Like many Tibetans, the old woman nurtured a fanatical desire to see her leader return to Tibet. But I could see that the chances of that seemed less likely with each passing year. As long as Beijing wielded firm political control over Tibet, Chinese leaders had little incentive to negotiate with the Dalai Lama, no matter how he impressed audiences around the world with his charisma and wisdom. Beijing has said publicly that they welcome talks and would be willing to discuss limited autonomy for Tibet. But before any negotiation can take place, Beijing requires the Dalai Lama to declare his allegiance to the Communist Party as the sole legitimate authority and to move to Beijing. Not likely.

Relations between Beijing and the Dalai Lama came to a head in the Panchen Lama dilemma, an intriguing chapter of Tibet's recent history. The Panchen Lama has traditionally headed a sect of Tibetan Buddhism that rivaled, and at times cooperated with, that of the Dalai Lama. If Tibetans saw the Dalai Lama as the holiest human on earth, the Panchen Lama was the second holiest. As with other prominent lamas, a Panchen Lama was selected as a young boy by Tibetan elders. In 1959, when the current Dalai Lama fled Tibet, the Panchen Lama was only twenty years old, a tall and quiet young man. As Mao tried to discredit the Dalai Lama, he decided to promote this young man, known as the tenth Panchen Lama, as the true spiritual leader of Tibet. The Panchen Lama was effectively strong-armed by the Chinese into endorsing their rule; he presided over religious ceremonies in Tibet but wielded no real power. Still, the Panchen Lama refused to denounce his spiritual confrere, the Dalai Lama, and he gradually grew embittered by what the Chinese were doing in Tibet. In 1964, addressing a large crowd in Lhasa on a traditional Tibetan holiday, he put aside the speech written for him and proclaimed, "Long live the Dalai Lama! Long live an independent Tibet!" He was immediately put under house arrest. While radical politics raged in China, the Panchen Lama spent eight years in jail, much of it in solitary confinement.

After Deng Xiaoping came to power, the Panchen Lama was released from prison and given a senior post in the National People's Congress, China's legislature. Beijing again wanted him to legitimize Chinese rule in Tibet, and this time the Panchen Lama agreed on the understanding that he would be included in devising Beijing's policy toward Tibet. He chose education, a politically neutral area, as a place to exert influence. He lobbied to expand Tibetan-language instruction in grade schools and became a power broker with modest influence. Ordinary Tibetans again admired the Panchen Lama as a holy figure, even though he was cooperating with the Chinese. I watched him at a convening of the National People's Congress in Beijing in 1988, appearing in a brown silk robe, with a shaved head and a fleshy face. He was an impressive presence, at six feet four inches and three hundred pounds. When he spoke, his voice ranged from a deep, gravely rumble up to a high-pitched screech.

By early 1989, the political mood in Beijing loosened to a degree that the Panchen Lama decided to take risks and push the boundary of what was acceptable in public speech, just as the physicist Fang Lizhi had done. The same week in January that Fang wrote his letter to Deng Xiaoping calling for a political amnesty, the Panchen Lama was touring Tibet and spoke pointedly about the atrocities that China had perpetrated there. "The Communist Party has done more harm than good in Tibet," he said in a public speech. That sounded like an obvious statement, yet it was a politically daring thing for him to say.

On January 28, 1989, the Panchen Lama died unexpectedly in Tibet. He was fifty years old. The Chinese said the cause was a heart attack, brought on by the strain of individually blessing thousands of worshipers during his daily appearances in Tibetan temples. Tibetan exiles speculated that the Chinese authorities had murdered the Panchen Lama for speaking out. While possible, that seemed improbable to me. The Panchen Lama served Beijing at the time of his death, and despite his criticisms of Chinese rule, he was enormously useful to Chinese leaders, acknowledging their legitimacy and serving as a buffer between Tibet and Beijing. After his death, no one could fill those shoes. When rioting erupted two months later in Lhasa, no one of the Panchen Lama's stature could mediate. Beijing imposed martial law.

The Panchen Lama's death provoked a political and religious crisis. Who would select his replacement? Traditionally, a successor was selected in the same secretive procedure used to choose a Dalai Lama, with elders consulting oracles and then searching the countryside for a boy with distinguishing marks, to be defined clearly only after they found a candidate.

Several Communist Party leaders were aghast at such an antiquated procedure and thought that no new Panchen Lama should be chosen. Yet moderates in the leadership saw no harm in accepting a traditional Tibetan practice, as long as the new Panchen Lama did not act too independently. Besides, if Tibetans were not allowed to choose a new Panchen Lama inside Tibet, exiles allied with the Dalai Lama would certainly try to choose one. The leaders decided that a new Panchen Lama, properly supervised within Chinese territory, was preferable to one chosen and raised outside.

Chinese leaders approved a search committee to be headed by Chadrel Rinpoche, the abbot of Tashilhunpo, the home monastery of the Panchen Lama. Chadrel Rinpoche was an intriguing figure. Though some Tibetans considered anyone who cooperated with Beijing as morally suspect, Chadrel was a respected cleric who helped build Tashilhunpo into a center of religious learning. Although Chadrel had compromised with Chinese authorities over the years, he would not follow Beijing's orders outright. In meetings in Beijing, Chadrel argued that the Dalai Lama must give his approval to the candidate for Panchen Lama. Without the Dalai Lama's nod, Chadrel warned, it would be hard to persuade Tibetans to accept the choice. Chinese leaders insisted that they alone could approve the choice and that the Dalai Lama would have to accept it. Chadrel knew he would have to handle the issue gingerly. Beijing and the Dalai Lama distrusted each other so deeply that even a small difference could escalate into a confrontation. If that happened, Chadrel feared, Tibet could lose the institution of the Panchen Lama altogether.

Chadrel devised a risky scheme. He wrote a secret letter to the Dalai Lama and gave it to a trusted monk who carried it overland through the Himalayas to India. In his letter, Chadrel proposed that the Dalai Lama approve a choice in secret, then let Chadrel try to push that choice through Beijing's selection committee. After Beijing announced the choice, it could be revealed that the Dalai Lama agreed. In this way, Chadrel hoped, Beijing could act as though it had been the final arbiter in the choice, while Tibetan worshipers could believe that the Dalai Lama had really made the selection. The Dalai Lama weighed Chadrel's proposal and studied the names of five boys secretly forwarded to him, including one favored by Chadrel. The Dalai Lama knew that by agreeing to allow China to announce the decision, he would be vulnerable to accusations among exiles that he was parroting Beijing. He called Isabel Hilton, a British journalist he knew, and asked her to film him as he made the choice. If she saved the footage and released it only after the Chinese announced their decision, then the Dalai Lama could plausibly claim that he had made his choice before the Chinese did. Hilton obliged.

It was a good plan, but no one knew if it would work. Word filtered out of China that Chadrel was under pressure from Chinese leaders to abandon the search committee in favor of a Golden Urn, an old ceremony used in times of crisis, akin to picking the name of a boy out of a hat. Meantime, pressure from the Tibetan exiles pushed the Dalai Lama to consider announcing his choice first. The longer he waited, the greater the chance that the Chinese would pick a different boy. The Dalai Lama told colleagues that he was only concerned with finding the "real" Panchen Lama. In this case, he apparently fell prey to political pressure in the exile camp. Though the Dalai Lama had promised not to betray Chadrel, he effectively did so by publicly announcing in May 1995 that he had selected Gedhun Choekyi Nyima, a six-year-old boy, as the eleventh Panchen Lama. Chadrel Rinpoche was immediately placed under house arrest, accused of leaking state secrets for his clandestine communication with the Dalai Lama. The boy disappeared as well.

The Dalai Lama evidently felt guilty about his role in the event. As he later confided to Hilton, "I feel," he said, "that I committed the crime here and they took the punishment there." Indeed, they did. China ordered a purge of leaders in Tibetan monasteries and orchestrated a campaign in every monastery to denounce the Dalai Lama and his choice for Panchen Lama. Chadrel was sentenced to six years in jail. In November 1995, Beijing went forward with the Golden Urn. It was a sad spectacle: Chinese officials presiding over a Tibetan religious ceremony, choosing a second six-year-old boy, Gyaltsen Norbu, whose parents both happened to be Communist Party members. He has been trumpeted as China's choice for the Panchen Lama ever since, but few people in Tibet seem to believe in his holiness. The original boy was held outside Beijing, under house arrest. As Chadrel Rinpoche originally feared, the institution of the Panchen Lama seemed to be finished.

During my visit to Tibet, I was curious about what monks would say about the split between Beijing and the Dalai Lama. One morning, Basang accompanied me to Sera Monastery, with its striking collection of old Tibetan buildings. The monastery was famous for having schooled many illustrious Buddhist clerics over the centuries. A middle-aged monk who tended to yak-butter candles and Buddhist statues in one room of the temple was murmuring tributes and fingering orange prayer beads when I approached with Basang. He smiled warmly, pulled out two stools, and poured two cups of yak-butter tea. Basang explained that I was a reporter from an American newspaper, and he nodded solemnly. I asked him my question in an indirect way: can traditional religion coexist with modern society? "Of course they don't mix," he answered. To him, modern society meant Chinese rule, which is continually described in Chinese propaganda as "modern," in contrast with the Tibetan rule that preceded it. The monk said Tibetan Buddhist worship could not really flourish under Chinese rule and pointed to the way Chinese police tightly monitored life inside the monastery. He seemed insulted at the way that the Chinese authorities constantly derided the Dalai Lama as evil and immoral. At one point, getting worked up and raising his voice, he yelled, "We had an independent country, we had our own ruler in the Dalai Lama, and he is a wise and holy man! He won the Nobel Peace Prize. Doesn't that show that he is a wise and learned man?" Basang tried to interrupt the monk, but he kept talking. She persisted, finally raising her own voice to warn him that it was not safe for him to say such things. He seemed surprised. "Are you unreliable?" he asked her. Basang did not answer directly. He resumed his rant in a firm whisper. He was pessimistic about the state of religious study at Sera. There were now 550 monks, he said, far fewer than the 5,000 who were there in the 1950s. Would it soon be 50?

When we got outside, I told Basang I felt moved by what the monk had said. She cautioned me to write about it carefully. "It may be best to write with two hearts," she said. "One is what can be printed now, in the *New York Times,* the other is what you can write later, yourself, about what you feel." If I used names in a newspaper article, she said, it might get people in trouble. "The people at the Chinese embassy in Washington read your newspaper very carefully.

Anything you write can come back here. They will go find the people you talk to, and it could be trouble. It is best to have two hearts. You can say one thing to some people, and other things to others. Sometimes this is the only way." It was terribly poignant. She was talking about herself.

Still, I had to puzzle over this moral issue. How much danger did I bring to ordinary Tibetans whom I interviewed? Would anyone I spoke with be noticed and later interrogated? I feared that if I limited myself to "approved" interviews, when I was accompanied by Basang, it would be like giving in to the authorities, watering down the accuracy of what I wrote. As a reporter, I felt a sense of mission, talking to as many people as I could, even if it meant skating close to the line of what was morally acceptable, reminding myself that doing journalism well often involves taking risks.

In China, when I sometimes worried that my mere presence could endanger someone, I often reassured myself that over the long run, a system run on persecution of free speech will inevitably fall, that I was on the right side of history. But I knew that the fall of the Communist authorities in Tibet might not come for a long time. Perhaps not in my lifetime, or that of the monk I spoke with at Sera Monastery. He had spoken to me as a friendly-looking person, not as a reporter. He did not guard his remarks or think about how they would look in a newspaper. He may have had no idea of what a newspaper in the West really was. If he did, I wondered, would he want his message broadcast? Probably, if it could be done thoughtfully. He had openly told me his name and had not asked that I keep it secret. I could go ahead and quote him by name, since attributing a comment to a real person is always preferable to a nameless one. I could make no mention of him, to play it safe. Yet I knew that day that I would take a middle path, using the monk's words to describe the situation in Tibet as best I could, without using his name. I was taking a calculated risk with someone else's life. I knew there was a chance that publishing his words would cause trouble for him, and that Basang was the only other person who knew his identity.

In the late afternoon on the day before my departure from Tibet, I happened to mentioned to Basang that I typed my notes on a small laptop computer each night in my hotel room. She seemed surprised that I had a computer, remarking that she had noticed I only carried a modest shoulder bag when I arrived. Basang soon went to a food store to use a public phone. After another fifteen minutes, she announced that our day together was over, that she was going home, and that I was free to wander in the market by myself. I was happy to stroll alone on my last evening in Lhasa. Yet something tickled my mind; Basang's phone call bothered me. Before long, I felt an urge to get back to my hotel room and make sure my computer was still there, in one piece, in case she had been relaying its existence to other authorities. I had known all along that agents might look through my belongings, and I had been careful to keep names and identifying descriptions of Tibetans out of my notes. Now I worried that they might break the laptop intentionally, just to harass me.

As I stepped into the hotel lobby, a Chinese man jumped to attention when he saw me, and ran to an in-house phone, no doubt calling the agents in my room. I ran, but had to climb a flight of stairs and get down a long hallway to reach it. When I got there, it looked undisturbed. I took a deep breath, assuming that I had just been paranoid. But then I checked my laptop: it was still warm, obviously in use a few moments before. Opening it up, I could see that the last eight files accessed were my phone lists and Tibet notes. Basang had told them to go look for it. I felt betrayed.

The next morning, Basang and her driver fetched me at dawn to take me to the airport. Once we were seated and moving, I told her that someone had illegally broken into my room and violated my private property. She acted as though she did not understand what a portable computer was. Yet when I brought it up a third time, Basang nudged me in a way that the driver could not see. She was warning me to keep quiet. I looked her in the eye. She nodded toward the overhead light. Was our conversation being taped? Basang suggested that when we got to the airport, there would be time to sit for a cup of tea. I took that as a hint that we should continue talking there, not in the car. We were silent the rest of the ride. Seated in the dingy airport cafeteria, Basang asked me pointedly what I had written in my laptop, saying she needed to know so she could prepare. Prepare? Under tough circumstances, she said, she might have to inform on "some people." She said she wanted to inform only on those who had already been implicated in my notes. My head swam. I couldn't believe she was admitting that she informed on anyone. I didn't know what to say. She asked me several times whether I had written down the name of the monk at Sera monastery in my notes. No, I finally told her, I had used no names in my notes, except in formal interviews. She asked again about the monk. I told her no, I never wrote down his name. She seemed relieved, saying it meant she would not have to inform on him. I realized that this was how Basang survived, by fingering those who have already been condemned. If the agents saw anyone in my notes quoted as saying something politically subversive, and asked Basang about it, she could get in trouble if she pretended innocence. The danger I brought to those I interviewed came via Basang.

Basang and I sat looking at each other. It was a painful exchange. She glanced over at a Chinese man who sat down at a nearby table, to make sure he was not eavesdropping. He looked like an ordinary traveler to me and was too far away to hear what we said. I asked her, "How many other people will you inform on?" Basang was silent a moment, then told me she lived in fear of the agents. "You don't understand," she said. "They interrogate me after each day with you. I'm already in trouble." I asked why. She grimaced. The day I arrived, she had told them I was not carrying a computer, since all I had was a shoulder bag. "And the box of mangoes," I added. She grimaced again. That was even worse. She had not told the agents about the mangoes. But her driver, interviewed by the agents separately, had mentioned that I handed her a box. "That made them suspicious," she said. "I had to give them something else." "So you told them about my computer when you called from the market?" She looked away.

After my plane left the ground, I stared out at the mountain peaks that stretched into the distance, partly hidden by plump white clouds. I closed my eyes. So much of my energy in Tibet had been concerned with monitoring and supervision. Tibetans lived with political oppression every day. Yet those who had made the deepest impression on me displayed a refreshing dose of that magical Tibetan spirit—wondrous, generous, laughing. Dawa and his wife, the pilgrims from Kham; the trinket seller outside the Potala Palace; the monk at Sera Monastery; Tashi the young clothing importer. Each of them seemed inspired, not defeated. In the face of tremendous difficulty, they remained stoic and uncowed. They took chances to curse their oppressors and to praise the Dalai Lama. They were solemn, they were joyful. I felt their sadness and their proud resilience. Tears spilled down my cheeks.

chapter seventeen

SKY BURIAL

left Tibet, but it did not leave me. Back in Shanghai, I continued to wear the ring given to me by the woman selling jewelry at the foot of the Potala Palace. I caressed it with my thumb a few dozen times a day. Sometimes it provoked a memory of the smell of burning juniper or yak butter, or a vision of the tawny and vermilion landscape. I left a pile of Tibet photographs splayed out on my desk, and glancing at them warmed me. I could not explain why exactly. I felt as though a small piece of Tibet lived on inside me. I didn't want to let it go; I wanted to nurture it. I had the sense that contact with Tibet would take me somewhere I needed to go. Eventually I decided to return to Tibet.

I knew the Chinese authorities were unlikely to let me go back to Lhasa anytime soon, so I needed to find a back door of some kind. My friend John Pomfret, the *Washington Post* correspondent in Beijing, suggested traveling together to eastern Tibet. Ever since 1965, when China redrew the borders of Tibet, eastern Tibet had technically been part of Sichuan Province and had remained inaccessible to outsiders, since special permission was required to travel there. But John had learned that Chinese officials in Sichuan had dropped the restrictions to eastern Tibet, hoping to lure urban Chinese tourists and their cash. Eastern Tibet was full of sparsely populated forests and mountains, and its unpaved roads and poor amenities did not make it an instantly popular destination for travelers. For me, the sleepy, underwatched nature of eastern Tibet was attractive. As no special visa was necessary, I might be able to wander unsupervised, to speak freely with Tibetans, and to follow my intuition on where to go.

Taking a rickety old public bus from Chengdu, the capital of Sichuan, John and I braved two long days of bumpy roads on our way to Garze, an old town with an impressive Buddhist temple, located in a remote corner of the province. It was physically painful, bouncing hard on a wooden seat for ten hours at a time and stopping at roadside stands with bad food. But traveling in Tibet once again, I felt the mixture of enchantment and sadness I had known in Lhasa. I was inspired by the irrepressible spirit I saw in Tibetan faces, and dejected by the relentlessness of the Chinese occupation. When John had to head back to Chinese civilization after a few days, I decided to stay on.

At the temple in Garze, I asked a monk whether anyone performed sky burials, a traditional way that Tibetans dispose of the dead. The monk said that many people did, but not at the temple in Garze. Instead, they carried a corpse hundreds of miles up north, to a place called Serthar, to perform the ceremony. In a sky burial, a corpse is cut into thousands of pieces. First the flesh, then the bone. Once the body has been decimated, its parts are consumed by vultures and recycled through the sky, at least through the body of a bird in the sky. Once the spirit has left the body, Tibetans believe, the body ought not be preserved. Fire burial, or cremation, was reserved for the well-to-do in traditional Tibet, since wood was scarce in a mountainous desert. Water burial, in which a body was chopped to pieces and dumped in a river to disappear into the mouths of fish, was common in Tibetan towns with access to a river. When I first heard about sky burial, it sounded medieval. The Chinese regarded sky burial as a bizarre ritual of a primitive people and banned the practice in the 1960s. But as Tibetans regained limited rights to hold religious ceremonies in the 1980s, sky burials were allowed to resume. After talking about it with the monks, my curiosity grew. If I could see a sky burial, I thought, it might open a window into Tibetan culture in a way that nothing else could. Outsiders were generally prohibited from attending a sky burial. In Lhasa, that rule was strictly enforced. But out in the wilderness of eastern Tibet, I wondered if the rules would bend.

Asking around, I heard that sky burials had once been performed at a temple in a village called Tingka, twenty miles away. I found a ride with a friendly man named Lhaso who drove a tiny van, shaped like a loaf of bread. As we passed through a village along the way, Lhaso pulled over to the side of the road where he recognized a friend. The man had a leathery face and tall black hat. They spoke in Tibetan, but as we pulled away Lhaso told me in Chinese that the man's sister had died recently and that he was just back from a long journey taking her body for a sky burial at a temple up north, at Serthar. I was still hoping I could find the burial ground in Tingka. When we got there, Lhaso pointed me toward a temple, up a steep hill. I walked up a dirt path. At its top, I saw a collection of flat rocks, with a few Tibetan prayer flags languishing in the soft breeze. It looked like a site that hadn't been used in years. At the temple nearby, one of the monks told me that no one performed sky burials there anymore. "They all go to Serthar," the monk said.

Serthar. There was that name again; I could not ignore it. Should I go there? I had already traveled about four hundred miles over unpaved roads to get to Garze. The idea of pushing on for perhaps another four hundred miles, without a clear idea of what I would find, was not appealing. I had already gone five days without a shower, a decent meal, or a clean bed. Emotionally, I was ready to head back to Shanghai. Yet the name of Serthar ricocheted in my head. I was mindful that my time in China was drawing to a close. I would not get many more opportunities to explore in Tibet. It was time to take a chance.

I studied a map. There was no direct route to Serthar and no bus. It was all long, winding roads through the mountains. I would have to persuade a Tibetan with a sturdy car to drive me there. I spent a day inquiring in Garze before I was directed to the home of a man named Luodeng, a former truck driver with a long, narrow face that reminded me of a collie. Luodeng took me outside to look at his car, an old Chinese-made sedan. He said the brakes were not so good but that the engine ran fine. That did not sound particularly safe, but I liked Luodeng and sensed I could trust him. We negotiated a price and agreed to set out the next morning.

On the road, Luodeng's car rattled and bounced as relentlessly as the bus I had taken to Garze. A dull, metallic stench of gasoline filled the car. When Luodeng pressed the car horn, it sounded like an old woman clearing her throat. The window handle on my side of the car had broken off, and when I wanted to open the window for fresh air, I had to struggle with a pair of old pliers, which were hard to grip in a bouncing car. Once the window was down, we would inevitably hit a dusty patch, filling the car with a layer of fine brown grime, forcing me to struggle with the pliers again to close it. Luodeng expertly steered us over rough patches of ruts or mud.

The road weaved through long stretches of dark pine forest, broad meadows of tall grass, and golden fields of ripening barley. We drove for hours and hours through unspoiled countryside, then passed through small villages where Tibetans in heavy black robes stared at our car going by. Hours more would pass before we saw another human. We dipped into deep valleys and then climbed successive mountain passes with breathtaking views of the wilderness below. I tried to look beyond the steep drops at the side of the road, since there was no guardrail. Each time we reached a long incline, Luodeng's car wheezed and grunted under the strain. I was afraid that if the car broke down, we might be stranded for days, but it kept going. In the valleys, swelling streams rose high enough to cut through the road at several places. At one I had to get out of the car and wade in barefoot to see if it was too deep to pass. The water rose to my knee. Luodeng thought we could make it. The car got stuck. Trying to push it myself, as Luodeng steered, did not work. After an hour or so, a pair of trucks came along, and the two Tibetan drivers got out and helped me push. They seemed to laugh the whole time, amused to see a Westerner get so muddy. Once we finally succeeded, they broke out a bottle of warm beer, which we shared, passing it around.

Back in the car, Luodeng told me a story that seemed to sum up Tibetan vulnerability under Chinese rule. His ten-year-old son, Tikka, was in school one day when his Chinese teacher told everyone in the class to stand and repeat the phrase *I am Chinese.* The boy refused, insisting that he was Tibetan, not Chinese. The teacher argued that everyone in the classroom was a citizen of China, but the boy stuck to his identity as a Tibetan. Tikka's teacher informed the school principal, who called the police. Tikka was handcuffed and taken to a local jail, where he spent four months. Luodeng got him released only by bribing a police officer. The officer, adding a final insult, warned Luodeng not to let it happen again. Luodeng's outrage was diluted by his sense of guilt. "It was my fault he got arrested," Luodeng said, shaking his head at the thought. "I taught him to be proud he is Tibetan."

By the time we got to Serthar, two days later, I was dazed and exhausted. We pulled up to a small crossroads where the mud road cut a path through a stunning valley, with deep green hills climbing in every direction, bursting into snowcapped peaks in the distance. Luodeng inquired at a general store and learned that a shack two doors down sometimes took boarders.

When we stepped through the door of the hostel I smelled the sweet stench of yak dung, burning as fuel in an old stove in the corner of the room. The main room was austere, with two wooden benches and a table. The place was run by a Tibetan couple, a tall man with a badly pockmarked face and his hefty wife, each wearing thick black cloaks. They spoke rudimentary Chinese, and when they could not think of a word, they would say it in Tibetan to Luodeng, who translated for me. The woman handed me a cup of yak-butter tea. It tasted rancid but was warm. She sat on a wooden bench and reached inside her cloak to pull out a breast, the size of a watermelon, to suckle her two-year-old child. I stared as I sipped my tea.

Luodeng told the couple I was looking for a sky burial. The man nodded and said that Serthar was becoming a popular place to perform sky burials because of its charismatic leader. People from all over the province wanted their dead to be blessed by him before the bodies returned to the earth. However, the man said, sky burial ceremonies were closed to outsiders. One needed to know some-one to get in. The man and his wife conferred, whispering in Ti-betan. They sent their young nephew out to fetch that someone.

Before long, a cheerful monk came into the hostel. His crew-cut hair was an inch long, and it gave him the quality of a furry bear. He wore a vermilion robe with a yellow silk tunic underneath. He had a big smile, like a devout Buddhist who saw joy in everyday life. His name was Tsering. He was no ordinary monk, Luodeng explained to me. He was a *tulku,* selected as the reincarnation of a ranking Ti-betan religious figure. It turned out that Tsering needed a ride down to Chengdu, several days' drive, where I was next headed. I looked at Luodeng, and he nodded. We made a deal. In exchange for a ride to Chengdu, Tsering would escort me to the sky burial. His presence would ensure that no one would object, even though I was an out-sider. The fact that I was a journalist, a problem in most of China, did not matter to the Tibetans. It was such a remote area, so cut off from the rest of the world, that the notion of what might or might not be printed in a newspaper far away seemed irrelevant. All that mattered was the rule of the local temple authorities. Tsering promised to take me to a sky burial the following afternoon.

Tsering asked if I was willing to go for a walk. There was some-thing he wanted to show me. He led me outside the hostel and up a twisting dirt path, winding its way between two steep hills. We saw a few dozen red-robed monks walking on the trail. The further we climbed, the more monks we saw. All seemed friendly and curious about what a big nose was doing so far from a city. We rounded a turn, and Serthar came into view against the side of the mountain.

It looked like a city of wooden shacks, a gold-rush town of Buddhist worshipers. There must have been five thousand new houses.
As we drew closer, we walked by crowds of monks and nuns buzzing
in conversation, their hair shorn and their gazes serene, as they gathered for evening prayers outside a rambling collection of meeting
halls, connected by muddy pathways.

Tsering explained to me that Serthar was one of many Tibetan
Buddhist temples thriving outside the main cities of Tibet, partly
because of growing donations from Tibetans making more money.
Chinese officials tightly controlled monasteries in cities and towns
but had a harder time governing a place like Serthar. Fresh recruits
were streaming into Serthar, lured by the growing reputation of a
master teacher, Khenpo Jigme Phuntsog who was determined to
revitalize the study of Tibetan Buddhism after decades of devastation by the Chinese. He established Serthar to train young monks
in 1980, when it was still a bare, uninhabited patch of land on the
side of a mountain. A half dozen disciples followed him there in
the beginning, and they slept under the stars or in makeshift tents.
Sitting outside each day, the master teacher trained his followers in
Buddhist classics and meditation. His reputation spread, attracting
more students. Students were inspired by his personal example of
strict celibacy and ethics as the best path to spiritual revitalization.
Hundreds more students came. The curriculum expanded to in-
clude history, painting, medicine, and poetry.

Khenpo Jigme Phuntsog banned any discussion of politics at
Serthar, insisting that everyone focus on religious studies. He was
careful to maintain good terms with the Chinese officials governing
the region, to try to keep them from curtailing his efforts at Serthar.
By 1999, when I got there, so many new recruits were arriving that
Serthar had nearly ten thousand monks and nuns, making it one of

the largest centers of Tibetan Buddhist worship in the world. It was only a matter of time before Chinese authorities would try to rein it in. (Serthar was virtually shut down two years later, and Khenpo Jigme Phuntsog was forced to relocate.) Yet in the long run, I felt sure, it would be impossible to restrain the Tibetan yearning for religious worship.

I returned to the hostel after dark. A candle burned in the kitchen, where the large proprietress was brewing tea. She poured and handed me a cup, the wooden floor creaking under her heavy frame. She gave me a woolen blanket for bedding. Luodeng was already asleep on the other wooden bench, and I lay down on mine.

I woke at dawn. A Tibetan herdsman shuffled noisily around the main room of the hostel, looking for breakfast. I could smell burning yak dung, chunks of it toasting inside an old iron stove in the corner. The herdsman gruffly pushed my legs to one side and sat down on the hard wooden bench where I lay. He stared at me as he ate a bowl of *tsampa,* barley flour with yak butter mixed in. His bloodshot eyes were expressionless, and his chestnut-colored skin looked thick and wrinkled. I was still sleepy and tried to roll over. My eyes were shut, but I could hear the herdsman chewing. My back and shoulders ached, and I was cold, with only one blanket for cover. I got up and pulled on my pants. The proprietress came in to set a black pot on the stove for tea.

I stumbled outside. A ceiling of tightly crocheted gray clouds loomed low in the sky, narrow strips of pink and blue peeking through at the edges. Another herdsman stood by the side of the road, relieving himself. I joined him. Our small puddles seemed like nothing, out here in the wilderness. Beyond the five or six shacks by the long dirt road, we were surrounded by hulking mountains that stretched to the horizon on all sides.

This was my day to see a sky burial, the mysterious ritual I had been seeking. I knew that Tibetan Buddhists traditionally approach death in a sophisticated way. Death is anticipated solemnly as a critical milestone in the passage from one state of consciousness to another. Tibetans believe that if one's karma can affect rebirth in the next life, one's emotional state or final thought at the time of death can influence one's path through the stairway of interim states that follow death. Those in-between states are intricately drawn in the *Tibetan Book of the Dead,* a classic that is studied carefully by Tibetan monks and scholars. It portrays death as the ultimate illustration of the idea that everything changes, that suffering comes from fear and attachment, and that enlightenment comes from letting go. A Tibetan scholar, Chogyam Trungpa, wrote in a forward to the *Book of the Dead:* "Continual contact with the process of death, particularly watching one's close friends and relatives, is considered extremely important for students of this tradition, so that the notion of impermanence becomes a living experience rather than a philosophical view." The Dalai Lama has said that his own daily meditation is ultimately a way to prepare for death.

Tsering came to the hostel to fetch me, smiling heartily. He too had studied death a great deal and had attended more than five hundred sky burials. So sacred and mysterious-sounding to me, a sky burial was a common occurrence for him. Tsering led me on a long walk through the valley, up one hill after another. He forged ahead, humming to himself. I lost my breath, panting hard in the thin air. It forced me to stop every twenty yards or so and take a look out at the green mountains that surrounded us. The air was misty, cool, and damp.

I caught up with Tsering on the crest of a hill, standing by a burial site. It was deserted. Several flat rocks were arranged together,

and Tsering nodded at the spot to indicate where the ritual was performed. A rugged stupa of piled rocks stood to one side. On the
other side, a field of prayer flags, thousands of pieces of colored silk,
fluttered in the light breeze, each one tied to a stick that had been
planted by the families of the dead. Pieces of old clothing and baskets lay scattered about, discarded like random gravestones. Mixed
among them, I saw broken sections of human skulls. Tsering said
that most skulls were destroyed during sky burial, but some were
evidently left behind. Tibetan monks sometimes make elaborate
cups out of human skulls and drink tea from them, an act that Chinese officials consider evidence that Tibet is still barbaric. For the
monks, Tsering explained, using a skull in everyday life was a way
to remain conscious of death.

It was noon, the appointed hour. No one else was there. We sat
to wait. Minutes ticked by; an hour passed. Raindrops started to
fall. I wondered if the sky burial would be held that day or not. I
felt impatient and wanted to tell Tsering to do something, but
knew he could do nothing. We were sitting on the side of a mountain. All we could do was wait. "Patience," Tsering said, as if he
had read my mind. Then he pointed to an enormous vulture
perched on a nearby hill. "He knows if they will come. As long as
he is there, we will wait." I looked over at the bird, and it made the
waiting easier. We sat in silence, staring at the hills, so soft and immense. I felt like a dot in the wilderness. I occasionally glanced
over at the hilltop where the vulture sat, to make sure he was still
there. He did not move.

At about 2 P.M., five men came into sight over the crest of a hill
in the distance, several hundred yards away. As they gradually came
into view, I could see that one of them was carrying a crude wooden
crate on his back, the size of a bale of hay. As the men drew closer,

I stared at the box. The men put it down next to the flat rocks and stepped away from it. Three of them looked like workmen, with faces darkened from laboring in the sun. The two others, one elderly and one middle-aged, were the husband and son of the woman whose body was inside the box. They sat for a moment as the three workmen circled the stupa, tossing flower petals over their shoulder and murmuring tributes of faith. Then the husband and son set off to find a place to sit on another hill, about three hundred yards away, so they could watch from a distance, too far away to see anything clearly but close enough to be aware of what was going on. The workmen struggled to open the box, which had been nailed shut. After some effort, they ripped it apart. An old blue bag rolled out onto the ground with a thud. They lifted it onto the flat rocks. Then they stepped away and took a seat on the side of the hill, near me and Tsering. A half dozen other monks also gathered to wait.

Soon a monk appeared, wearing a sleeveless gold silk top and a thick red robe. He carried a large butcher's knife and spent several minutes sharpening it on a rock. His name was Lobsang. He had a short goatee and a fierce-looking frown, and was all business, as though this was something he did every day. He ripped a piece of burlap and wrapped it around his waist as an apron. He dumped the woman's body out of the old blue bag. It looked inhuman, though long, stringy hair framed a pasty white and bloated face. The woman had been sixty-seven years old and had died three days before. Even from where I sat twenty-five yards away, it smelled stale and sour. I covered my nose.

Lobsang turned the body over, surveying it slowly. Then he raised his knife. There was no ceremony, no music, no group prayer. He just started cutting. First he sliced away tendons in the woman's neck. Then he picked up an arm and sliced away the flesh in one long strip, throwing it on a nearby rock. He sliced away one breast, then the other. One of the monks tapped my shoulder and pointed up the hill behind us, where about four dozen vultures had gathered. They watched intently.

As Lobsang worked, we watched too. I was mesmerized. It was like a meditation, watching an expert artisan at work. My mind ventured through moments in the life and death of this old woman. I imagined her as a baby, born in some poor and run-down Tibetan shack, her own mother lucky if a midwife had been available to help. I imagined her as a little girl, as a teenager making love for the first time out in a barley field. I thought of her as a mother. I thought of my own mother, at the time of my birth, beginning the path that had led me to this hillside, on this day, contemplating the death of another. I thought of the death of my mother, when I was nineteen, and of her cremation. I did not see her body after her death, as I was seeing one now. I sat there watching, surrounded by immovable mountains, sensing how small this woman's life seemed. As did my own. All my anxiety, the kinds of daily worries and fears I carried in my frenetic work life, seeped out of my mind like wisps that floated away into the sky. Nothing mattered.

I felt keenly conscious of my own body, sitting there cross-legged as I watched, with blood flowing through my limbs. I would not care if I were cut to pieces once I was dead, or burned in a brick oven. Out on the mountainside, reducing this old woman's body to pieces, on its return to nothingness, seemed natural and fitting. Her spirit had gone already. In this desperately poor region, with impassable mountains, with few roads and little electricity, human life followed the brutal rhythms of nature. It was peaceful, not ghoulish, watching Lobsang cut the woman to bits. The last stage in a cycle of life. The sun will rise, the rain will fall. Old women will die. As will I.

Lobsang worked diligently, throwing flesh on one pile, bones on another. Eventually, he dropped his knife and picked up a hammer. He raised the hammer overhead, and as he swung it down to strike the woman's skull, I jumped slightly in my seat. It was as if my last wisp of sympathy, my innate connection to another human, was now gone.

Lobsang methodically smashed the bones into small pieces. It was hard work. He paused occasionally to catch his breath. When he finished after an hour or so, Lobsang wiped his hands on his apron and looked up the hill at the vultures. He waved us spectators to step off to one side, to clear the path between the vultures and the human remains. Once we were out of the way, Lobsang yelled out sharply and threw a long stringy piece of flesh toward the birds. The vultures began moving down, some opening their wings as they walked. Their bodies were enormous, the size of humans. They struggled to fly, overweight from hearty feeding each day. Their broad wingspans made a loud whooshing sound as they flapped their wings. Eventually they all came down the hill, about fifty of them, feasting on the human remains, which disappeared in minutes. Once the last scrap was consumed and the flat rocks were picked clean, the vultures waddled back up the hill in a long single file. There was no trace of the woman's body, except the memory of it, fading slowly in my eyes.

I walked back down the mountain with a deep sense of peace and acceptance. I felt tiny and inconsequential, my life as fragile and impermanent as the old woman's. I felt connected to the mountains, the soft rolling hills, the clouds in the sky. All the travails of my journey to this place seemed irrelevant now. I knew I would try to describe to others what I had seen, and I knew that no words would convey the depth of what I felt. The thought of talking about it seemed to belittle the day, the woman's life, and her death. I felt a firm sensation on the bottom of my feet, touching the ground through my worn leather boots, alternating steps, walking down the mountain.

epilogue

I went back to Shanghai and resumed my work as a journalist. My daily life there, and the news stories I pursued, seemed inconsequential after what I had witnessed in Tibet. I told friends about my trip, showing photographs and describing the treacherous roads I traveled to get to Serthar. Yet I found it hard to explain the deep sense of peace and acceptance I had found on the mountaintop, contemplating the death of another. It felt as though my mind had stepped through a passageway to a new realm, where I had a broader sense of perspective. It gave me a palpable notion of my own mortality and a feeling of exhilaration at simply being alive to see the colors in a sunset, to smell the fragrance of a woman, to taste the delicate flavors of a carefully prepared Chinese meal. It made me want to spend each day in a meaningful way.

For years, I had been searching for the secrets of Chinese culture, as though getting past all the thick walls and closed doors would deliver me. I had snuck into temples and military compounds. I had pursued politicians, chief executives, and criminals. I had visited schools and factories and cemeteries. I had been to almost every province in China and had met people from virtually every station in life. Whatever particular piece of information I sought, there always seemed to be more that was unknowable, just out of reach. There were always more secrets. I felt compelled to go onward, traveling with an unspoken belief that if I could penetrate just one more layer of society, I would somehow gain the keys to the kingdom.

What lies at the heart of most secrets is, in the end, utterly human. When I witnessed a Tibetan sky burial, all that lay before me was the corpse of an old woman. The lesson I took from watching her body disappear was a simple truth; about the preciousness of life, available to anyone on any day. I had to travel a long way to be able to see its meaning.

A friend in Beijing, Shao, often spoke to me about how everything changes, how nothing is permanent, how one needs to let go of daily anxiety and accept life as it unfolds. I had heard him say that countless times. He often chastized me for working too hard, urging me to find more depth in my life. Although on some level I knew he was right, I never listened closely. Nothing he said connected with my daily life as a journalist in China, which centered on fighting for snippets of information, testing limits, and constantly questioning the established way.

When I saw Shao after my trip to Tibet, I found myself telling him about the sky burial and what it meant to me. He broke into a broad grin, as though I was finally getting his message. Shao told me he wanted to show me a Taoist temple outside of Beijing. We went on a hot summer day, and the air was hazy and thick. When we got out of my jeep and walked up a hill toward the temple, all we could hear was the loud buzzing of crickets. Although it was a Sunday, a day when urban residents liked to escape the city's heat, there was no one around.

The temple was a simple yellow structure with a sloping roof. Inside, a monk tended to a small collection of figurines. He had a long, wispy gray beard. I noticed that his fingernails were several inches long, except for one that looked like it had accidentally broken. He wore a long gray and yellow robe. He smiled as he saw us approach, nodding in greeting.

The monk showed us around, patiently answering Shao's questions about when the temple was built, how it had fared in various waves of political upheaval over the past century. The monk had a roiling laugh, which came easily, and he exuded a deep sense of calm and acceptance. To many of our comments, he rejoined, "And so it is."

Shao and I left the monk and walked the temple grounds on our own. Shao told me that Taoists teach that all of life is in a state of change and that attachment to wordly things is temporary and ultimately futile. The essence of Taoism, for Shao, was zeroing in on the mysteries of life. To him, fulfilment came by keeping alive a sense of wonder, a true excitement at being alive, and an acceptance that much lies beyond our control. It is the same with all religions, Shao observed. The deepest truths are universal.

Shao and I talked about the secretive nature of Chinese society. The reason for secrecy, Shao believed, was that many Chinese people felt insecure about their culture. It seemed quite obvious, once he said so. The mind that holds onto secrets is an unhealthy mind.

The culture that overprotects its secrets is unhealthy. This was a dark side of Chinese culture that no one liked to talk about. Yet it has been that way for longer than anyone can remember. Like any cultural habit, it is taught and learned from such an early age that it is embedded in the worldview of most Chinese people.

Beneath the secretive habits of China, however, lay an age-old wisdom about what was important in life. In the teachings of Chinese culture—the devotion to family, to mealtime, and to tradition—a man like Shao was able to find his own sense of meaning. He lived with a deep sense of acceptance about the direction of things, without giving up his free will. He exuded compassion and understanding. A dose of the spiritual truths of Taoism and Buddhism and Confucianism helped him find the way. His was a road less traveled, available to anyone, yet chosen by few. He centered his life on living each day and each hour to its fullest. "Keeping my eyes open" was how Shao liked to put it. It was a lesson I had heard many times. I only truly listened after my trip to Tibet.

In the months that followed, I let go of my desire to uncover any more secrets. After many years of exploring, my thirst for adventure had been fulfilled. I lost my aching desire to fit in, as a Westerner in China, always wondering whether I belonged or not. The excitement of journalism, which had seemed so thrilling to me at one time, no longer held the same allure. The long shadows of Chinese culture were still there, but I felt sure that it was time to let others carry the searchlights. I needed to find balance and deeper meaning in my own life. My journey was over.

I was not sure where to go when I left China, but I knew somehow that if I kept my eyes and ears open, an answer would come to me. It appeared as a voice, and a face, on my television set. It belonged to a correspondent for CNN named Siobhan Darrow. I found myself mesmerized by her voice every time one of her stories came on screen, from Russia or Northern Ireland, or elsewhere in Europe. I loved her manner and her name, Siobhan, pronounced "Sha-von." Something about her suggested to me that we were kindred spirits. I asked around, finding out a little more about her from fellow journalists who knew her. Then I took a leap. I wrote her a message, letting her know how she had charmed me. When I pressed the SEND button, I envisioned my message whirling off into cyberspace like a shot in the dark. I imagined Siobhan reading it, laughing, and pressing DELETE. I did not expect to hear from her. To my everlasting delight, however, she wrote back. Two weeks later, I flew to meet her in Los Angeles. That day, I knew I had finally met my partner. I left China to embark on a new stage of life.

And so I ended up "crossing the river by feeling the stones," as a Chinese proverb put it. I followed my intuition and took chances when they presented themselves. The riches of my voyage did not lie in a grand conclusion or summing up at the finish line. They were hidden in steps along the way. The first light of dawn breaking over a Chinese rooftop. The steam rising off a bowl of watercress soup. The late-afternoon sun reflecting off the wheat fields as I rode a bicycle beside a new friend. The sight of student protesters in a midnight march on the streets of Beijing. The smell of braised spareribs in an elegant Shanghai restaurant. The soft hum of murmured prayers by pilgrims inside a dark Tibetan temple. These are the moments that linger in memory, in the crooked recesses of my soul.

Acknowledgments

Two writers, Lynn Pan and Nicole Mones, said the right things to me at the right time, when I was vulnerable to the suggestion that I try writing something longer than a newspaper article. Their timely encouragement tipped me in the right direction.

In the years I spent in China, I made friends who offered me concrete help and emotional shelter in circumstances that often required courage and ingenuity. I benefited from countless acts of kindness and bravery. A few of these friends are named in my narrative, and many are not. I am grateful to them all.

When it came time to sit down and write, I relied on uncommon sympathy and criticism from my friends in the Monday Night Writing Group, led by the incomparable Nancy Bacal, with her remarkable ability to steer her writers directly to the emotional heart of things. My writing also benefitted from the wisdom of Jack Rosenberg, whose lessons on life and love are unmatched.

A handful of special friends were willing to wade through early drafts of my work and gently point out shortcomings: Paul Florsheim, Stephen Grynberg, James Harding, Martha Huang, Christopher Hunt, and Adi Ignatius. Three particularly close friends, Larry Zuckerman, Joseph Kahn, and John Pomfret, offered particularly insightful advice with intellectual scope and factual specificity.

Several editors at the *New York Times* inspired me to go further in my travels than I would have otherwise: Bernard Gwertzman, *acknowledgments*

Joseph Lelyveld, Bill Keller, Susan Chira, Andrew Rosenthal, and the unmatched China hand Jeanne Moore. As a newspaper man, I spent some days wanting to kill one of my editors and spent many more feeling honored to be a member of their club. I am grateful to Patrick Tyler, colleague extraordinaire, who showed me secrets of the craft and the true romance in foreign correspondence, and to James Bennet and Steven Lee Myers, my favorite reporters at the newspaper, for their enduring friendship.

The Pacific Council of International Policy kindly granted me a fellowship in Los Angeles to help me start writing. Sam and Marie made me feel welcome all day at the Eighteenth Street Coffeehouse in Santa Monica, where most of this book was eventually written.

My agent and friend, David Black, displayed wonderful patience and faith, looking through innumerable drafts and outlines and insisting that I try just a little harder. George Witte, my editor at St. Martin's Press, blessed me with expert guidance and advice.

I would like to thank my parents and my sisters for their steady love and support, even when I was far away for years at a time.

More than anyone, I thank my wife, Siobhan Darrow, who persuaded me to write this book, read countless drafts, talked me through moments of despair, and came up with its title. Siobhan showed me how to follow my intuition, how to decode the symbols hidden in my dreams, and how to find elements of the divine in steps along the way. She offered love in many forms, most beautifully in two young souls, Lane and Sasha, who arrived together just after I finished writing this book.